SKEPTIC, INNKEEPER, BELIEVER . . . NOW SHE'S YOUR INSIDE GUIDE TO AMERICA'S MOST HAUNTED HOTELS!

When Frances Kermeen purchased the old Southern mansion in Louisiana, she was sure it would make the perfect quiet period hotel. But after seeing a candelabra floating up the stairs, hearing voices coming from a stilled gramophone, and learning about an irate foreman who stalks the grounds a century after his death, she soon discovered that The Myrtles was "America's Most Haunted House." And when The Myrtles became front-page news across the country, her business boomed.

Fascinated by ghost stories from other hoteliers around the country, Frances began researching some 150 haunted inns, hotels, and bed-and-breakfasts. From Maine's rugged sea coast to the Rockies' windswept lonely plains, she's collected spine-tingling true ghost stories about fascinating past owners, visitors—and others—who even now make these houses their otherworldly homes. The author also includes useful information from pricing to location—and sometimes the blood curdling accounts of her own firsthand . . .

GHOSTLY ENCOUNTERS

GHOSTLY ENCOUNTERS

TRUE STORIES OF AMERICA'S HAUNTED INNS AND HOTELS

FRANCES KERMEEN

WARNER BOOKS

An AOL Time Warner Company

WARNER BOOKS EDITION

Cover design by Diane Luger/George Cornell
Cover photo by Ludovic Moulin
Book design by Charles Sutherland

Warner Books, Inc.
1271 Avenue of the Americas
New York, NY 10020

Visit our Web site at
www.twbookmark.com.

An AOL Time Warner Company

Printed in the United States of America

First Printing: October 2002

10 9 8 7 6 5 4 3

ACKNOWLEDGMENTS

First of all, I would like to thank my wonderful agent, Jodie Rhodes. I'd also like to thank my editor, John Aherne, and his assistant, Megan Rickman, for all their creative genius.

A special thanks for all the hotel and inn staff who, like I, find themselves searching for a meaning to their ghostly encounters; and all those who gave help and encouragement along the way: Aldine West, Mike Scheck, Greg Proffit, Sharron Gammel, Marina Rosario, Dr. Larry Montz of the International Society for Paranormal Research (ISPR), psychic Peter James, Ghost Tours of St. Augustine, David Sloan and the Key West Ghost Tours, the Nebraska Office of Tourism, and all the many many people I've had the pleasure to meet along the way.

Contents

GHOSTLY
ENCOUNTERS

Introduction

❦

On April Fool's Day, 1980, I bought an old mansion in St. Francisville, Louisiana, known as the Myrtles Plantation. It was my dream to live in this magnificent southern mansion, furnish it with period treasures, and turn it into a wonderful romantic inn. Little did I know my first guest would be a ghost.

I certainly did not really believe in ghosts and tried to convince myself my eyes had deceived me. But more and more ghosts appeared. Wondering if someone was trying to play a nasty trick on me, I went to the local sheriff with my problem. He and his men came and checked the house out. They saw ghosts too. Police Chief Larry Peters ran out of the house and vowed never to return. I went to respected people in town and heard frightening tales about the old mansion. In the local library I found stories about the ghosts at the Myrtles dating back over one hundred years. So why hadn't someone told me before I purchased the place and moved in?

The next thing I knew, national media picked up the story from the local paper, and I was big news. My haunted plantation made the front page in the *Wall Street Journal,* earned a cover story in *Life* magazine and the *Star,* and was featured in *USA Today, Time* magazine, *Playboy, Glamour, Good Housekeeping,* the *Robb Report, US* magazine, the *National Law Journal,* the *Los Angeles Times,* the *New York Times,* and almost every other major newspaper in the United States.

I was interviewed on the *Today Show,* the *CBS Morning News, A Current Affair, Ripley's Believe It or Not, CBS Nightly News, NBC Nightly News, PBS, Eye on L.A.,* the Discovery Channel, and TV shows in Australia and Japan, just to name a few.

It was the worst thing that could have happened, I despaired. My inn would be avoided like the plague. No one would ever book a room, or host a wedding. My dream would be crushed. I'd go bankrupt.

How wrong I was. Rather than hurting the business, as I feared, stories of the hauntings brought people by the droves. Thousands of people overwhelmed me with room requests. Ghosts turned out to be the greatest possible attraction. People came from all over the world, hoping to experience the ghosts at the Myrtles. And experience them they did. Over the years I collected more than one thousand personal ghost accounts from the guests.

Over time, I learned that people seek a haunted hotel for many different reasons. Many, of course, go for the thrill and sensationalism. However, there are more profound reasons. More and more people are seeking a deeper meaning to life itself. The Myrtles is a spiritual vortex. Still others seek out a haunted inn because they lost a loved one, and they desperately want proof that life transcends death. Encountering a ghost gives them that proof.

I began to hear from other inn owners from all over the country who also had ghosts. Most of them harbored the same fears. I was fascinated by their stories, and I began to visit other haunted inns. Wanting to share this information, I wrote a travel guide of haunted inns for people who'd love to have a ghostly encounter. But this, I promised myself, would not be any ordinary travel guide. Haunted places have very special personalities and unusually fascinating histories. What was needed was a travel guide that gave a personal narrative about these places, along with the essential information about location, prices, amenities, and so on.

Since I now felt I owed ghosts a lot, I promised that I wouldn't allow any fakes to creep in. So I spent over two years traveling the country and personally researching each and every haunted inn and hotel in this book. Did I meet any ghosts along the way? You betcha.

The Myrtles Plantation

St. Francisville, Louisiana

I didn't always believe in ghosts. But you cannot live at the Myrtles for long before you encounter the unimaginable. My experiences at the Myrtles deeply affected me, and changed me forever.

Multiple visits or an extended stay at the Myrtles Plantation will almost guarantee some sort of paranormal experience. The site of at least ten murders (and many more deaths), this antebellum mansion is host to literally hundreds of "ghosts," at least one of which is bound to manifest on any given day. Dubbed "America's Most Haunted House" by various sources, including the *Wall Street Journal* and the *National Enquirer,* the Myrtles harbors a multitude of spirits.

Ethereal parties keep guests awake until the wee hours. A servant carrying a candle makes her way from room to room at night, tucking in little boys and girls. A beautiful Indian maiden sits naked beside the pond. Two little girls, poisoned in 1824, romp and play outside, stopping occasionally to chat with an unsuspecting guest. The ruthless overseer, brutally murdered in the 1920s, confronts visitors and brusquely orders them away.

A warning about the ghosts at the Myrtles was found in a book published in 1882. "The lights are never extinguished at the plantation," it admonishes. "When the lights are all out, something always happens." To this day, a light is always left on inside the mansion at night.

Lights, however, are no guarantee. As the sun drops and the shadows beckon, voices from the past call out your name; and a disembodied candelabra floats up the stairs; or you hear a tapping at your door; or the bone-chilling sound of a child calling, "Mommy, Mommy." These things always make your heart beat a little faster and the long night ahead seem even more foreboding. Darkness looms larger than life at the old plantation.

The Myrtles Plantation sits gracefully among ninety-one century-old oak trees, ten crape myrtle trees, and dozens of pink and fuchsia azalea bushes, a deceptive setting for what lies inside. With lacy French ornamental ironwork encompassing its hundred-foot galleries, the rococo home is the antithesis of the massive, austere Greek Revival architecture so prevalent in that era.

Hand-painted French glass sparkles in the double entry doors, casting a dancing kaleidoscope of colors throughout the entry hall. Baccarat crystals the size of pigeons' eggs dangle from the shimmering chandeliers, leaving droplets of light on the floor below. Ornate plaster friezework adorns the ceilings in patterns of grape or acanthus leaves. These intricate creations, up to twelve inches wide, are so thick in the icy-peach double parlors that you feel like you are inside a richly decorated wedding cake. Woodwork throughout the house was painted to look like oak, granite, or marble. This process, called *faux bois,* "false wood," has become popular recently, but once was consigned only to highly skilled European artists.

The history of the Myrtles is steeped in passion and romance, tragedy and intrigue. General David Bradford, who led the Whiskey Rebellion in Pennsylvania, built the plantation in 1796. Barely escaping George Washington's troops, he hopped aboard a river barge and fled to what is now Louisiana. With a Spanish land grant he purchased 500 prime acres at $1.40 an acre, and built his home atop a rolling hill.

His daughter, Sarah Mathilda, inherited the plantation and married Judge Clarke Woodruff. Sarah suspected that her husband was having an affair with one of the servants, a beautiful mulatto housemaid. Such an affair was an unspoken but widely accepted practice among some slave owners, including Woodruff. To confirm her suspicions, Sarah waited and watched as her husband led the young maid up the back staircase and into the children's nursery. With the children out playing, the nursery would be empty for several hours. Sarah quietly paced outside the door, her tear-filled gaze fixed on the doorknob. With all her courage, she flung open the door.

The wide-eyed young slave panicked. Would Sarah send her away, or would an even worse punishment await her? If only she could make herself indispensable, then maybe Sarah would forgive her. She devised a desperate plan to save herself. If the family became sick, she could nurse them back to health, and they would realize they needed her. The unwitting slave baked poisonous oleander flowers into the dessert, intending that the family would suffer mild flu symptoms. In her naïveté, she poisoned them. Sarah and her two little girls died that night; the pathetic slave was hung in the morning.

In 1834 the plantation was sold to the Ruffin Gray Stirling family of Scotland. By then, St. Francisville was a bustling river city. Accounts of Ruffin portray him as a kind and jovial fellow, most remembered for the time he fell off a steamboat and almost drowned. Stirling increased the acreage to over 5,000 acres and bought several hundred more slaves. Planted mostly with cotton and indigo, the property extended all the way to Bayou Sara. The Stirlings had nine children, eight boys and one girl, Sarah. It was a happy and prosperous time at the Myrtles.

Until the war. Death and tragedy soon became no strangers to the Stirlings.

The War

In 1864 the War between the States erupted. The Yankees annihilated ill-prepared southern river communities. Horror stories were reported from nearby Vicksburg, where mothers and children were forced to leave their homes and live in caves while death and pilfering ravaged on around them. Gruesome hand-to-hand struggles ended in agonizing deaths. Soon bloody battles erupted on the waters of Bayou Sara as Union troops fired upon St. Francisville. With attack on homes imminent, every man old enough to carry a gun joined forces, passionately committed to protecting his wife and children from the aggressive slaughter. Seven of the eight Stirling sons bravely left home to join the Confederate army. Tragically, only one, Lewis, returned. As if the family hadn't suffered enough death, a year later Lewis was gunned down in the dining room as the family watched in horror.

Sarah led a deliciously sheltered life before the War. Her eight doting brothers all watched over her. When she met and fell in love with William Winter, an attorney from St. Louis, she believed that life was perfect. Her wedding celebration, held at the Myrtles, was the social event of the decade. It was the day she had been dreaming of her entire life. The couple settled into wedded bliss. Sarah and William had three beautiful children.

Tragedy struck yet again in 1871, when William was brutally gunned down while tutoring his young son. Gasping, he clutched his chest and desperately tried to reach Sarah. He staggered up to the seventeenth step of the main staircase, where he collapsed and died in Sarah's arms. For 114 years, every single night, heavy, labored footsteps were heard going up the stairs, stopping at the seventeenth step. It was unnerving if you were on the staircase; the footsteps trudged forward up the stairs, right through you, to the seventeenth step.

Tortured Spirits Released

In the 1980s the Myrtles Plantation was host to Murder Mystery Weekends, re-creating the life and death of William Winter. Meticulous efforts were made to ensure that everything, from the antebellum costumes to the music, and even topics of conversation, were exactly as they had been in 1871. Guests attended the nuptial gala, waltzed to a string ensemble, and feasted on foie gras and whole roast pig.

The weekend progressed as guests relived major events

in the Winters' lives. Saturday night, January 24, 1985, the production climaxed with an eerie reenactment of William's murder, played to the exact day, hour, and minute of the real event 114 years earlier. Caught off guard, guests scurried to the gentlemen's parlor as a voice called out from the darkness beyond, "A visitor to see the lawyer."

As the actor playing William Winter stepped out onto the veranda, shots rang out. With crimson blood oozing from his starched white shirt, a mortally wounded William crashed through the doors, stumbled through the double parlors, and dragged himself up the stairs, desperate to reach his beloved Sarah. They met for the last time on the seventeenth step, where he collapsed in her arms. As she tearfully stroked his face, he died in her embrace.

Immediately all the lights went out. Guests thought it was a dramatic conclusion to such a heartrending scene, but it was not part of the production; the main fuse to the house had somehow blown. The fuse box was locked. At the exact moment of William's death years before, as the desperate scene was re-created, who turned off the lights, and how?

When the power was restored, we found that all of the paintings in the home were off-center or upside down. A nineteenth century portrait of a young woman hanging above the piano was crying. If one of the guests had tampered with the paintings, someone would have seen. The portrait above the piano was inaccessible, yet drops of clear fluid were streaming from the subject's eyes.

In the wake of the weekend, we noticed another phenomenon. The labored steps ascending the stairs, which had been a nightly occurrence for 114 years, ceased that night. Is it possible that this reenactment of the life and subsequent brutal slaying of William Winter, and attempt to solve his murder, had released his spirit? Could the plot of the murder mystery have solved the real murder, setting William free?

An Historic Pattern

Although not everyone who was murdered at the Myrtles became a "ghost," and not every ghost is a murdered soul, many of the restless resident spirits can be historically accounted for. Some have their own particular room to haunt, or appear at a specific time of year or even a specific day, which correlates somehow with their past physical life at the plantation.

One example of this is in the entry hall. Throughout the house the thick cypress floors shone like glassy water on a still pond. To achieve this, once a week Lilly May, who had worked at the Myrtles for twelve years, would polish and buff the floors. One spot on the shining planks, just outside the dining room, was always dull and hazy. No matter how hard Lilly May persisted, she could not get the buffer to go over that one spot. Even if she got a good running start, her entire weight behind it, the buffer would stop dead, "like running into a wall." When the history of the house was researched and archived newspaper articles were scoured, it was revealed that when Lewis Stirling was shot, he died outside the dining room, on that very spot.

In January 1868 little Cate Stirling lay dying of yellow fever in the room that we called the Peach Room. The Stirlings did everything possible save their daughter. In secret, Sarah begged her handmaid to get the Voodoo Queen. It was rumored that through her voodoo spells, she could take away sickness and even raise the dead. That night after dark, the frantic, rhythmic beat of drums sent an urgent message to the slaves at neighboring Solitude Plantation.

The Voodoo Queen arrived before dawn. She locked herself in Cate's room and began her chanting and gris-gris (or incantation). For three days she feverishly danced, wailed, and cajoled the listless child, but Cate finally succumbed. Every January, the month Cate was ill, the smoky figure of the Voodoo Queen looms larger than life over people sleeping in that room. She may appear as a shadow dancing across the walls, or you may awake to find her working her voodoo over you.

The Green Room was where the Stirling family hid a frightened sixteen-year-old Confederate soldier during the Civil War. His leg was badly mangled, but his mental wounds were far worse. Sarah and the house servants watched over him, bringing him hot pabulum and changing his bandages. When neighbors from Rosedown Plantation discovered the lad hidden away, they were angry that he hadn't gone right back to the front lines after his leg healed. They broke down the back door of the Myrtles and chased him down to the bayou, where they lynched him for deserting.

Most men who sleep in this room have strange, vivid dreams about war, or of being chased. These hallucinations escalate in May and June, the months the soldier hid out. Sometimes you can actually catch a glimpse of the frightened soldier lounging on the bed or crouching in the corner, looking as solid as you or me.

A newlywed couple from Desterhan, Louisiana, spent their June honeymoon in that room. Knowing nothing about the ghosts at the Myrtles, they came to spend a romantic weekend lolling about in a southern plantation. When they didn't show up for breakfast the next morning, no one was concerned. About an hour later, the staff received a strange call. It was the bride. Around two in the morning, they had left the Myrtles. In their frenzied haste to get out, they hadn't taken the time to pack their suitcases. "Could someone please pack up our things and bring them to town?" she politely requested. When asked why they didn't come back, enjoy their breakfast, and get their things, she put her new husband, obviously shaken and agitated, on the phone.

"I am not going back up into that house," he stated. "I was on my honeymoon, but I kept having horrible nightmares about being chased. They seemed so real. I finally fell asleep, but something woke me up. Someone was messing with my leg. At first I thought it was my wife. I looked up, and a black lady was putting bandages on my foot. I grabbed my wife, and we left."

Safe Sex

Can ghosts have sex? Many female visitors to the Myrtles are convinced that they can. The old nursery upstairs, once a favorite trysting place for the judge, is now a guest room. Single female guests sleeping in that room have confessed that at some time during the night an invisible phantom slid into the bed. Slowly and passionately the ghost skillfully seduced her. It is believed that this ghostly lover is none other than the judge himself.

The Blue Room, located upstairs in the middle wing of the house, is known as the "eye of the storm." While fantastic sightings and unbelievable events are reported in every other room, occupants of this room are not bothered. However, every night at exactly 2:00 A.M., the room's occupants awake with a start. This waking hour changes to 3:00 A.M. during daylight savings. Obviously, something corporeal occurred in that room at that hour, though we don't know what.

The room known as the Bridal Suite once belonged to Sarah and William Stirling. That room is active most of the time, as are the rooms downstairs. Voices, footsteps, and the scent of perfume are common throughout the house. In the spring and fall, the ball seasons, guests hear parties going on at night. But if you try to find the source of the merriment, it seems to move. Every Thanksgiving, we can hear the soft music of a string quartet.

The house itself is not the only place where spirits manifest. Ghosts are also seen on the grounds, in broad daylight. A caretaker murdered in the 1920s wanders the property, and has ordered tourists to leave. People would call and ask when the plantation was open for tours. When we told them that the house was open every day, they would tell us that a man had told them to go away. They always described him in the same way—an older, nondescript man wearing khaki pants. They thought he worked there. He did, just not this century.

The two little girls who were poisoned in 1824 still romp on the plantation grounds. They walk up and talk to people, who don't realize at first that they are talking to ghosts. Sometimes people sent photographs which showed these children. "There was no one there when we took the photo," they write.

One of the black gentlemen who greeted people at the gate walked off the job and never came back after a lady in an antebellum gown strolled across the grounds and vanished into thin air.

The Squeamish Need Not Apply

At times, because of the ghosts, it was hard to find people willing to work at the Myrtles. It was even harder to keep them. Several employees walked off the job after encountering a spirit. The ghosts usually get to a new employee right away. Typically, on someone's first day, they hear their name called. This indicates to me that "they" are aware of us; that they can see us, and they know us by name.

The Ghost in the Green Turban

I hadn't even been at the plantation for a week when I had my first encounter. The house hadn't closed yet, but I came out early for the annual Audubon Pilgrimage. Mr. John L. Pearce, the previous owner, had friends staying over to help with the event. He put me in the suite. I was so excited I could hardly contain myself. Even so, I was a little bit nervous about the huge house, and about being in strange surroundings. I was glad that there were other people upstairs, even though they were across the house, in the other wing. For comfort, I set the dimmer switch to low, leaving a slight glow in the room. I drifted off, only to be awakened by footsteps in the hall. I figured it was just the other houseguests taking the long way to their room. When I opened my eyes, the lights were on bright. I dimmed them again, and fell back to sleep. The bright lights woke me again. I thought to myself, "This is weird. I could have sworn I turned the lights down." Lowering them once again, I drifted back to sleep. When I woke up again to find them on, I'd had enough. I knew this time it wasn't my imagination. I grabbed my pillow and blanket and retreated downstairs to the sitting room where I lay down on the sofa.

Before long, I had the distinct feeling that someone was watching me. Nervously I looked up. Standing next to me, staring down, was a heavyset black lady, her square, angular face framed by a turban wrapped around her head. She had no ear, but an earring was dangling down from her headdress. I could see her clearly from the light she was carrying—an old-fashioned tin candleholder with a loop so you could grab it. I was terrified to look in her eyes. I started to scream.

It seemed that I was screaming for hours, though it was probably just a matter of minutes. When I finally resigned myself to the fact that no one was coming to rescue me, I peeked back up to see if she was still there. She was. Timidly I reached out to touch her, to see if she was real. As my hand passed through her, she faded away.

I jumped up and switched on every light in the room. I remember I snuck out to the cupboard and found some cherry brandy. It tasted like cough syrup, but I didn't care. I sat up with the brandy waiting for daybreak.

I couldn't wait for John L. to wake up to tell him what happened. "Frances, don't be ridiculous," was all he said. I felt embarrassed. It wasn't until several days later, after the closing in which I legally bought the place, that I learned the truth. John L. took me to meet his mother. The first thing she said to me was, "John L. tells me that you saw the ghost in the green turban. That's really exciting. She hasn't been seen in years."

When I finally got John L. alone, I jumped on him. "You didn't tell me you knew about the ghosts," I accused. "You tried to make me believe that I was imagining things." Sure enough, John L.'s friends and employees later confided that he had instructed them not to tell prospective buyers about the famous ghosts.

Another evening I sat in the plush velvet chairs in the gentlemen's parlor, happily daydreaming, long after everyone else had gone to bed. In an instant, the room turned icy cold, and I felt terror in the air. I looked through the ladies' parlor and into the entry hall. I saw a silver candelabra, aglow with candles, floating up the stairs, one step at a time. It hovered at the same height it would have been, had someone been carrying it. My mind boggled. I could barely force myself to turn out the lights before fleeing the room.

After the festivities of the pilgrimage and the closing celebration, John L. moved out, and I was left alone. Not wanting to stay alone in the house, I decided to stay with my real estate agent, Betty Jo Eschete—who is first cousin to Jimmy Swaggart and Jerry Lee Lewis—for a few days until my friend Charles Mandrake arrived to become the Myrtles' curator. Betty Jo was at the Myrtles, gathering a few items to take to her house. When I went to leave, the door was locked! Now this is impossible, because the only locks are on the inside. Thinking it must be some kind of hardware defect, I went to the front door. It was locked too! I couldn't get out! I started to panic, running from room to room, trying each exterior door. I was locked in! I tried all the huge floor-to-ceiling windows, then all the windows. They were all locked. I was trapped inside the Myrtles!

Terrified, I raced for the phone. Thank God that worked. I dialed Betty Jo's number, and I was sobbing and screeching at the same time into the phone, begging her to come right over. When she understood the magnitude of what I was telling her, she raced right over. She was there in a matter of minutes.

Betty Jo came running up to the house, hollering my name. I sobbed back, "I'm here, help me!" Betty Jo reached the back door, turning the handle with all her might. It wouldn't budge. Next she tried the double doors into the entry hall, which could not even be locked. She shook them frantically. They were locked as well. She raced down the gallery, trying every door. Finally, not knowing what else to do, she just stood there outside my door, beating on it, screaming frantically, "Let me in, let me in."

Inexplicably, the doors just suddenly unlocked and Betty Jo tumbled in. She raced in and grabbed me, and we made a run for the car. We didn't even stop to gather my things. When we reached the car, we hugged each other tightly, then silently stared deep into each other's eyes. We drove to her house without speaking a word, afraid even of our own thoughts. I didn't step foot back in the Myrtles until Charles arrived more than a week later.

With another human in the house, I tentatively moved back in and actually began to enjoy the plantation once again, at least during the day. Nighttime was another story. It seemed that every night, something else would happen. One night Charles set up his gramophone, and we listened to his collection of antique records. At the end of each and every song, we heard voices coming through the speaker, voices that were not part of the recording.

On another occasion, we walked down the winding road to lock the outer gates, a nightly ritual. When we turned to go back up to the road, the house glowed an eerie iridescent gold. It looked as if hundreds of candles were illuminating the house, both inside and outside. I ran back down the road, through the gates, to the old garçonnier, where I sat there sobbing. "I never want to go back to that house," I cried.

Charles came up and put his arm around me. "You have to," Charles insisted. Finally we looked back to find the house returned to its normal appearance. Step by terrifying tiny step, we made our way back in.

Mrs. Michaud

One of the most troubling encounters happened several days after Charles arrived. I slept in the sitting room, and I put Charles in the French Bedroom next door. I always left the door open between the two rooms, just in case. On this particular night, I heard noises coming from his bedroom. I peeked through the door and saw a short woman dressed in black twirling around the room like a ballerina. Startled, I called out to Charles. He darted into my room and told me that he had seen the lady too, and she had spoken to him.

A shaken Charles piled into my bed, plumping a pillow between us. We sat up talking about all the strange things that had been happening. I don't know why I looked out the window, but when I did, I saw an old oak wheel chair slowly making its way through the rose garden and up to my bedroom window. There was no one in the wheelchair, but it continued coming towards me. Beyond terror, I clutched for Charles. "Look!" I screamed. "It's coming to get us!"

Charles reached for his glasses, which he had placed by the bed. They were gone. Practically blind without them, he felt around the bed. His glasses were nowhere to be found.

I clung to Charles, hysterical, knowing I was the only one who could see the empty wheel chair inching closer and closer. It stopped right in front of my window, and remained there, taunting me, until daybreak thankfully arrived. Afraid to look, yet afraid not to look, we held on to each other until dawn.

Several weeks later, I made a welcome trip to San Jose to visit my husband and family. I have to admit that I was relieved to get away from that place. One day Ruth Reed, wife of the bank vice-president and one of the Myrtles tour guides, called me in California to tell me that the Michauds, who owned the Myrtles for twenty-five years between 1950 and 1975, had moved to San Jose. She wasn't sure if they were still living, as they were very old. Excited about the possibility of meeting this couple, themselves an integral part of the history of the home, I looked them up, and called them. They invited us over that very day.

My first shock came when I realized that they lived exactly six blocks to the number behind the house where I grew up. Very odd.

Mr. Michaud greeted us at the door. He ushered us into the living room, explaining that Mrs. Michaud was ill, but that she would be out to visit shortly. My eyes bounced around the room, fixing on an old photograph on the étagère. I felt my chest tighten, and I couldn't breathe. The lady in the photograph was the same lady who had been dancing in the French Bedroom. My mind boggled as I tried to comprehend this.

"Who's that," I was finally able to squeak out.

"Oh, that's Mrs. Michaud. She's coming out now."

I wanted to run away. I was terrified to come face to face with the woman who had been a ghost in my house just a few days before. The only thing that kept me sitting there on the couch was the sweet openness displayed by Mr. Michaud. After all, we are socialized to be polite. So I sat there, petrified, waiting.

She was much older than she had appeared in the French Bedroom, and obviously at death's door. As terrifying as the meeting was, I also felt so grateful that she had even gotten up to receive us. We spent several hours visiting with the couple who once owned our house, prodding them for every bit of information they could remember. They finally opened up about the ghosts, with whom they had many encounters.

I could hardly wait to get back to my parents' house and call Charles. I knew he would be blown away by this startling revelation. "Charles, you'll never guess who the dancing ghost was!" I shouted into the phone.

"Mrs. Michaud," he replied.

"What? How did you know?" I asked.

"I found some old postcards and saw her. I wanted to say it first, since I knew you had visited them and you knew too."

This unexplainable experience kept me up at night for quite some time. How could Mrs. Michaud be alive, yet be a ghost at the Myrtles?

Months later, I watched a television show where Gary Collins interviewed some expert guests from UCLA, who were doing a study about life after death. They explained how people in nursing homes sometimes leave their bodies and do the things they loved to do when their bodies were intact—walk, run, or even dance! Sometimes these elderly souls sported huge smiles, with their eyes shut tight. They talk about going to a party, or talking to deceased friends.

That would explain how Mrs. Michaud could be in San Jose and at the Myrtles at the same time. She appeared at the Myrtles, happily dancing and talking, as her frail body was failing and she was close to the other side. It was only frightening because our minds were not prepared to accept this phenomenon. I know that Mrs. Michaud's family might read this, and I certainly don't want to upset them. But I feel it's an important fact that as she neared death, her spirit was freed, and she was able to return to the place that she had lived and loved.

Kerri

My friend Kerri was too afraid to come up to the door. She'd drive in and honk her horn, waiting like a princess for someone to come out and escort her up to the house. Like so many others, when she finally had an encounter, she didn't even realize it until afterward.

Kerri was in charge of public relations at the nearby nuclear plant. One year River Bend and the Myrtles put on a joint fund-raiser for the American Cancer Society, a mystery garden party. The attendees all came in turn-of-the-century costume. Kerri encountered a little girl dressed in a long white dress, and had a conversation with the child. Afterward, at the cast party, she told everyone about the cute little girl. "Kerri, there were no children at the garden party," cast members told her. At first Kerri thought we were kidding her, but she soon realized that she had met one of the little ghost girls.

One time I was talking on the phone with Kerri when someone knocked at my door. "Hold on, Kerri, I have to get the door," I said. When I got back to the phone, Kerri was talking away. I listened for a while, then I said, "Kerri, who are you talking to?"

"You."

"No, you're not. I told you I had to get the door."

"Yeah, but you came back and started talking again."

I told Kerri she had just been had by the ghost!

The Floating Bed

Over the years I was at the Myrtles, I asked everyone who encountered a ghost to write down their experience. I've collected over a thousand of these supernatural reports, and I'm sure there were many more people who didn't tell us about their encounters. These following stories are but a few of those reports.

When the entourage from the *Star* came to visit, the photographer stayed in the Bridal Suite. In the morning she reported that the bed had lifted off the ground and floated. "Sure," I thought. "Sounds more like the spirits in the tavern." But every once in a while after that, someone would tell me that the bed had lifted off the ground. I never believed it, until an older couple from Texas stayed with us for three nights. They didn't know anything about the ghosts, and we didn't tell them. He was a diabetic, so they kept his insulin in our refrigerator, and we got to know them. The third morning, she came down and told us that the bed lifted up off the floor in the middle of the night. "*&#^$," I thought to myself.

It was probably my last year at the plantation when it finally happened to me. I was staying in the suite with several friends. I was entirely awake when the phenomenon occurred. I was sitting on the bed as it floated up and hovered about twelve feet off the ground. "So this is what it's like," I thought to myself. Luckily, I had heard the story so many times that by then it was anticlimactic, or I might have been scared out of my wits.

Sam

Sam Moore, a cameraman for the Baton Rouge CBS affiliate, had visited the plantation many times, and was feeling slighted because everyone else had seen a ghost, and he hadn't. When he had his wedding at the Myrtles, even his mother saw the two little girls running up the stairs.

Sam eventually became the star of our Murder Mystery Weekends, re-creating the part of the soon-to-be-slain William Winters. The first night of the event starts with the wedding of William and Sarah. The party goes on into the early hours, as actors and guests sip champagne and dance to a traditional string ensemble. The group was doing the Virginia reel, a lively, historic line dance. Sam casually glanced up and saw two little girls dressed in long white dresses, their tiny noses pressed to the panes of glass separating the ladies' parlor from the entry hall. He did not fully grasp the momentous implication of this event—that he had actually seen the famous "ghost girls"—until he looked back up, and they were gone.

I was in my room when several of the actors started banging on my door. I went out to find a pale and shaken Sam sitting limply on the back veranda. "I saw them," he choked. "I really saw them."

Saved by the . . . Ghost?

It was my first winter at the Myrtles. Since I had first seen the plantation, I had dreamed about Christmas, the house decked out in Victorian Christmas attire. I started planning in November. I had a wedding booked in early December, and I wanted everything to look spectacular.

A week or two before the wedding, I looked out my window and saw a man walking across our property. He was carrying a gun. I got very upset, and ran out to tell him to leave. When I got outside, he was gone. When I went back in, I could see him again. Upon closer inspection, I saw that he was dressed in a gray uniform, with a gray pillbox hat. Later I learned that his attire was a Confederate uniform. I watched him walk the property for several days, but didn't tell the members of the upcoming wedding party about him or any of the ghosts.

The night of the wedding, one of the guests parked on a pile of leaves next to the tavern, and the car's catalytic converter caused the leaves to catch fire. It had become a full blaze by the time my employees banged on my door. The flames were higher than the building. The pipes melted from the wall, and a mink coat in the backseat of the car burned beyond recognition. The fire should have burned the house down—a similar fire, started in the carriage house of one of my Victorian fixer-uppers in California, had jumped to the house in a matter of minutes, totally destroying everything. Fire was my biggest fear. Somehow, the main house was spared. I couldn't stop shaking.

Later I learned that the first person to arrive at the house after the wedding was the father of the bride. He walked through the historic home. In the gentlemen's parlor, he looked up in the gilded mirror above the Italian Carrara marble fireplace. Behind him was a Confederate soldier, dressed in gray, with a gray pillbox hat. Not wanting to frighten his guests, he didn't tell anyone until the next day.

We didn't see the soldier again after that. It was as if he was keeping guard. The Myrtles could have burned down that night, but it didn't. If it was somehow that soldier, I am very grateful.

Who You Gonna Call?

When you hear heavy footsteps coming up the stairs, or feel a clammy hand on your shoulder, don't bother to call the police. When former police chief Larry Peters was summoned to the house, in the daytime, a young lady wearing a hoop-skirted gown greeted him. Assuming it was a tour guide in costume, he followed her into the house and up the stairs. When they got to the top, she vanished. The police chief turned and ran. Chief Peters says he wouldn't go back for a million dollars.

I tried to arrange it so I was never alone at the plantation. If I was alone, I used to bribe my friends to come stay with me. However, there were a few times in the middle of winter when I found myself totally alone with the house. My bedroom was downstairs, chosen because it had two windows and three doors, in case I had to exit fast.

I'd no sooner turn out the lights than the dreaded clamoring would begin. It sounded like men in heavy boots, coming up on the back veranda. Then I would hear the double doors to the entry hall crash open. They were in the house! Before long, I would hear pounding on the door to my quarters. Barely able to breathe, I crouched on the floor next to my bed and dialed the police. I would dial every number except the last, listening and waiting. I didn't want to seem like a crazy lady if it was the ghosts. Besides, I knew that if Chief Peters was on duty, he wouldn't come out here. I would just sit there, frozen, as this group of men continued pilfering my home just beyond my door, silently praying over and over, "PLEASE BE A GHOST!"

Indian Burial Grounds

Why are there so many ghosts at the Myrtles Plantation? There seem to be as many explanations as there are ghosts. One is that the home sits on sacred Indian burial ground, a definite no-no. I think possibly that the Indians chose that spot because it already possessed mystical qualities.

The house was haunted long before a previous owner paved over the graveyard to make a parking lot, which might have just added to the turmoil. Another theory is that the intensely passionate emotions of the people who lived, loved, and died there, bound these souls to the plantation, or maybe they simply just wanted to come visit, or stay on.

I experienced many things during my eight and a half years at the plantation, far too numerous to write about in this short chapter. Many of those things I didn't believe in, nor could I comprehend. Some of them I don't want to believe in to this day.

But my experiences have left me with proof that the physical world that we live in and believe in is not the whole picture. There is something more that transcends time and space. To me, it's proof that there is a God, and that life goes on beyond this physical world. It's oddly comforting.

Best Rooms/Times

Every room, all the time.

The Inn

There are six guest rooms in the plantation house, including the suite. For those not so brave, a new wing is available outside by the pond, offering four more guest rooms. These rooms offer the best vantage point to catch a glimpse of the naked Indian maiden.

All have private baths. A full plantation breakfast consisting of bacon, eggs, grits, homemade biscuits, and fruit is served each day in the Carriage House Restaurant, which also serves lunch and dinner. Beyond the plantation is a picturesque island sitting in the middle of a one-acre pond, surrounded by irises. With the beautiful weeping willow leaning over the gazebo, it looked so much like Monet's garden at Giverny that I painted the bridge blue.

Dining

The original carriage house is now a restaurant and tavern, and guests can enjoy a cool mint julep while relaxing in one of the white wooden rockers on the veranda.

Don't Miss

The historic tour is offered every day from nine to five. An entertaining ghost tour is presented every Friday and Saturday night.

The Myrtles Plantation
P.O. Box 1100
St. Francisville, LA 70775
225-635-6277
www.myrtlesplantation.com

Historic Argo Hotel

Crofton, Nebraska

Most of the restless spirits at the Historic Argo Hotel are in the basement. It's not known exactly how many human bodies might be buried down there, and even on the grounds. The "doctors" who operated a popular bogus health clinic there in the 1940s and '50s did not want anyone to know that their patients had died. It would have been bad for business. So bodies were quickly carried out the back door in the middle of the night, or buried in the basement.

Employees refuse to go down there alone. During the renovation of the Argo Hotel, workmen dreaded having to go down to the basement, claiming that they felt like someone or something was down there. A telephone employee, sent to set up the hotel phones, knew nothing about the history of the hotel or its ghosts when he began his chore. He wasn't down there long when he bolted upstairs and absolutely refused to go back down. He reported that he felt as if his every move was being watched, even though he was the only person there. Then "someone" started messing with the lights, turning them off, then back on. He turned to see who it was and came face to face with an apparition.

Intrigued, I went to experience the basement for myself. It was late at night. The owner unlocked the door. I took a few steps down into the darkness, and every hair on my body stood up. I felt afraid. "No, thanks," I said as I backed up out of the stairwell. "I changed my mind."

As a New Age retreat half a century ago, the center became very well known, and boasted of "miracle cures" and "spontaneous healings," as well as one of the very first X-ray machines in the nation. However, of the forty "doctors" who practiced at the center, not one was a licensed physician. These so-called healers used methods including potions, massage, mud baths, and miracle cures to heal the sick, many of whom were deathly ill. Patients flocked to the center from all over the Midwest, often as a last resort. Many patients actually did walk out well, though some didn't. Those who died were quickly buried in the basement or quietly carried out the back door in the middle of the night so as not to tarnish the center's bogus reputation.

The operation was finally shut down in 1954 by the health department. The hotel remained closed for six years, until Dr. Charles Swift Jr. bought it as both his home and his office. Dr. Swift was often called "the most colorful doctor in the land." Serving in the cavalry during World War II, Major Swift was awarded the Silver Star in 1945 for gallantry in Luzon, where he was regimental surgeon. The doctor was known for prescribing a "shot" of this and a "shot" of that. Today, the bar at the hotel is called "Doc's Place" in his honor, where guests come for their "shots."

The Argo has a long history of both prostitutes and movie stars. Aspiring actress Leslie Brooks, voted as

having the best figure in all of Hollywood in 1940, lived at
the Argo for several years before moving west to Hollywood. She became a Ziegfeld Girl, and appeared in thirty-
three movies.

Jerry Bogner, who once managed the Hotel Monte Vista
in Flagstaff (also featured in this book; see page 250), and
his sister, Sandra McDonald, bought the place, which had
been vacant for several years, in 1994. The property was
run-down, and the interior had to be gutted. Jerry admits he has
had several experiences in the hotel. Often during the restoration, when he walked through the front door, he would catch
a shadowy image and feel a draft rush past him as he walked
in, even when there was no wind outside. He later had
trouble with his computer, which began to send strange messages.

Sightings

Baffled about the strange happenings, Jerry contacted
a professional ghost hunter. He purposely didn't tell
her the gruesome stories about the basement.

The psychic examined the hotel from top to
bottom. She determined that the upstairs was usually
"clear," and that most of the ghostly activity was con-
fined to the basement. She saw many distressed
spirits down in the basement and cautioned, "They
do seek light, and will probably move on upstairs."

She also picked up on old Doc Swift: "He is here in
the hotel. He is here to see what is going on. He wanders freely through the hotel."

Best Rooms/Times

Definitely the basement, now the Speak Easy night-club. The ghosts are active any time of the day or night.

The Hotel

In 1912 in Crofton, Nebraska, there were forty-two businesses, four lumberyards, five freight trains passing through daily, and over a hundred prosti-tutes. Nick Michaelis, a Greek immigrant, convinced the town board that he would build a nice hotel if they would put in a sewer. They did, and he named his pristine brick hotel the Argo after the ship that car-ried him to America. The Argo enjoyed its well-earned reputation as the finest hotel in town, until it was sold in 1940 to Dr. Wiebelhaus and began its new life as the natural healing center.

The outside of this very plain, square brick struc-ture, built on the original Lewis and Clark Trail, doesn't hint at the size or grandeur that lies within. Listed on the National Register of Historic Places, the turn-of-the-century Argo Hotel is an imposing three-story redbrick building with 3,600 square feet on each floor, very large crowned windows, lace curtains, ceiling fans, and oak chair boards and moldings. The interior has been restored to its early 1900s ambi-ence, featuring a magnificent oak staircase, fire-places, and tin ceilings. Upstairs are twenty guest rooms, all appointed in period decor, many with brass beds, chandeliers, and pedestal sinks. All rooms include a continental breakfast and a tour of the property.

Dining

Candlelight dining is offered on the main level in an elegant dining room that seats 120 people. Specialties include charbroiled steaks, prime rib au jus, and seafood. Doc's Place, the bar named in Dr. Swift's honor, is also on this level.

Don't Miss

The dreaded basement, now renamed the "garden level," houses the Speak Easy nightclub, complete with a hundred-year-old bar, dance floor, cigar room, and two fireplaces. Hermenia Bogner, nearly ninety years old, who happens to be Jerry and Sandra's mother, plays piano several nights a week, pounding out all the old favorites from the 1920s, '30s, and '40s.

Don't worry too much . . . three staircases lead out of the basement.

Historic Argo Hotel
211 West Kansas
Crofton, NE 68730
402-388-2400 or 800-607-2746

Artist House

❧❧❧

Key West, Florida

The evil doll Chucky in the cult horror flick *Child's Play* has nothing on this real-life demonic doll, who plays sinister tricks and forces people to do nasty things. Robert, a creepy three-foot-tall straw doll with darting beady eyes from which he glares if he doesn't get his way, is said to be possessed by an evil spirit. Through some evil force, he is able to manipulate and control people, making them do things they don't want to do. He drove his owner, Gene Otto, crazy with his demands, each one becoming more and more wicked. But try as he might, Gene could not get rid of Robert. Over and over, he would lock the doll in the attic, only to race downstairs and find him sitting in the rocker in the Turret Room, waiting for him. If he threw him in the trash, Robert would be back upstairs before Gene even got to the stairs. There was just no escaping Robert or his wickedness.

The doll was made by a servant girl who had been abused by the Otto family. It's said that she put a curse on the doll, invoking a series of rituals as she created him. She dressed him in a child's crisp white sailor's suit and gave him to Gene, who named the doll Robert.

From the moment he received the doll, Gene's life began to change—and not for the better. He began to experience a never-ending series of misfortunes. Robert was always to blame, and many people who knew the family agreed that the malicious doll was indeed responsible for a host of evil deeds.

Neighbors would cross the street, eyes focused straight ahead, rather than walk by the magnificent Queen Anne Victorian mansion, with numerous graceful columns and verandas, and a lot of gingerbread detail, highlighted by the magnificent presence of its turret. It wasn't the imposing structure they were afraid of, but its malevolent occupant, whose reputation for evil had spread like wildfire through town.

Gene's parents, Mr. and Mrs. Thomas Otto, built the home in 1898. The youngest of three sons, Robert Eugene Otto would inherit the family home. Gene, as friends called him, studied art at the Academy of Fine Arts in Chicago and the Art Students League in New York before traveling to Europe, where his work created quite a following. In Paris he met Annette Parker, a native of Boston, who was studying music there. They fell in love, and were married in Paris.

Anne was making a name for herself as well, as an accomplished pianist. After she finished her studies in Paris, the couple moved to New York, where Anne performed at the famous Rainbow Room at Rockefeller Center.

They should have stayed in New York. Little did they suspect that back in Key West, the evil Robert was patiently waiting for his owner to return. When the couple moved back into Gene's family home, their lives were changed forever.

As Robert demanded more and more of Gene's time, Anne became deeply distraught by her husband's unsettling behavior. It was almost as if he were possessed by Robert. He would spend hours locked in the Turret Room, alone with the doll. It almost seemed that Gene preferred Robert's company to hers. Many nights Anne would hear Gene sitting alone in the Turret Room, talking and pleading. He blamed Robert for everything bad that happened to him, including his deteriorating relationship with his beloved wife. Anne feared for her husband's sanity.

Robert's reign of terror did not end with Gene's death in 1972; the doll still held his evil control over the house and those in it. Although Robert was stashed in the attic, neighbors began to report hearing an "evil giggle" coming from next door. Some even claimed to hear the doll walking up and down the stairs from the attic, or see him leering down at them with an evil grin through the attic window.

Several years later, a new family bought the house. Robert had a new playmate! Their ten-year-old daughter became Robert's next target. She claims that Robert tortured her. Even today, in her forties, she is tormented by memories of Robert and his sadistic powers. She refuses to talk about the unspeakable horrors she was forced to endure.

Eventually the satanic doll was removed and placed in the East Martello Museum. But the attic of Artist House was not freed of its ghostly presence. Soon after the doll's departure, the ghost of Gene's wife, Anne, took up residence, standing guard against the return of Robert's evil spirit!

Sightings

David Sloan, who runs Key West Ghost Tours, says people frequently report seeing the ghost of a woman dressed in white:

Anne is the protector of the house, and Robert's spirit hasn't been back. Lots of people tell me they have seen a woman in white who goes up and down the staircase. I talked to one lady who felt someone sit on the bed next to her. Then the pillow went down, like someone's head was lying there. Another guest complained that a woman had come through his room.

On one of our tours, we stop across the street from the Artist House. Recently one of our tour guides, Joannie, told me she had just finished talking about the Turret room when they saw a shooting star go right behind the house. I thought to myself, No big deal. Several nights later, I was leading one tour, and there was another tour right behind us. I heard a little boy from the other group say, "Look, a shooting star!"

I looked up to see. This was no shooting star! It was a large orb, slightly bigger than a basketball. It was glowing a greenish blue, about ten feet to the left of the Turret. It went down at about a forty-five degree angle, by the tree line. It lasted for a good five count. Everyone on the tour saw it, and everyone was at a loss for an explanation.

We've seen it several times since. It has always appeared right after we talked about Anne. It's unlike anything I've ever seen.

I asked David if he had ever seen Robert. "Robert is at the East Martello Museum. Sometimes he looks like a regular doll, but I've seen the transformation too. It's just—boom. You can see that something enters him. A lot of people have problems taking photos of Robert. Batteries drain in his presence—watches, Walkmans—and when they leave, the batteries work fine. One guy, who didn't believe, videotaped the museum. When they watched it, the sound cut out when they got to Robert. Very weird."

Mattey Casey manages the ghost tours. He talked about his initial visit to see Robert:

> The first time I went to the museum, the docent began talking to Robert as she approached the case: "Hey, Robert, this is Mary. I have brought someone who wants to see you—"
>
> I thought, What a freak. She is talking to a doll!
>
> Now I do it too. If you saw Robert, even if you didn't know anything about him, you would have the need to say to him, "Hey, Robert, I'm not going to hurt you." It's a very strong presence.
>
> I don't believe that he can kill me, though there are people who believe he can. He is one of the only spirits I've ever encountered who has an oppressive feel. He is very angry.
>
> Robert is beginning to show his age. He is, after all, over a hundred years old. He has that moth-eaten appearance on his face, and his eye-

brows and lips, which were painted on, are starting to fade. He really is incredible craftsmanship. He's missing the little flappy cloth ear on his right side, which just adds to his eeriness.

His hair is a weird yellowish brown. Sometimes it looks like paint, but other times it looks just like an Afro! It really freaks me out. It's wacky. He looks different every time I see him.

What's really creepy is that Robert has a constant companion, a little stuffed lion that he carries around with him wherever he goes. The doll is one thing, but HE's got a doll. It's really weird for one doll to "have" another doll! He has been carrying around that little lion for at least fifty years.

During Key West's Fantasy Fest they close down the Martello and move Robert (and his doll) to the Custom House in Old Town, where they lock him under a Plexiglas cube. They always put a bag of peppermints at his feet, to try to bribe him into being good. They swear that the mints are always gone in the morning.

Robert shares his display case with a red sports jacket that belonged to the first fire commissioner of Key West, and a doll made in the image of the Mallory Square Cookies girl (they keep her in there to keep Robert company). There he sits all day, leaning back in his chair, with his little toy lion in his lap. Many of the people working at the museum believe that he gets out on his own. They say that he hides the key to his case, and at night he lets himself out and walks around. Recently, they cleaned him up and sewed his neck back together. The day after they cleaned him, the bottoms of his feet were dirty again, and there were tiny little footsteps leading down the hall to the door!

Every Christmas, the museum puts Christmas trees up and down the wide hall where Robert is displayed. Late one evening, Lois, who works there, was walking down the hall, turning off every light individually. When she got to the end and turned around, several of the trees had been lit up again. Then she heard a rapping on the glass—*knock, knock, knock.* She went over to Robert's case, which is brave, in my opinion. His hand was at the glass! There is no way to explain how his hand could have been hanging up there at a forty-five-degree angle. She went out of there pretty quick.

I had a chance to go visit Robert. I passed.

Best Rooms/Times

Robert spent most of his time in the attic, where he had his own little room above the Turret Room, now called the Turret Suite. This room has the following description in the inn's brochure: "Turret Suite. The lower level includes a King bed, private bath with antique claw-foot tub/shower, private dressing room, French doors to the Veranda and fairytale stairs that ascend to the upper mezzanine. Here you will find a double bed, dresser, desk and seven tall, magnificent windows that look out over Old Town. There is no other room in Key West quite like this one."

But don't be fooled by the flowery prose. This was the spot where the evil Robert plotted and planned all his wicked misdoings.

The Hotel

Formerly the home of the celebrated Key West painter Robert Eugene Otto and his wife Anne, a concert and jazz pianist, Artist House is an architectural gem. It was built in 1890 by Gene's father, Thomas, a surgeon in the army. Dr. Otto was famous for his work during the devastating smallpox epidemics in Key West.

Today, there are six guest rooms and suites in this elegant Victorian mansion. Filled with period furnishings, the rooms have twelve-foot ceilings, richly detailed original wall coverings, splendid woodwork, fireplaces, and private baths, some with claw-foot tubs. Continental breakfast is served in the lush and intimate tropical garden, by the quaint antique fishpond. The old cistern is now the site of a huge, ten-by-twelve-foot in-ground, heated spa with fountain, surrounded by the original hundred-year-old bricks.

Dining

An outing to the haunted Hard Rock Café is a must for ghost hunters. It's haunted by a startling entity with yellow, glowing eyes, believed to be Robert Curry, Florida's first millionaire. He received the house, and all his money, as a gift from his family. Despondent after he squandered his fortune, he hung himself in the second-floor bathroom. The estate was sold to the Key West Order of Elks. The Elks soon realized that Mr. Curry had never left. Today the staff watches in amazement as drawers systematically open and shut or things float through the air. Passersby have seen the apparition, with its glowing yellow eyes, wandering through the place after hours.

Fogarty's Restaurant is also haunted. It was once a Hooters restaurant, and the third floor was converted into a dorm for the girls. They would wake up to find their shoes arranged in bizarre patterns. Subsequent restaurants on the site failed, until it was learned that Fogarty himself had put a curse on the place. Since it has been renamed after him, the ghost seems appeased.

Don't Miss

David Sloane's Ghost Tours. "As Florida's second oldest city, Key West has more ghosts per capita than any other city in America," claims David. "When Key West was discovered in the sixteenth century, the beach was covered with bones, with skeletons hanging in the trees. Spanish explorers named it Cayo Hueso, or Island of Bones. Cayo eventually became Key, and Hueso evolved to West, or Key West. Ghosts of Indians, explorers, pirates, cigar makers, fishermen, artists, and poets continue to be seen around town."

Tour guides are dressed in Victorian mourning attire: men in black tuxedos, capes, bow ties, and top hats, ladies in long black dresses and capes. They carry a lantern in one hand and ghost repellent in the other, just to be safe! Two tours are offered, the traditional Old Town ghost walk and the Bone Island ghost walk.

"We take you to the sites of many of the Key West ghosts," says David. "Each tour visits ten different haunted locations. In the hour and a half walk, you'll discover the dwelling places of ghosts, ghouls, and benevolent protectors. And you'll learn the stories behind many of the legends of our haunted island paradise: the deadly Key West Cemetery; a Voodoo curse placed on Klansmen after a lynching; the La Concha Hotel's suicide roof, where no less than thirteen jumpers have ended their lives; or the lady in blue at the hanging tree. One of the most famous Key West legends involves a doctor who married a corpse, consummated the marriage, and even crawled into the coffin each night to sleep with the lifeless remains of his wife. And then, of course, there is Robert." For reservations, call (305) 294-9255 or visit *www.hauntedtours.com*.

Artist House
534 Eaton Street
Key West, FL 33040
305-296-3977 or 800-582-7882
e-mail: info@artisthousekeywest.com
www.artisthousekeywest.com

Balsam Mountain Inn

❧

Balsam, North Carolina

The folks on Balsam Mountain have been whispering tales for generations about the strange goings-on at the old Balsam Mountain Inn. Townspeople who once worked at the grand hotel, years before the restoration, tell stories reminiscent of *The Shining*. They talk about how they would meticulously shut down the grand lady for the winter, room by room, then say their final good-byes and drive away, only to turn and look back up from the bottom of the hill to find every light burning brightly again. Weary, they would have to return to the hotel to shut them all off again, only to find them back on as soon as they got to the bottom of the hill again. Children, lured by the spooky, vacant structure, would bravely dare each other to peek through the windows, to be scared out of their wits by the ghostly images of people inside the dining room and lobby.

Standing like a sentinel on a high ridge above Balsam Gap, the three-story Balsam Mountain Inn welcomed its first guests in 1908. For decades visitors arrived by rail at the old Balsam Depot, the highest railway station east of the Rockies, at an elevation of 3,500 feet. Passengers from this era would disembark on cool, starry summer evenings and take a slow stroll or carriage ride up to the inn.

"If you are coming to the mountains, come all the way up," read the advertising slogan of the Balsam Mountain Inn when this Colonial Revival structure was first opened by two brothers, Joseph and Walter, who had been so successful with their boardinghouse that they decided to expand into the hotel business. Wanting everyone to see what a grand place they built, they erected the majestic monument at the top of the highest hill, overlooking the town. After framing the first two floors, the brothers raced to the bottom of the hill to admire their handiwork from the train depot. When they saw that it wasn't visible from that point, they added the third floor, so that both townsfolk and train passengers could not help but notice the palatial retreat.

Not much exists of the town of Balsam today except for the grand old wood-frame hotel sitting high on the mountain. Once a bustling mountain retreat, with three inns, several general stores, and a Baptist church, the town practically vanished in 1959, leaving a single grand reminder of a time when people came from all over the country to this mountain haven.

The lonely hotel had sat vacant for many years, and according to architects only inertia and beaded board were holding it up, when Merrily Teasley purchased the ailing property in 1990 and painstakingly restored it to its original grandeur.

Shortly after she reopened the Balsam, Merrily started hearing reports from guests that someone had tried to enter their rooms. Occasionally, the guests would inquire if there were a ghost. Merrily scoffed at the idea that her hotel was haunted, and figured that someone had just gotten lost on their way to their own room— That is, until one night in the dead of winter, when she was the only other person in the hotel. When the sole occupants reported the next morning that someone had turned the door knob of Room 205, Merrily knew it could not have been a human hand, and she started taking the reports more seriously.

"The first few times I didn't pay attention," Merrily admits. "I figured maybe someone was trying the wrong door, but then, when no one was here but me, that's pretty hard to explain."

Interestingly, the reports only come from Rooms 205 and 207, in the southwest corner of the hotel.

Today, a blank diary is left in each room for guests to record their impressions of the Balsam. The diaries in Rooms 205 and 207 are filled with ghostly accounts.

Sightings

Some guests have actually heard footsteps walking across their room as they lay in bed. Although they could not see anyone in the room, the footsteps continued for hours, pacing back and forth on the wood floors.

Probably many others have heard the phantom at their door, but did not think enough of it to report it. When I stayed, there was only one other couple in my wing at the hotel. They had received their night as a wedding gift from fellow workers at the North Carolina Office of Tourism. They didn't know that the inn was haunted, but realized they too had experienced the ghost.

In the morning, as they were dressing, the doorknob began to turn and jiggle.

"I really didn't think anything of it, until I heard the reports from the others. I was more afraid that the maid would walk in and find me naked," she mused, eyes wide.

The ghost also hangs around the kitchen. Jennifer, a waitress in the Balsam restaurant, reports stories she has heard from other workers. "Sometimes the door to the kitchen suddenly swings wide open, and then closes slowly, as if someone is walking through. The door is so heavy, there is no way it can open on its own. I've also heard talk about footsteps in the dining room, and the smell of perfume. My friend used to work here years ago. She saw the lights go on after they turned them off."

Best Rooms/Times

Ask for Room 205 or 207. Many guests don't even realize they have experienced the ghost, blaming the boisterous noises outside on a drunken guest looking for his room. To date, no one who hears the commotion has opened the door to investigate, so if you hear someone (or something) outside your room, rattling the doorknob and trying to get in, open the door if you dare, and solve the mystery of what awaits on the other side.

The Hotel

The splendid Victorian structure, built in 1905, is perched atop a 6,000-foot mountain. On the National Register of Historic Places, the hotel boasts a one-hundred-foot lobby, a restaurant, a gift shop, and a library with over 2,000 books. Over the years, the inn experienced only minor changes until an extensive restoration was undertaken in 1990 by owner Merrily Teasley, who restored the beautiful hardwood floors, the beaded-board walls, the original artwork, and the Victorian furnishings. Outstanding features include the massive Greek columns throughout the lobby and the two huge porches that encompass both the first and second floors. These are a favorite place for guests to relax and enjoy the magnificent mountain scenery.

The warm, inviting lobby is full of wicker furniture and runs the full hundred-foot length of the hotel. In the fall and winter, guests snuggle up to the huge fireplace in the lobby to warm their toes.

Although each of the original hundred rooms had running water, there were two large public baths, one for ladies and one for men, on opposite wings of the hotel. If your room was on the other side of the hotel, you had a long walk. Today there are eight suites, sixteen rooms with sitting areas, and twenty-six regular rooms. Each has a private bath, some with antique claw-foot tubs.

The inn is perched upon twenty-six glorious acres, with trails, creek, springs, a pond, and lawn games.

Tennis, golf, whitewater rafting, and fishing are nearby.

Dining

The original grand dining room and kitchen are once again open and serving Smoky Mountain specialties to guests. Some evenings, diners are entertained by live piano music. Merrily also hosts dinner theater and murder mystery weekends. Breakfast, as well, is served in the dining room. Early-morning coffee is served in the library, which boasts more than 2,000 volumes of classic books.

Don't Miss

At various times throughout the year, the hotel becomes very lively, as both local and nationally acclaimed musicians make both scheduled and unscheduled performances. You might run into Sheila Adams, Paul Craft, Muriel Anderson, or Tony Ellis Washington strumming a banjo or guitar in the lobby.

Balsam Mountain Inn
P.O. Box 40
Balsam, NC 28707
828-456-9498 or 800-224-9498
e-mail: BalsamInn@earthlink.net
www.balsaminn.com

1843 Battery Carriage House Inn

❧

Charleston, South Carolina

The grotesque, disembodied torso floats off the ground where it might rest, if it had arms, legs, and a head. If startled, it unleashes a horrific sound, much like a deep, guttural growl. Known as the "Headless Torso," the ghoulish entity has been encountered on countless occasions by unsettled guests at the Battery Carriage House. These guests breathlessly recount an unspeakable horror, totally unaware that countless others have witnessed the same beast.

The shocking sight made a believer out of at least one guest. Several years ago, an engineer slept in Room 8. He woke up with a creepy feeling that someone was watching him. He looked up, and next to his bed was the torso of a broad, barrel-chested man hovering in midair between his bed and the wall. The entity was so close to him, he could hear its raspy, labored breathing. Not believing his eyes, he reached out to touch it. The headless torso let out a horrid "guttural growl," then "moaned or uttered some angry sound."

The disturbed engineer checked out, but he could not get over his haunting experience. At his wife's urging, he returned to the scene eight months later to recount his experience and learn more about the history. He was shocked to hear that many others had encountered the strange phenomenon. He kept repeating that he felt threatened, and that the being really frightened him.

The historical explanation for this headless entity is not known. It is possibly the broken remains of a man who "fell" to his death from the mansard roof of the five-story mansion in 1904, or maybe a Confederate soldier, blown apart by the blast of a Yankee rifle.

Not all of the ghosts encountered at the 1843 Battery Carriage House are hostile and grotesque. A well-dressed Victorian gentleman hangs out in Room 10, and a lost Confederate soldier roams outside.

The Battery Carriage House is part of the palatial Stephen-Lathers estate. Built in 1843 during Charleston's golden age, the elegant mansion next door was the childhood summer home of the owner's grandmother, who lived there in the 1890s. Sara Calhoun Simonds grew up in the house. As a spunky young girl, she nearly died when she climbed a tree up onto the roof, where she was playing before she slipped and came tumbling through the ballroom skylight, her fall broken only by the huge crystal chandelier. Her parents, hearing her desperate cries, raced to the room to find her dangling upside down from the chandelier.

The Stephen-Lathers House is a rambling, five-story antebellum mansion complete with double piazzas and a fish-scaled mansard roof. A large ballroom and an extensive library were added after the war. Just across the street, the pristine White Point Gardens was once an oceanfront fortress, the site of ramparts and pirate hangings. Original Civil War cannons dot the sidewalks.

The guest rooms are a part of what used to be the out-buildings, the servants' quarters, and the carriage house, the site of some of the more lurid incidents in the house's rich history. It is rumored to have been a favorite hangout for call girls and strippers in the 1920s and 1930s.

Sightings

May Reynolds, a longtime employee at the Battery Carriage House, has heard so many strange things at the inn that it no longer fazes her.

I don't see them, but I hear them, and I see the results of whatever spirits are here. When I first started, I was here by myself one day. I wasn't scared, because it was the middle of the afternoon. The door was closed to the upstairs staircase. All of a sudden something took the doorknob handle and rattled it back and forth. I thought it was the owner of the house coming down. The door handle turned, and the door swung open wide, all the way back to the wall. I waited for her to come out. I called, "Kat, Kat, are you there?" There was no response, so I went around to the stairs, and there wasn't a soul there. I realized then that I had just en-countered the ghost.

Jennie [who also works at the inn] was here one Thursday night. The lady who brings in the flowers each week was here too. She and Jenny heard keys rattling from the same door, by the stairs. This has happened many times.

Several times I heard two men talking. They seemed to come from the back of the room, but I didn't pay much attention to it at the time. It wasn't until the door incident that I put the two together. The next day I told the owner of the house, "You never told me you had a ghost here! I have heard things."

"Was it the ghost of a man?" the owner asked. He confessed that there were two male ghosts here. One of them is purported to be a young boy who committed suicide by jumping off the piazza. The other one is a soldier in the civil war. Since the war ended, he's been hanging around this end of town, not knowing what to do or where to go.

The things that he told me frightened me, because I didn't expect it.

Eduardo serves the breakfasts. One morning he came in early, and heard voices. He went to investigate, thinking the maids must have left a radio on. There was no radio, and no other was up yet. Another time, he was working in the kitchen very early. The lobby was locked, and the room was dark. Suddenly Eduardo heard someone ringing the bell on the desk in the lobby. They kept banging on it like they were very impatient. Startled, he unlocked the door and turned on the lights. No one was there.

Jenny has heard the bell ring, too. Believe it

or not, she was sitting right at the desk, and it rang, a shrill ring. She jiggled the desk to see if she could duplicate the sound, but there was no way. She screamed, "Ghost, go away and leave me alone." So although I am not afraid, I do talk to them. My thinking is that they want someone to know that they are here hanging around. They've certainly let me know.

We get a lot of letters from guests, telling us about their experiences. They say they felt silly talking about it, or they were afraid we wouldn't believe them. We would have. We received one letter from a guest who wishes to remain anonymous. Her story is the same one told by others staying in Room 10. She woke up to find a man in the room. He was well dressed, with a topcoat and top hat. Scared to death, she screamed for her sister, who was sharing the room. When her sister woke up, the ghostly intruder had vanished.

"I think there are lots of spirits that live in these houses down here," May laments. "Whoever they are want you to know they are here. I have heard if they are bothering you, just tell them to leave you alone and they will. It's just all very strange.

"I'm not so scared anymore, but I do worry about ghosts going home with me. I don't want ghosts at my house."

Best Rooms/Times

The gentleman ghost welcomes ladies to Room 10. Avoid Room 8, unless you are prepared to meet the Headless Torso.

The Inn/Hotel

Built in 1843, the Greek Revival mansion was remodeled in 1870, with the addition of the slate mansard roof, bracketed cornices, ballroom, and library. In the 1980s the historic outbuildings were converted into eleven guest rooms and one suite. Each room has a private entrance and is decorated in an antebellum theme.

Dining

Don't miss the chance to dine at one of Charleston's most famous haunts, Poogan's Porch Restaurant (72 Queen Street; 843-577-2337) in downtown Charleston. Poogan was a feisty Yorkshire terrier who spent much of his life dog-napping on the front porch. When he eventually died of old age, he was laid to rest under his favorite tree, with a headstone befitting the precocious pooch. But he isn't the only one to haunt the establishment that bears his name.

Inside the restaurant, a reticent old lady is frequently spotted dining alone in one of the less conspicuous booths. Evidently she hopes that no one will notice her, but restaurant diners and staffers often see her, and even guests at Mills House Hotel next door have observed her. If she sees you take notice of her, she vanishes. Her name is Zoe St. Ammand, or just Zoe, as she is referred to at Poogan's. She was a lonely child (her mother died when she was just six), and she grew up to become a spinster schoolteacher. She lived in the old building with her sister until her death in 1954. Ever since Poogan's opened in the mid-1970s, Zoe has been a regular, sitting shyly at her table. On more mischievous days, she amuses herself by playing pranks—opening doors, setting off the alarms, and spooking the dog.

Don't Miss

After dark, tour the haunts of this historic city, and hear about the many ghosts from Charleston's colorful past. Ghosts of Charleston's tour guides lead you on a tour of the city's most haunted sights, and weave ghostly tales of haunted houses, restaurants, pirate hangouts, battlefield ghosts, and the deep-rooted superstitions of Charleston's Gullah culture. Ghosts of Charleston Walking Tour, (800) 854-1670 or *info@tour-charleston.com*

1843 Battery Carriage House Inn
20 South Battery
Charleston, SC 29401
843-727-3100 or 1-800-775-5575
e-mail: info@batterycarriagehouse.com
www.batterycarriagehouse.com

Ben Lomond Historic Suite Hotel

❦

Ogden, Utah

One of the toughest and most stressful jobs around is that of a housekeeper in a haunted hotel. You are required to walk, all alone, down dark ominous corridors, and bravely enter rooms known to be occupied by ghosts. You never know who (or what) might be lurking behind that door.

"It's scary," admits Gerdi Curran, who has worked at the Ben Lomond for over ten years.

I didn't believe in all these things. They scared me to death. When I started, they gave me the second floor and the eleventh floor. On my very first day, when I went into the bathroom in 1102, I felt a very cold chill . . . a very cold chill. When I stepped out to get a rag, it felt like someone pushed me hard from behind! I said to myself, "What is going on here!"

I went to talk to the supervisor. They were laughing and giggling. "That's the ghost," they told me. I knew if I wanted to keep my job, I had to go back up there.

When I got to room 1102, I said out loud, "Okay, leave me alone!" And they pretty much did, after that.

One time, I was vacuuming underneath the bed. The bed is high, so you can vacuum under it. The vacuum got stuck. I pulled it, thinking it had caught on something. I pulled it real hard. It would not budge. I said to myself, "Whoa! They are at it again!" I didn't want to go downstairs and tell the supervisor, because I knew they would laugh.

A week later, my supervisor came to me and said, "You left water in 1102 in the bathtub." I said, "No way." I went up there, and sure enough, there was water in the bathtub. The next thing I know, the phone in the room starts ringing. Every time I answered it, no one was there. So I went downstairs to tell the supervisor that I did not leave the water in the bathtub. Again, they were laughing. I learned that someone drowned in 1102 on their wedding night, and now they are a ghost, that's what they told me.

A lot of guests had problems with the phone ringing, too, especially at night. The manager asked the telephone company to come look. The man was down in the basement, where the main controls are. On my way down to help him out, I heard a voice saying, "Gerdie." It was a woman's voice. When I got to the repairman, he accused me of banging on the walls. He thought it was me, but I had just gotten there. He said he heard voices, and lots of banging. But it wasn't me.

Sometimes you can smell perfume. It smells like lilacs. What's interesting is that when you go on the elevator, it stops on the fifth floor, even if you haven't pushed that button. When it stops, you can smell that same light perfume.

I learned that the ghost in 1106 is also a woman. She came from out of town and stayed at the hotel during World War II. Her son was injured during the war, and she was waiting to see him. My general manager said she never left the hotel. She is still waiting, hoping to see her son. No one told her that her son died.

The ghost in 1101 is a male ghost. He is supposed to be the son of the lady ghost in 1102. He came here and found out his mother was drowned on her wedding night, so he killed himself.

I go to work at four every morning. Sometimes I've seen what looks like smoke on the staircase. I know now that is the lady ghost. It's like the smoke lingers, then it forms a shape. It's the shape of a woman.

A lot of times when you go into the rooms, there is an imprint on the bed, like someone had laid down, so the supervisors started watching us to see if any of the staff pops in for a nap while we are supposed to be working. They watched for two or three months, and nothing. It's amazing.

I don't like it when the ghosts push me. I haven't fallen down, but they push hard. One time I had to set all the clocks ahead. Everything was fine until I got to 212. Then I felt something, like someone had come up behind you, pushing you.

There is a tunnel underneath the hotel. It used to go all the way to the Union Station on Twenty-fifth. It was underneath the whole town. They used it to smuggle booze. There was a lot of crime in this city.

At one time, this hotel was a rooming house. Madames, prostitutes, gangsters, they all lived here.

I give tours here to school kids. Once I had a group from junior high. We experienced something very interesting. We went up the stairs to an isolated place on the second floor. All the rooms were dark. We were waiting for the rest of the group to come up when we felt a big nasty chill. All of a sudden the bathroom door to the men's room swung open and then banged shut. No one was close to it. The kids got it on video. They were really scared. I said, "Wait a minute, maybe someone went in there." So I went in to check it out. But there was no one there.

After that, we went down into the basement. The kids were still taking video. When you looked through the video camera, you saw orbs, just floating everywhere. Orbs are ghost energy. They were just floating on the video camera. The kids still have the tape.

Another time I took forty kids down into the tunnel. We were just standing there, and I felt someone behind me. I turned around, but no one was there. Suddenly someone grabbed me! I jumped. One little girl screamed, "Oh my god, I just got grabbed!" She was grabbed too. It was like long bony fingers grabbing you.

Then I saw legs . . . no arms, no stomach, just legs, moving, just moving. It was very interesting. I think it's that guy from 1010. No head. Nothing. Just legs, then three orbs, just floating. The kids saw it too. They were scared.

Now, I won't go down there by myself, uh-uh, nope!

I never believed in ghosts. Never. Till I start working here. My son worked here for a while too. He got chased on the fifth floor. But he couldn't take it. He works at the Marriott now. Before I go into a room, I always announce myself. I say, "I'm here." After so long they probably know me now. It's really amazing.

Sightings

Don Flink managed the hotel in the 1980s, prior to its current ownership. It was part of his job to investigate when the staff made complaints. He said many of the construction workers walked off the job during the 1984 restoration because of the ghosts.

Don worked at the hotel for six years in various capacities. He saw a lot of unexplainable things during his tenure here. "The middle elevator in the lobby would suddenly start up and stop at the tenth floor, like someone up there had pushed the call button. One time it stayed up there twenty minutes. With the programmed wiring, that's impossible.

"The night crew was hearing loud sounds and doors slamming upstairs. They called me to check it out. We looked around, but there was no one upstairs. It was then that I made a management decision for the night crew to get a radio!"

Another time, when working with the night auditors, he heard sounds that sent a chill up his spine. "Those were not normal building sounds," Don claims. He says his entire experience at the hotel was very eerie and more than a little chilling.

As I was finishing this chapter, the phone rang. It was Chad Vander Kolk. He had been a guest at the hotel, and when he told the clerk his experiences, she suggested he call me.

"When were you there?" I asked.

"Last weekend," he replied.

We were down there with my buddies' band, Illusion 33. We heard about this haunted hotel, and decided to stay there. We were pretty pumped up, but they put us on the fourth floor, so we didn't think anything would happen. I changed clothes to go to the guitar shop nearby. My clothes were thrown all over the floor. When we got back, all my clothes were folded neatly on the bed. I said it must have been the maid, but my buddy said he had seen them folded before we left. That was the first thing.

Later on we went on the ghost tour, and we were in the room where the man stabbed his wife. There was a mint on the bed. I could see my friend reaching for the mint. I said, "Oh, no, Jesse, don't mess with that, the ghosts will get you!" But he took the mint anyway. The next morning when he was in the bathroom, the faucet blew off the shower and hit him in the leg. Later, we were sitting around the room listening to a CD. It was really warm, so I had my shirt off. All of a sudden it felt like someone opened a thirty-degree freezer right next to my neck. It was unreal. Jason, the lead singer, was sitting on the floor. His eyes got real big, and he said, "Dude, can you feel that?" I felt it, that's for sure. We were like, "No way!"

I heard on TV that you can catch ghosts on camera. I took about sixty pictures with my digital camera. In lots of them, there were these glowing silver balls. They showed up all over the place. I even caught one of the balls moving. I took two pictures in a row, and the balls had moved across the room. In one shot, there were fifteen or twenty of them. We think they were following us around the hotel!

Best Rooms/Times

The most haunted guest rooms are 1101, 1102, and 1106, though incidents have occurred on every floor. The lobby and the basement are also hot spots of activity.

The Hotel/Inn

Making its debut in 1891, the high-rise portion was added in the 1920s to accommodate passengers from the new Transcontinental Railroad and Union Station. Today this thirteen-story Second Renaissance Revival hotel has been transformed into an all-suite hotel. On the National Register of Historic Places, the hotel has maintained many of its original art deco features. Every suite has a separate living room and sleeping area and is equipped with a wet bar, a refrigerator, and two televisions. Many of the rooms have a Jacuzzi tub. The hotel also accepts pets.

There is a cardiovascular fitness center and spa at the hotel, and great skiing nearby. An evening "Manager's Social," with complimentary cocktails, soda, juice, and hors d'oeuvres, is held in the lobby on weekdays. "Lately, the conversation has been about ghosts," claims reservation manager Karen Galloway. "Just this week we had some people who were taking pictures with a digital camera, and caught several orbs. They were very excited."

Dining

Yesteryear's Victorian Restaurant is located on the main level, serving breakfast, lunch, dinner, and a complimentary breakfast buffet to overnight guests.

Club Esquire, a lively jazz and blues club, serves lunch and dinner. In the evenings guests enjoy live entertainment by nationally touring bands.

Don't Miss

Although Ogden began as a religious Mormon community, with the completion of the Transcontinental Railroad and Union Station, all sorts of characters came into town. On Twenty-fifth Street, near the train station, one could witness gambling, prostitution, drug sales, robbery, rape, and even murder. Ogden grew and became a rough city. Even crime boss Al

Capone commented in the 1920s that Ogden was too wild a town for him.

Today you can stroll down the once-notorious street, laden with the ghosts of a wilder time, not so long ago, and enjoy the modern-day mix of restaurants, boutique shops, antique stores, and art galleries.

Ben Lomond Historic Suite Hotel
2510 Washington Boulevard
Ogden, UT 84041
801-627-1900 or 888-627-8897
e-mail: tgalloway@benlomondhotel.com
www.benlomondhotel.com

Biltmore Suites Hotel (formerly the Shirley Hotel)

Baltimore, Maryland

One of the most decorated officers in the English Royal Navy built this hotel as a trysting place for his affair with a dance-hall floozy named Shirley. The notorious affair between Shirley and Sir Charles Madison, a shipping tycoon and a member of Her Majesty's Royal Fleet, was a source of embarrassment to the queen.

In 1890 Sir Charles built an entire hotel to facilitate his affair, and set his mistress up as the innkeeper. That way, when he was in America, he could live with her without suspicion. To further accommodate his liaison, he added two secret stairways that allowed him to reach her boudoir unnoticed.

Sir Charles's wife, Lady Madison, herself a direct descendent of the royal family, insisted that her husband take her to the New World. Finally, he gave in and allowed her to accompany him on a trip. He was so consumed with lust for

Miss Shirley, he foolishly checked his wife into his mistress's hotel. Each night, he waited patiently until his wife was sound asleep, then quietly retreated to Shirley's waiting arms. They got away with it for several nights. On the third night, he became careless. With his wife sound asleep, or so he thought, he openly embraced Miss Shirley in the courtyard of the hotel. Lo and behold, his wife woke up, found her two-timing husband missing, and caught the adulterers in the act. Enraged, Lady Madison grabbed a fireplace poker and brutally struck Shirley until she lay mortally wounded in the courtyard.

Shirley has stayed on at the hotel, waiting for her lover to return. She greets guests on the stairway and in the halls, or in her room.

The indecent hotel no longer bears her name. It has been renamed several times this century and has housed a variety of tenants, even becoming an all-women's dorm for one of the local colleges. When the current owners purchased the hotel several years ago, everything was painted pink. Restoration continues on the grand Victorian hotel, which still bears traces of crimson in its carpets, paint, and wallpaper.

Sightings

Bruce Dalrymple, general manager of the Biltmore Suites, says that although he has never personally seen Miss Shirley, he has encountered "a lot of strange things," including footsteps, voices, and music coming from Shirley's room.

Bruce tells about one of his guests who was at the hotel for a hardware convention:

The man was staying on the fourth floor. A few hours later, he came running back down to the lobby, white as a ghost. He could barely talk. He told us that as he walked up to his room, he looked up the staircase to the top floor and saw a lady dressed in white looking back down at him from the ledge. When he got to the third floor, he saw her step away from the rail. He kept coming up the stairs. When he got to the fourth floor, she vanished into thin air, right in front of him.

Another young lady, attending a wedding at the hotel, came down to the desk about 10:30 P.M. and asked me if a woman had ever died violently at the hotel. Before I told her anything, I asked her why she asked. She told me that when she got to the second floor, it was real cold, and she could feel a disturbed presence, but as soon as she got down to the first floor, it passed. Shirley's room was 214.

When I first came to the hotel, I inspected the rooms after the maids had cleaned them, and they would be immaculate. When guests would check in, the rooms would be in a shambles. I know they were made up, because I had checked them myself. We are a secured hotel, so there is no way anyone could have gotten in.

Sedonia Taylor, who has worked at the hotel for many years as a maid, concurs. "I cleaned those rooms, and went home. The next morning, they would tell me that the room hadn't been made. I started to show them every room I made up, so they would see that they had been done. I would hear her, too. I would never hear the room door open; the doors inside her room would go crazy, opening and closing."

Other guests report hearing voices and laughter coming from Shirley's room.

Best Rooms/Times

Miss Shirley still occupies the same room she has kept for over a hundred years, Room 214. Keep your eyes on the upstairs banisters as you ascend the Hitchcock-style staircase. Most sightings occur in the middle of the night.

The Hotel

The Biltmore Suites Hotel is a truly grand nineteenth-century Victorian Hotel, in the heart of the Mount Vernon district of historic downtown Baltimore, in walking distance of Antique Row and the Inner Harbor. Its original architecture has been historically preserved, as is evident in the main stairway. The stairs were completely dismantled, cleaned, and re-assembled on steel beams. The hotel's interior wood-work, all made of ash, is original. The original thirty rooms were converted into seventeen rooms and eight suites, each with opulent Victorian furnishings and private baths.

Nearly a century ago, an elevator was installed in the secret stairwell. The elevator is unusual in its tiny size (just three by four feet) and style, reminiscent of a typical European elevator.

Dining

Accommodations include a full European breakfast of breads, pastries, cereals, fresh fruits, and an assortment of juices, teas, and coffees. Occasionally an evening reception features international wines and lagers, with complimentary hors d'oeuvres, served in the infamous courtyard where Miss Shirley was bludgeoned to death.

Don't Miss

A visit to the USS *Constellation* is in order. Just a short walk from the hotel, this World War II memorial is haunted by a young gunman who lost his life on the battleship. He appears on the gun deck, where the acrid smell of ghostly gunsmoke occasionally permeates the air.

Biltmore Suites Hotel
205 West Madison Street
Baltimore, MD 21201
410-728-6550 or 800-868-5064
e-mail: contact@biltmoresuites.com
www.biltmoresuites.com

Historic Broadway Hotel
and Tavern

Madison, Indiana

Charles, the resident ghost at the Historic Broadway Hotel, is a feisty spirit who loves to gamble. He is credited with winnings of over $18,000!

Perky hotel owner Libby Hancock says she "wasn't scared of no ghost," so when the previous owners warned her that the hotel was haunted, Libby was undaunted. It wasn't long before she encountered the ghost at first hand. This ghost likes to play with electrical mechanisms. The jukebox will play in the middle of the night, lights go on and off, and phones ring off the hook. When they are answered, no one is there.

One time, Libby claims, "They tried to save my life." During her first winter, shortly after the central heat was turned on, everyone working at the hotel became ill, and even Libby took on a chalky cast and began passing out. At the same time, the ghostly antics seemed to reach a peak.

One night when she was working on her computer, no matter what she typed, when she printed it, the computer only printed the words *Historic Broadway Hotel* over and over, in different fonts and angles. On one of these strange printouts was the phone number of her brother. His phone number had never been entered into the computer, so there was no way this was a computer glitch.

That's weird, she thought—maybe I need to call him. So she called, and everything was fine. But Libby was still feeling spooked, so she ran downstairs to join her sister and a friend, Tom, in the bar. As soon as she sat down, the phone started ringing, chairs started scooting around the room, and the jukebox blared by itself. "Okay, I've had enough," shrieked Libby's sister. "Let's get out of here."

But Libby didn't want to leave her hotel. Determined to find out who, or what, was trying so hard to communicate with them, she ran up to get her ouija board. As soon as she got it out of the box and placed it on the table, the pointer started racing on its own, jerking from letter to letter. Tom, a big, strong guy, uttered a garbled "whoa."

Libby took charge: "Who are you?" she demanded.

"C-H-A-R-L-E-S M-O-R-G-A-N."

"Why are you here at the Broadway Hotel?"

"T-O H-A-V-E F-U-N," it spelled. That was the last coherent answer the group could make out. The pointer spun furiously, stopping on the same two letters, C and O, over and over. Not being able to make sense of it, they finally put the board up and forgot about it until the next day.

The next morning, Libby felt so bad she went to the hospital. When she got back, she smelled gas, so she called a repairman. He found a carbon monoxide leak in the heating system that could have killed everyone in the hotel, and almost did. They had finally found the cause of everyone's weird sickness.

That night Libby and Tom were talking about the events of the night before when Tom yelled, "That's it. That's what the spirit in the ouija board was trying to tell us. He was trying to warn us. The symbol for carbon monoxide is CO!"

Libby is very grateful to Charles for trying to save her life. She finds herself walking around talking to him, although now he gets the blame for most everything that happens. Charles is also credited with a lucky gambling streak.

Sightings

After all her hard work, Libby needed a much-earned vacation, so she booked a flight to the Bahamas. She wondered why the plane was so empty, and why there were no other guests at the hotel. Then she learned that hurricane Erin was about to hit. Even the employees of the hotel vacated, rushing home to save their possessions. They left Libby alone in the hotel with just one large candle, no electricity, no food, and no water. The hurricane was raging outside, wreaking havoc on the island. There was no way off, and there was no one to help her. Abandoned, and giddy from fright and starvation, Libby passed the time by chatting to "Charles." After two harrowing nights, the storm finally passed, and the hotel staff returned. Libby went down to the casino, happy to mingle among the crowds of gamblers.

"Charles, if you're here with me, I need $1,000 to

pay the phone bill," she requested as she sat down at a blackjack table.

"I couldn't lose after that," she claims. As people gathered around the table to watch, Libby gathered in $1,700.

"You must be a professional," the man to her right remarked.

"No, it's 'Charles,' the ghost of the Broadway Hotel. He is here with me," she explained as she scooped up another handful of chips.

The dealer agreed. "Ya, she do had de spirit."

Soon, every time the cards were dealt, the growing crowd of onlookers chanted, "Charles, Charles." After each subsequent winning, Libby made sure to thank Charles out loud. By the end of the evening, Libby had won over $1,700.

"I have no doubt it was him," claims Libby, and she thanked Charles after each win.

Libby told all her friends about Charles and her lucky streak. One friend, on the way to Las Vegas, called Libby from the airport, asking to borrow Charles.

"I don't know if you can send a spirit through the phone or not, but if you can, I'll send him over," she offered.

The friend was blown away when he won $17,000 that night. He called Libby to say thanks. "Just be sure to bring him back, and I get half," she quipped. Hmm, maybe a lucrative new side business at the Broadway—ghost rental.

Best Rooms/Times

"Sensitive" guests claim that Room 10 is haunted, though most action occurs down in the tavern. "We hear all kinds of things at the bar," says chef Kathy. "The music goes on and off all the time, and we hear footsteps, and chairs being scooted up, like someone bellying up to the bar."

The Hotel

The Historic Broadway Tavern Hotel is the oldest continuously operated hotel and tavern in Indiana. During the Civil War, it became a haven to slaves traveling on the underground railway. Traveling north from Kentucky, the newly freed slaves found respite at the hotel. Since then, the hotel has accommodated a number of famous and notorious characters traveling the Ohio River, including John Wilkes Booth.

On display in the lobby is the original deed dated 1834, as well as the original bar application, made official by the signatures of thirty upstanding citizens of Madison, vouching for the character of Jacob Smith, proprietor.

There are seventeen guest rooms on the top two floors, small and sparsely furnished, designed for the riverboat traveler. Many are furnished with the hotel's original oak or iron beds, dressers, and armoires. All have new paint, ceiling fans, and private baths. Several of the rooms on the second floor look out over the courtyard.

Unique features at the hotel include a beautiful locally carved oak bar, a unique oak corner front lobby desk, and a New Orleans–style courtyard where weekend guests enjoy live jazz or blues.

Dining

The restaurants are a family affair, run by Libby's sister Kathy, a classically trained chef. There is a formal dining room, as well as a casual café off the bar. The carriage house behind the hotel hosts a sports bar. On weekends, brunch and blues are served up in the New Orleans–style courtyard. The original livery stable is used for receptions and banquets.

Don't Miss

Several times a year the hotel hosts "Saloon Days," recreating the hotel's bawdier days. Actors dress in vintage attire and mingle with guests, hosting poker games while cancan girls put on a show. Other weekend entertainment includes a robbery and a gunfight.

Historic Broadway Hotel and Tavern
313 Broadway Street
Madison, IN 47250
812-265-2346

The Brookdale Lodge

✿

Brookdale, California

Nestled deep in the haunted redwood forests of the Santa Cruz Mountains, the rustic Brookdale Lodge is vaguely reminiscent of the secluded gingerbread house in the story of Hansel and Gretel.

After a 1920s feature in *Ripley's Believe It or Not*, the lodge became world-famous, and was host to a long string of celebrities, politicians, and gangsters. It became a world-class retreat, attracting international celebrities who arrived by railroad on the old logging lines. Others camped in tents or stayed in cabins. Guests would come to fish, swim, ride horses, and play horseshoes or tennis for a week at a time. Marilyn Monroe, Clark Gable, Joan Crawford, and Mae West all vacationed at the famed Brookdale. Shirley Temple and Johnny Weissmuller had homes nearby. Herbert Hoover loved to fish off the bridge.

The original lodge was built in 1890 for the local judge on the site of the Grover lumber mill. The mill's headquarters, built from logs, were converted into a hotel, and the extensive acreage became campgrounds and summer cabins.

In 1922, after Dr. F. K. Camp purchased the hotel, Clear Creek changed course, cutting a channel through the lodge. Camp hired architect Horace Contin to construct a dining room around the natural brook. For seventy feet the creek passed through the dining room, beneath a large atrium skylight that allowed sunlight to nourish the indoor trees, ferns, and other foliage that lined the stream. At night, colorful underwater lights illuminated the sparkling waters, and people could watch fish swimming by as they dined. From Honeymoon Bridge, a rustic canopy built over the falls, people could catch their own dinner.

In the 1940s gangsters and bootleggers found the Brookdale to be an ideal location with its quiet, out-of-the-way location, isolated in the redwood forests. During this time secret passageways, hidden rooms, and an underground tunnel were added. It's rumored that bodies are buried beneath the floor.

Ghost stories at the Brookdale Lodge abounded long before the gangsters took over. In the 1920s Dr. Camp's young niece, Sara, fell into the creek and drowned. Her childlike spirit began appearing shortly after her death. Later reports center around another little girl who drowned in the hotel swimming pool in the 1960s. Reports of loud splashing sounds and a dancing shadow are common, even when no one is in the pool area.

When the logging company was in operation, many of its employees lived in company cabins on the site. There are grisly reports of a man who brutally shot his wife, and of a little boy who met his death in another cabin. Some of these cabins were later converted into Brookdale's motel rooms, while others are rented month-to-month.

Sightings

Jim Mangin, a software systems engineer at Sun Microsystems, says he still gets the shivers each time he relates his ghostly encounter:

I grew up in that area. Everyone knew that the place was haunted, but I really didn't know by whom. When I was in high school, it was all closed down, and we would go in and explore. If you went to the back you could get to the old dance floor, and the old indoor pool. It was empty then. It was really creepy. We never went at night.

Many years later, I went back with a friend to the bar. I didn't know about the little girl. We were standing in the lobby, and I noticed a little girl sitting alone in the bar. She had blond hair, tied in a ponytail, and she was wearing a blue-and-white dress. I was wondering why someone would bring a little girl to a bar and then leave her all alone. I was looking around for her parents.

My friend was at the display case, reading old newspaper articles about the ghosts. I wasn't really listening until he started talking about a little girl. All the hair on the back of my neck was standing straight up, and I had goose bumps all over my body. I stepped toward my friend and then turned back to look again at the little girl. She was gone. I went into the bar and asked the bartender about the child. She said, "Yeah, right." There were several other people in the bar, but none of them had seen the girl. There was no way for her to leave without being seen. It was just the most bizarre feeling. When I told my friend that I had seen the little ghost girl, it freaked him out too. She was real, she was so real. She wasn't see-through or anything. It's definitely something I will never forget.

Edith Spears, Brookdale's manager, was once the desk clerk. "I have never actually seen anything, but occasionally I get creeped out. It just never feels empty to me. I never feel like I'm alone, even when I am. I used to hear a lot of reports when I worked at the front desk from guests or people just visiting."

Her son, however, has conversations with one of the ghosts. "Recently we moved into one of the old cabins on the property. My son has seen a girl around sixteen, inside the cabin. He has seen her several times now. He says that she looks just like a real person. She told him she is here just to let him know that she is here."

Best Rooms/Times

The lobby, the bar, and the pool area have the most sightings. The two motel wings, originally cabins, sometimes get reports of hauntings, especially of the young boy who died in one of the cabins during the time of the logging camp. Of these, Rooms 31, 32, and

33 in the building behind the pool have the most sightings.

The Hotel/Inn

The impressive log lodge is decorated with rare, unusual, and often hand-made adornments. Tanglewood gingerbread hangs from the log verandas. The chandeliers are welded from horseshoes from the old mill. The forty-six rooms at the lodge are primitive and sparsely furnished. The Creekside Cottage is outside in a lovely, secluded creekside setting. It features a Victorian bedroom and sitting room with a fireplace in each, antique furnishings, a Jacuzzi tub, a full kitchen, and complimentary champagne.

An indoor swimming parlor is off the main lobby.

Dining

At the world-famous Brookdale dining room, guests are seated on balconies and terraces above the babbling brook, where cool bubbling water tumbles just inches away. There are still plenty of trout and crawdads swimming by, though guests no longer fish for their dinner.

Three fireplaces, made from massive river rocks, lend a cozy atmosphere to the lounge and Fireside Room. There is live entertainment on Friday and Saturday, and guests still dance on the original "retro" black-and-white-checkered dance floor.

Don't Miss

The secrets of the majestic Santa Cruz Mountains have held the public captivated, not just by the Indian myth and local legend. For years the beckoning forests have been a source of mystery and fear. For all the beauty of the redwoods, the hills supposedly host a large percentage of Santa Cruz's satanic rituals and murders.

Nestled in those hills is the historic Roaring Camp and Big Trees Narrow-Gauge Railroad (831-335-4484). Tracing its heritage as far back as 1857, the train is a rare reminder of that colorful era when gold miners, lumberjacks, and other early pioneers chugged over the mountains of the American West. Today it takes visitors between Roaring Camp and the Santa Cruz beach and boardwalk. It hosts a variety of special events, including western hoe-downs, robbery reenactments, and a Halloween Ghost Train.

As the train twists and turns, carrying tourists along the mountain tracks, a lone woman has been spotted stepping from the woods onto the tracks in the path of the oncoming train. Each time, the startled conductor quickly jams the brakes, bringing the train to a screeching halt, only to find no one there.

Another haunt, well known to locals, is the Red, White, and Blue Beach (831-423-6332), a private nudist beach on Highway 1. One ghost is that of an old sailor who walks around the camp and into the owner's farmhouse. He is believed to be the sea captain who built the clapboard house in 1857. When sunbathers approach, he just stands there and stares, and he does not respond if he is spoken to.

The other ghost is a young girl named Gwendolyn, who is spotted strolling along the beach in turn-of-the-century clothing. When the current owners built a barbeque pit, they dug up a skeleton. Thinking they might have come upon an old Indian burial ground, they called experts at UCSC. The bones were analyzed and determined to be those of a young woman buried eighty to ninety years ago. Gwendolyn mysteriously disappeared while visiting her uncle, who owned the place in the early 1900s.

The Brookdale Lodge
11570 Highway 9
P.O. Box 903
Brookdale, CA 95007
831-338-6433
e-mail: manager@brookdalelodge.com
www.brookdalelodge.com

The Buxton Inn—1812

❧

Granville, Ohio

A group of people who call themselves "the Towns-people" frequent the sidewalks in front of the Buxton Inn, watching the daily activities of the inn and its guests. Sometimes just one or two stand peacefully, watching, and sometimes a large mob marches back and forth, almost as if in protest. These people do not rest until they get their way. Luckily, most of us cannot see the Townspeople, but they are there, watching. Sometimes they come in.

The Buxton Inn is comprised of several different buildings. At the core of the main building is a wooden structure that was built as a tavern in 1812. It housed the first post office in Granville and eventually became a stagecoach stop, where weary travelers could sleep on primitive straw beds and cook their food in open fire pits.

In 1865 Major Buxton purchased the inn, named it after himself, and ran it for forty years. He added a ballroom on the second floor, where it is rumored that one local citizen, being "high of spirit," rode his horse up the main staircase and into the midst of a party.

In 1905 another colorful character, Ethel Bonnie Bennel, bought the inn. Ethel loved to party, had a flair for big hats, and always wore blue. She had performed at the opera in New York, and loved to throw elaborate parties. When she died in 1934, she bequeathed the inn to one of her employees, Nell Scaller, who then ran the Buxton for thirty-eight years.

Today Orville Orr, a Protestant minister, and his wife, Audrey, graciously share their inn with its past inhabitants. When the Townspeople speak, they listen.

Renee Rivers, a close friend of the Orrs, has been instrumental in helping the couple understand what was going on in their inn. Renee has known for years that she has "the gift."

Renee tells her story: "When I was a child, I didn't know I was different. I always knew things before they happened. My mother used to punish me because I knew things that I had no business knowin'. I didn't know why they even bothered to ask me questions, because I just assumed that everyone knew things the same way I did.

"Sometimes it makes you nervous, but you learn to live with it," she confides about her "gift." Renee has had "hundreds" of experiences while visiting the Buxton. "I have seen people in the tavern, the Stagecoach People, sitting around a fire in the fireplace, and I didn't even know the history of the place. They would be laughin' and jokin', having a good time. Once in a while one of them would notice me, and start talkin' to me."

It was on Renee's advice that the Orrs bought the house next door.

I would see groups of people, they called themselves the Townspeople, marching up and down the street outside the home, as though they were picketing. I told them [the Orrs], "The spirits want you to buy this house and restore it." This went on for months. Finally I told the Orrs, "Go over today with a check, or it will be too late and you won't be able to get it." They did, and sure enough, another offer came the very next day.

The spirits tell me, "Do this, and do that," naggin' me all the time. I beg the Orrs to please do what they ask, so these people will just leave me alone. I see them a lot in the ballroom. I can hear the music down the hall. I saw Major Buxton, too. I saw his spirit trying to enter Mr. Orr's body.

I've seen a dark-haired woman on the balcony outside Room 7, shaking a rug as if she was cleanin' up. One day I had to sleep in that room. She tried her best to force me out. She succeeded. I have never slept in her room again. You don't get much sleep in that room if you're at all sensitive.

Every time I come, I have some brand-new experience. If I came right now, before the day was over, I'd have an experience. If I sleep in Room 9, I usually leave with a new recipe. In Room 10, I get healing formulas. Each room does a different thing with me. It's all good. A lot of information has come through here, a lot of direction and support. This place is conducive to clear messages; spirit comes more forcibly here.

Sometimes I wonder why they chose me. I have talked to a lot of people from all over the United

States, and I have heard a lot of spiritual revelation. I know that as people go to the other side, they do come back to support you and offer guidance.

There are a lot of ghosts at the Buxton. Some are just hangin' around, like they don't know time has passed. Some of them can see us. Some of them come to tell us things.

Sightings

The Buxton Inn is one of the few places, among all those I visited, where I actually had a full-fledged ghost experience, and believe me, while staying in and writing about haunted hotels and inns, my goal was to report and not to encounter.

I was so taken by the ambience of this inn that I forgot all about ghosts. As I walked out of my courtyard room, someone slipped an arm around my shoulder, in a very warm, welcoming way. I turned my head to see who it was, and no one was there. It happened so fast, and seemed so natural, that I wasn't afraid—until afterward.

When I told the Orrs, they smiled, and told me that when Nell owned the inn, she confided to her sister that she often felt a supportive arm around her when she was in the courtyard!

The Orrs told me about their own experiences. Things started happening as soon as they moved in. While working late on restorations, they heard footsteps and "coins falling," even though they were alone. Audrey recalls her first sighting: "I was painting in the dining room. Suddenly a man popped into my peripheral vision, like he was ducking around the corner. This happened three or four times. I called out, but no one answered. I thought it was my husband playing a trick on me, so I went down to confront him. He was in the lobby, talking to his mother. So I went back up. The next time, the figure came closer. He was dressed in dark clothes. I was scared. I said out loud, 'I don't know what's going on, but you're scaring me, and I don't like it.' That's the last time that I actually saw anything."

Gloria Demasko came to the Buxton with a group of nurses. She heard papers rustling, looked up, and saw a young woman in a long white dress standing in her room. She spoke to the woman before realizing she was talking to a ghost. The next morning Cecil, who manages the inn, showed her a picture of owner Ethel Bennel, the "Lady in Blue." Gloria became hysterical. "It's her, it's her!" she screamed.

Most of the employees have experienced the ghosts. During an employee meeting in the dining room, "three men just materialized, like you see in a movie. It looked like George Washington and General Grant, all dressed in old-time clothing. They were just standing there, solid, looking back toward the kitchen." The head chef claims that the ghost of a woman kicked him in the hip when he was in Room 9. Tamme, who tends bar, says that the lights in the tavern blink in strange patterns.

Best Rooms/Times

According to Renee, the ghosts are everywhere. "Each area, each room, has its own spirits," she claims. Room 9 is where the "Lady in Blue" is seen, along with the ghost cat. Maybe you will even get a new recipe. Nell is most frequently seen in Room 7, her old bedroom. The old tavern in the basement is loaded with spirits. Other spots in the inn that seem to have the most activity are the main dining room, the courtyard, the main hallway, and the sidewalks outside, where the Townspeople gather.

The Inn

As Ohio's oldest continuously operated inn, the Buxton has exquisitely maintained its historic past while offering guests modern-day luxury. The inn is actually a complex of five historic buildings. Every building is painted pale peach, and at night the complex is bathed in thousands of tiny, twinkling white lights. The inn offers twenty-five guest rooms, all furnished in period antiques. Each room has its own charm; even the television, telephone, and hair dryer do not intrude on the historic ambience. Most of the employees sport bright period costumes, which give the inn a festive feel.

Dining

Fine dining is offered in one of five elegant dining rooms, served by staff in period costume. Specialties include beef Wellington and lobster Thermidor.

Downstairs in a dark, dungeonlike cavern is the original tavern. Here, where the Stagecoach People hang out, you can join them for a sandwich or a beer.

Don't Miss

The immaculately landscaped grounds with fountains, formal gardens, and a New Orleans–style courtyard. At night the property is transformed into a fairyland as the inn glows with hundreds of tiny lights.

The Buxton Inn—1812
313 East Broadway
Granville, OH 43034
684-587-0001
www.buxtoninn.com

Casa Monica Hotel

St. Augustine, Florida

Though reopened just a few years ago, the landmark Casa Monica Hotel has had literally scores of ghost sightings.

"Nearly everyone who works at the hotel has had their own ghost experience," says John Stavely, manager of Ghost Tours of St. Augustine. "Every time I go in, one of them will say, 'Hey, let me tell you what happened.' It seems like every day I hear a new story."

Casa Monica was built by magnate Henry Flagler over a hundred years ago. When it fell upon hard times, it was converted into government offices and served as the county courthouse for a number of years. Maybe the ghosts are happy that it once again welcomes guests.

Sightings

The strangest sighting at the hotel is that of footprints that appear on the carpets. "Every maid in the hotel has witnessed this phenomenon," claims John.

They will vacuum the room thoroughly and enter the bathroom, only to come back and find fresh footprints across the newly vacuumed carpet. Several times they even reported footprints imprinted across freshly made beds.

Then there's the usual hauntings . . . frequent electrical glitches, lights going on and off, doors locking and unlocking. But sometimes a distinguished-looking gentleman is seen walking through the hotel, only to vanish when he is approached.

One unsuspecting couple had a visitor in the middle of the night. They were in bed, wide awake, reading and watching television, when they both heard footsteps out in the hallway, which paused in front of their door. Seconds later, they both heard footsteps enter the room. They both looked at each other, paralyzed. The footsteps continued, walking from the door across the room to a side chair. They watched silently as the cushion of the seat sank down. They were both just frozen to the spot, speechless. After a few minutes, they both saw the cushion seat rise, and heard the footsteps go back to the door and proceed down the hallway. They were pretty shaken up.

Another male guest heard noises that woke him up during the night. When he opened his eyes, he saw a woman in a green dress standing by the door. She stayed about a minute, then turned around and left through the door. The guest felt strongly that he should not be in that room. He politely called the front desk and requested another room.

Best Rooms/Times

Although sightings occur throughout the hotel, the Henry Flagler Suite is the most haunted guest room. One of five imposing tower suites, it rises high above the hotel. Often people will see a man looking out of the very top window of the tower when no one is in the suite. He is thought to be Franklin Smith, the architect who built the house, or possibly even the ghost of Henry Flagler.

The Hotel

Built in 1888 and restored in 2000, the Casa Monica Hotel is a charming example of Spanish architecture, and is listed on the National Register of Historic Homes. Rising out of the quaint downtown area, the Moorish Revival castle boasts intricate balconies, an arched carriage entrance, hand-painted Italian tile, five majestic tower suites, and a red tile roof.

No two rooms are alike. The 138 guest rooms, many of which are suites, feature Spanish-style furnishings, including wrought-iron beds, mahogany tables, and wicker lounge chairs. The towers were made into suites, which occupy two or three stories. The majestic corner tower, named in honor of the hotel's owner, Richard Kessler, is a spectacular four-story, three-bedroom penthouse suite that offers a striking panoramic view of historic St. Augustine and the bayfront. It has proudly hosted the king and queen of Spain.

Dining

St. Augustine's most haunted restaurant is Harry's Seafood Bar and Grill (46 Avenida Menendez; 904-824-7765). A ghost named Catalina haunts the place, which was once a residence. Catalina lived there in the early 1760s. When the English took over from the Spanish, she was forced out of her house and into exile in Cuba, where she lived for twenty years. She dreamed of coming back to America and reclaiming her house. This dream came true in 1784, but it was short-lived: she died in her beloved home just three years later.

She remains in her house to this day. People see her upstairs, especially in the upstairs dining room and ladies' room, dressed in very old-fashioned clothing. The temperature drops suddenly, and paintings are turned upside down. One lady came running out of the bathroom screaming after something grabbed her.

A photograph was taken recently that captures Catalina peering out the second-story window of the restaurant. "It's really creepy," John admits. "She looks like she is looking for something."

Don't Miss

Four uniquely different, spine-tingling tours are offered by Ghost Tours of St. Augustine (888-461-1009 or 904-825-0087; www.ghosttoursofstaugustine.com). The original is a one-hour walking tour of America's oldest and possibly most haunted town. A second tour begins under the beacon of the haunted St. Augustine lighthouse. On the Ghosts of the Matanzas River Cruise, adventurers board the seventy-two-foot schooner *Freedom* and set sail for dark, haunted waters. A theatrical ghost host lights the way with his lantern through ancient and strange tales of centuries past, legendary stories, folklore, and ghostly experiences. The fun-loving ghost proceeds to spin tales, sing songs, conduct contests, and attempt to frighten the passengers. Grog and rations are included on the cruise.

Ghost Tours of St. Augustine has recently partnered with the American Institute of Paranormal Research (AIP) and Dr. Andrew Nichols, who brought his team of researchers to investigate St. Augustine. As a result, a "Haunting St. Augustine" tour invites people to learn about the tricks and trade of paranormal research and actually have a chance to go out "ghost hunting" with real ghost investigators and scientific equipment, including electromagnetometers, used to pick up electronic or magnetic activity, devices to detect temperature variations, and infrared videotape.

Sandy Craig, who founded the tour company, is of Minorcan descent, a group of Spanish settlers who ventured to St. Augustine over 400 years ago and still inhabit the ancient city today. Maybe this explains her interest in the old spirits of St. Augustine.

Casa Monica Hotel
95 Cordova Street
St. Augustine, FL 32084
904-827-1888 or 800-648-1888
e-mail: info@casamonica.com
www.casamonica.com

Chateau Sonesta Hotel

New Orleans, Louisiana

The body of D. H. Holmes, founder of the legendary Holmes department store, mysteriously disappeared after his death; to this day it has never been found. His ghost, however, has been frequently spotted at the site of the famous department store that bears his name, now the Chateau Sonesta Hotel.

"Meet you under the clock at Holmes," locals shouted, until the famous Louisiana department store closed its doors in 1989 and the legendary clock stopped keeping time. In the opening line of John Kennedy Toole's Pulitzer Prize–winning novel *A Confederacy of Dunces*, the comic main character, Ignatius J. Reilly, waits for his mother at this very site.

One of the most famous pre–Civil War landmarks in New Orleans, the D. H. Holmes department store dominated the corner of Canal Street and Bourbon Street in the French Quarter. It has been elegantly resurrected as the Chateau Sonesta Hotel, and the grand clock is once again keeping time outside.

Holmes ran the store until his death in 1898, when he was

interred in the Metairie cemetery. Several years later, when family members opened the tomb to place him in another casket, his body was missing.

"I think this man's reputation is more lasting than stone, that this building is a monument to the man. He looked over every detail of its construction, of the business," says Kristen Gaglione, director of public relations for the Chateau Sonesta. "Maybe he is still here watching over things."

At least that's how the talk went. As construction crews encountered obstacle after obstacle during the store's transformation into a hotel, there was a certain amount of speculation that Mr. Holmes was indeed still in charge. "There goes D. H. again" was a frequent remark, and it was apparent that these big burly construction men were legitimately unnerved by the ghostly occurrences. Rumor had it the project might even be cursed.

Soon after the hotel opened, the staff of the Chateau began to receive complaints about voices coming from the walls. The hotel sent a host of specialists, including contractors, electricians, and phone servicemen, to determine what could be causing the phenomena, without success.

Patrick Werner, a former bell captain at the hotel, says he has witnessed many an irate guest on the fourth floor complaining about the noises from the next room. When he assured one couple that there was no one in the next room, they hurriedly checked out. Werner also reports that a six-foot-four security guard ran off his shift after encountering the voices, and that several of the maids have refused to clean the rooms on the fourth floor after encountering the chatter. "Every now and then I just look over my shoulder. You can just sense that someone is watching you. It's weird," Werner admits.

Sightings

During my visit, Kristen arranged to have famed parapsychologist Larry Montz, founder of the International Society for Psychic Research, investigate the hotel. As we walked the halls, Larry would pause and remark, "I see all the racks. We are in the men's department now," or "I see hats, lots of hats." Maps of the old layout confirmed that we were indeed exactly where the men's department and hat department once were. In the lobby, Larry described a man in a gray uniform, possibly a security guard, who was jumped and murdered just outside the building. Although no records of a murder have been uncovered, a charcoal gray shirt was part of the Holmes uniform.

Best Rooms/Times

Rooms on the fourth floor have received the most ghostly complaints, though D. H. himself observes everything.

The Hotel

In 1849 Daniel Henry Holmes opened one of the most important dry goods emporiums in New Orleans, which gained a national reputation as one of the outstanding retail establishments in the United States. Holmes offered the finest lace goods, fans, ribbons, leather goods, jewelry, parasols, gloves, and a large fabric selection. Here, it was advertised, "a lady could procure a complete summer, winter, bridal, mourning, or traveling outfit from the fitting department in a matter of days."

The store grew during the Civil War and Reconstruction. In 1913, the original four-story Gothic architecture gave way to a large neoclassic design; this facade was restored and now adorns the hotel's Iberville Street entrance.

The 150-year-old store closed in 1989, and the building reopened as the Chateau Sonesta Hotel following a $23 million historic conversion. Each of the hotel's 251 opulent guest rooms, designed and built inside the walls of the famous store, is uniquely different, with nooks and crannies and impressive twelve-foot ceilings. Many have balconies overlooking tropical courtyards, world-famous Bourbon Street, or the illustrious Holmes clock.

In honor of the rich New Orleans literary tradition, two luxurious themed suites have been created. The Toole suite, named after the Pulitzer Prize–winning author of *A Confederacy of Dunces,* is located on the second floor, overlooking the clock. The Tennessee Williams suite bears the theme "Southern and madness," with brass beds, ceiling fans, sunflowers, and bold, brazen colors.

Dining

The huge Chateau Sonesta complex, occupying the entire city block, offers a variety of dining options, including the Red Fish Grill, a world-class seafood restaurant owned by Ralph Brennan of the famous New Orleans restauranteur family.

"Meet me under the clock" takes on a new meaning at the Clock Bar, named after the famous clock. When the hotel first opened, the landmark clock was placed in the Clock Bar, then moved back to its original spot on Canal Street in 1997. A bronze statue of Ignatius Reilly now resides under the clock.

Don't Miss

Even though the buildings that housed the bordellos and bars are long gone, the ghosts of the legendary Storyville district continue to haunt the streets of New Orleans, America's most haunted city. Storyville made its own contribution to the emergence of jazz over a hundred years ago.

When state legislation made prostitution legal in one area of town, newspapers quickly dubbed the new bordello district Storyville and the area flourished for the next twenty years. At its peak, Storyville employed as many as 2,200 prostitutes, 70 professional gamblers, and 30 piano players, nestled in as many as 230 houses, cabarets, houses of assignation, and cribs. A hotbed of colorful characters and activity, personalities such as Jelly Roll Morton, King Oliver, LuLu White, French Emma, Madame Piazza, Marguerite Giffin and Josie Arlington rose to prominence during the Storyville era. For visitors new to Storyville, a lavishly printed "Blue Book" was the ultimate guide, including advertisements from illustrious madams boasting of their houses' grandiose architecture, gorgeously appointed furniture, and melodious beauty, and of the specialties of the girls inside.

From 1897 to 1917, New Orleans musicians honed their skills at the various bordellos existing within Storyville. At virtually any hour, music could be heard wafting through the air in the original Storyville district one hundred years ago. The cabarets, cafés, dance halls, and bordellos fostered a fledgling style of music called jazz, allowing it to take root and develop. The district proved to be a receptive venue for musical experimentation and innovation, as its clientele was more tolerant (and slightly preoccupied). The laissez-faire attitude that permeated the district via sex, gambling, and drinking also encouraged creativity and freedom in music. A young Louis Armstrong, too young to enter on his own, used to make drugstore deliveries into Storyville just to hear some of the great jazz musicians perform.

Sadly, the Storyville era came to an end when the federal government banned it at the start of World War I. The new Storyville district captures the wonderful architecture and atmosphere of the original Storyville, allowing people to travel back in time and experience the music of old N'Awlins at its finest.

Chateau Sonesta Hotel
800 Iberville Street
New Orleans, LA 70112
504-586-0800 or 1-800-SONESTA
e-mail: reserv@chateausonesta.com
www.chateausonesta.com

The Colony Hotel and Spa

Delray Beach, Florida

The ghosts at the Colony Hotel are not spooky at all. They are, in fact, the dearly departed relatives of Justina Boughton, the third-generation owner of this trendy art deco hotel.

The complex was built in 1926 by Charles "Charlie" Bowden, Justina's grandfather, and George Bowden, her father. Father and son were equal partners in the hotel, but they had very different attitudes when it came to running the hotel. Charlie was a dapper dresser and a big spender. In contrast, George was much more conservative, always worried about cutting costs and saving money. The two argued over what to spend money on, and how to run the place.

They are still arguing, their voices heard rising in a passionate debate inside their former office.

The hotel has long held a reputation for being haunted. When Justina first moved back to the hotel in 1995, locals asked her if she heard the ghosts, and if they frightened her.

"At first, I was a little taken back," she says. "I felt safe in my bedroom, but I always felt like they were watching me downstairs, especially in the office. Sometimes I catch a fleeting glimpse of Charlie's jacket when I turn around.

"I have realized that they are not here to hurt me, or scare me, but to watch over me. In fact, they have really helped me. I spent twenty years as a landscape architect. I had no idea how to run a hotel. Their grave advice has been invaluable."

And just how do they give this advice?

"They just start talking out loud, out of the blue. They tell me what to do. Other times, I hear their voices raised in some kind of debate. Sometimes I ask them a question, and I can audibly hear them answer. Those times, I feel like my spirit is asking their spirit for advice. And they are happy to help out. If only they could agree it would make my life a lot easier."

Sightings

Justina spent her childhood at the hotel, which was seasonal, open only in the winter months, attracting northerners who flock to the warm sunny Florida beaches to avoid the freezing weather back home. During the off season the huge empty hotel became a summer residence for extended family members.

"In the 1950s John Banta, my father's cousin, was the general manager. In the summertime, I played with his children, John and Carol. It was really creepy. There were all these empty rooms. We would hear whisperings about the ghosts. I can remember that we were afraid to go into the rooms on one side of the hotel, Rooms 102, 104, and 106. At that age, our imaginations ran wild. We would scare ourselves silly."

It seems that not just human spirits enjoyed a grand afterlife at the hotel; the young cousins swore that the ghosts of two pet scorpions, Scorpio and Scorpiana, returned to haunt the hotel after their death.

Though other spirits linger at the hotel, George and Charles are reported the most often. Portraits of the two partners are scattered throughout the lobby, their eyes seeming to observe all that goes on.

"My grandfather was a very handsome man," says Justina. "I have a four-foot-high portrait of him, taken in the 1930s, hanging right behind my desk in the office. He looks very dapper in his white spats, cuffed pants, and blazer, standing in front of the hotel. His eyes seem to follow me." Indeed the smiling face in the portrait has actually frowned, expressing his disapproval.

My father told me when I recently renovated the hotel to keep all the original furniture. He was such a penny pincher. Even the guest rooms sport their original 1920s furnishings. We have had to add a few things, like TVs, but the rooms are basically the same. He says he is very happy about that, because he never wanted to throw anything out.

I found some really boring chandeliers in the attic of our hotel in Maine. [Justina's family also owns the Colony Hotel in Kennebunkport.] They had been hanging in the rafters for decades, and were painted a really ugly brown. I heard my father's voice telling me to fix them up. I had them painted and sent them down to Delray to be installed. When I came back to see them, the contractor told me the date 1925 was stamped inside each of them. I was amazed that they were an identical match to the wall sconces. Apparently, they were the originals. My father had been saving them all these years. My father led me to them, and insisted I put them back up. He told me afterward that he is pleased.

Sometimes they want to discuss my personal life, but I tell them it's none of their business.

Charles and George are always here when I have a serious decision to make. In 1995 we had horrible rainstorms and hurricanes. The roof was leaking like crazy. I had these buckets all around the hotel, collecting the water. We had the original coal-tar pitched roof from 1926. I was seriously considering replacing the roof. That's when I heard my father tell me to use the same kind of roof. He said that's what the building wanted. I'm not going to argue with him.

Best Rooms/Times

George and Charles like to walk around and keep an eye on things in their hotel. The lobby and Justina's office have the most sightings, most often after dark. Guests in Rooms 102, 104, and 106 also report ghostly activity.

The Hotel

The 1920s art deco hotel represents the Mizner era of Florida's Mediterranean architecture. Claiming the honor of being Delray's oldest hotel, the Colony is situated on Atlantic Avenue, just five blocks from the beach. In those days, the city was known as an artist's colony. Today Delray remains a haven for art enthusiasts, and chic Atlantic Avenue is home to dozens of galleries, boutique shops, sidewalk cafés, and trendy restaurants.

The spacious lobby of the hotel has retained its original airy feel, complete with French doors, potted palms, skylights, wood-burning fireplaces, and the original manned elevator, still in use. Also in the lobby is the complete collection of rare Fixx Reed white wicker furniture, which has sat in the hotel since the day it opened.

The sixty-six guest rooms retain their original tropical hues and Dade County pine floors. The original headboards and matching bureaus show off delicate old hand-painted red roses. A large display of fresh foliage and ferns gives the hotel a bright and breezy feel.

A complimentary continental breakfast is included with the room, served on an original 1926 children's dining room table. Pets are welcome!

The Porch Bar overlooks vibrant Atlantic Avenue. Deep red awnings shade the hotel's arched veranda, where guests can sip tropical refreshments while listening to live music.

In the grand style of an old Floridian beach club, the Colony Cabaña Club offers guests and members a private beach with cabanas, and one of the largest heated saltwater swimming pools in Florida. Located two miles from the hotel, the Cabaña Club offers a putting green, snack bar, tropical cocktail service, and a weight room. Regular shuttle service is provided.

Dining

Two blocks down the street is the actual nineteenth-century Olde English pub, the Blue Anchor (804 East Atlantic Avenue; 561-272-7272), where two of Jack the Ripper's victims are said to have spent their very last night alive! Elizabeth Stride and Catherine Eddows were seen drinking with a well-to-do gentleman at the Blue Anchor on that fateful night in 1888. Their drinking companion may very well have been Jack the Ripper himself.

The tavern was built in London in 1864 on the site of an ancient seventeenth-century inn. The rich, famous, and notorious passed through her doors for almost 150 years until the pub was torn down to make way for a parking lot. But she was to rise again—this time in Delray Beach. The entire exterior of the original pub, with its beautiful dark oak doors and paneling and unique stained-glass windows, was carefully dismantled in England and shipped across the ocean in 1996 to become a landmark on trendy Atlantic Avenue.

The ghost at the Blue Anchor is the spirit of Bertha Starkey, who was stabbed to death while sitting at the bar after her enraged seafaring husband caught her in the arms of another man. She has been haunting the place for over a century. When the tavern was torn down and moved to Delray, she moved with it, refusing to leave. Her footsteps and spine-chilling wails have been frightening the staff and customers since her death. Even today at its Delray Beach location, the haunting continues.

"How do you explain the eerie sounds of footsteps in the ceiling late at night or the sudden shattering of a half-inch-thick reinforced glass shelf behind the bar on the anniversary of Bertha's gruesome demise?" quips British owner Lee Harrison. "And how do you explain table candles extinguishing themselves and then reigniting seconds later? Or heavy kitchen pots lifting themselves off meat-cleaver-size hooks and crashing to the floor? It's all very creepy!

"In fact, experts in the field of paranormal studies have told us they are not aware of any previous case where a ghost has traveled more than 4,000 miles to set up residency in another country," adds Harrison.

Don't Miss

Board the 140-passenger *Hannah Glover* or the 70-passenger *Susannah* (561-243-0686) and enjoy a lazy hour-and-a-half narrated cruise down the picturesque Intercoastal Waterway. The tours glide past historic sites, opulent homes of the rich and famous, and an occasional manatee. Special themed cruises are offered at Christmas, Valentine's Day, and of course, Halloween. "We are headquartered out of Salem, Massachusetts," says sales manager Alice Appel, "so we know a lot about ghosts and witches."

The Colony Hotel and Spa
525 East Atlantic Avenue
Delray Beach, FL 33483
561-276-4123 or 800-552-2363
e-mail: info-fla@thecolonyhotel.com
www.thecolonyhotel.com/florida/

The Crescent Hotel and Spa

❖❖❖

Eureka Springs, Arkansas

Known as the Queen of the Ozarks, this opulent hotel, once a playground for millionaires, hides a dark past from the days when its rooms were used to house desperate, dying patients, and its basement became a morgue and crematory. It's rumored that human bones are buried in the walls.

Built to be the grandest hotel of the Ozarks, the Crescent was completed in 1886. The magnificent structure was adorned with the finest draperies and furniture. It was truly a showplace, boasting the most modern of accoutrements: Edison lamps, central steam heat, and a hydraulic elevator. Visitors could enjoy tea dances during the afternoon and ballroom dancing each evening, with music provided by an in-house orchestra. A stable with one hundred sleek-coated horses was provided for the guests' riding pleasure, for early-morning canters along the mountainside.

But the good times did not last forever. When the Great Depression hit, the hotel was converted to an exclusive girls' boarding school. One student became so depressed, she jumped to her death from the hotel's rooftop. By the 1930s the Crescent Hotel had become an experimental cancer hospital operated by "Dr." Norman Baker, who had been run out of Iowa for passing himself off as a licensed physician and conning desperately ill patients out of their life savings. He set up examining rooms on the fifth floor, and the basement was used as the morgue. His claim that he could cure all cancers brought people by the droves.

It is alleged that Dr. Baker cremated bodies in a large walk-in furnace below the hotel. When word of his arrest reached Eureka, residents, not wanting to tarnish the reputation of their pristine resort town, came and destroyed all papers they could find relating to the hospital. They also removed all traces of the furnace. Dr. Baker's autopsy table and walk-in freezer are still in the basement today. Up until 1985, one room in the hotel contained a wall of shelves, lined with jars of formaldehyde and preserved body organs.

It was also rumored that many deceased patients were buried under the floors and in the walls. Though it has never been proven, a woman visited the hotel recently and said that her family owned the hotel in the 1940s. She recounts that one day the workmen were instructed to remove a wall. She was only six at the time. From behind that wall skeletons tumbled out. The workers fled, and it took weeks to get more people to come back and finish the job.

Sightings

One of the most famous ghosts at the hotel is known as Michael. One of the Irish stonemasons who built the hotel in 1886, he plunged to his death and died on impact in what is now Room 218. Guests in this room have heard his final cry, and witnessed a hand coming out of the bathroom mirror. The door to the room opens, then slams shut, often locking its inhabitants inside the room.

Many of the apparitions in the hotel are from its hospital days. "Dr. Baker" has been seen in the hotel lobby. He is described as a man in a purple shirt and white linen suit. When guests are shown his photograph, they exclaim, "That is him."

A nurse pushing a gurney down the halls is another frequent apparition. You can actually hear the squeaks and rattles as the gurney clamors down to the operating room. Housekeepers and workmen have reported meeting a "Theodora" in Room 419, who introduces herself as a cancer patient of Dr. Baker's, and then vanishes after courtesies are verbally exchanged.

Ken Fugate and Carroll Heath conduct ghost tours. Once when Ken was working in Room 419, stenciling border at the top of the wall, he heard a woman's voice say, "It's so pretty, what you are doing to my room." He looked around, but no one was there. Then the ghost repeated the statement. He asked her name: "Theodora." She told him she was a patient in the cancer hospital and loved her room so much she just couldn't bear to leave it. "She is a sweet little lady," says Ken.

But if you say you don't like her room, she gets angry. She has actually taken guests' clothes and thrown them out in the hallway, as if to say, "If you don't like my room, then leave."

We channeled Theodora a few months ago in Room 419. Carroll has a special gift for channeling entities. She revealed she knew she had left her body but stays in the hotel because she has many friends there who were also patients, and they enjoy being together there. She seems in no hurry to leave.

We have communicated with many of the patients and some of the staff of the hospital. Baker is still in the building and actually materialized to one of our customers on a tour, holding an autopsy on one of the autopsy tables that is still in what was used as the morgue.

On the fifth floor is the room referred to as the North Penthouse. This is very active, and the energy is quite unsettling. We have had people report eerie colored lights flashing in the middle of the night. It was the private quarters of Norman Baker.

Not all of the ghosts are from this dark era. Throughout the hotel's history a formally dressed gentleman ghost has descended the main stairway, pulling on his gloves as if to attend the nightly ball that was held in the hotel's legendary Crystal Dining Room in the 1880s. The descriptions are now thought to match that of Dr. Ellis, the physician for the Crescent Hotel, who maintained an office in what is now Room 212.

There is also activity in the main dining

room. Both staff and guests have seen a gentleman dressed in Victorian attire. He is very friendly, and talks to people. He says he is waiting for someone—a beautiful young lady. He saw her the night before at a party in the dining room but was too shy to introduce himself. He is still there, waiting for her!

Other employees tell about hearing noises in the dining room after hours. When they investigate, there is a party of guests in the corner. When they are approached, they just disappear.

Another popular ghost at the hotel is the "Lady in White." For decades she has been seen floating through the gardens or standing alone on the balconies.

Best Rooms/Times

So many spirits are here that they seem to manifest anywhere in the hotel. The scariest room is probably 218, where Michael resides. I don't know about you, but I would be terrified if I saw a hand coming out of the mirror. Dr. Baker haunts the North Penthouse. Theodora is in 419, but she is a happy spirit.

The lobby, stairways, restaurant, and basement of this hotel are also very active.

The Hotel

The grand hotel has sixty-eight guest rooms, eight suites, and two penthouse suites. All the rooms have

balconies offering breathtaking views of the village or
the Ozarks. The rooms have been fully restored with
Victorian authenticity. Just steps outside are twelve
acres of formal Victorian gardens, hiking and nature
trails, and a swimming pool.

The New Moon Spa offers everything you need to
bring your mind and body to a state of blissful relax-
ation, including massage, a workout center, a medita-
tion garden, crown chakra cleansing, and spiritual
development. Protein shakes, smoothies, sushi, and
hummus are offered at the New Moon Spa Café, recognized as "the best vegetarian restaurant in the state."

Dining

At the Crescent's historic Crystal Dining Room, guests
enjoy the grandeur of yesteryear. Music is an integral
part of the hotel's culture, and live jazz or blues enhances the dining experience.

The art deco Dr. Baker Lounge is a tribute to the
"crazy" doctor. As the highest point in Eureka Springs,
it offers exquisite views.

Don't Miss

Ghost tours are conducted nightly by a team of
trained psychics. Guests are guided through the hot
spots of the hotel, and finally down the dark halls
below the hotel that housed the morgue, the realm of
the sinister "Dr." Norman Baker.

"Because of the enormous activity at the Crescent

Hotel," says researcher Carroll Heath, "we have made it our business to investigate the phenomena, and we host informative ghost tours seven days a week." Carroll and her partner, Ken Fugate, are professionally trained psychics and members of the International Ghost Hunters Society. They pride themselves on offering an experience to visitors without the props of a showman or the sensational lingo. "We prefer to give straight information without the drama that many people use as a distraction. As trained clairvoyants, we take our sensitivity, as well as others', to psychic phenomena very seriously."

The Crescent Hotel and Spa
75 Prospect Avenue
Eureka Springs, AR 72632
501-253-9766 or 800-342-9766 or 800-678-8946
e-mail: crescent@arkansas.net
www.crescent-hotel.com

Hotel del Coronado

❧

Coronado Island, California

The entire nation was captivated by the tragic newspaper accounts of the Hotel del Coronado's "beautiful stranger," a mysterious young woman who checked into the hotel alone on Thanksgiving Day and was found dead on the steps of the hotel five days later of a single gunshot wound to her head. Because she checked into the hotel under an assumed name, it would be weeks before her true identity was learned. Rumors and speculation ran rampant as to what drove her to such a desperate act. Perhaps that is why she still occupies the room in the grand hotel where she spent the last few days of her short life.

Kate Morgan, a pretty woman in her twenties, checked into the Hotel del Coronado on Thanksgiving Day, 1892, as "Lottie A. Bernard, Detroit." Five days later she was found dead on the exterior stairs leading to the beach.

Authorities knew nothing about her, other than the name Lottie, so local newspapers ran stories referring to her as the "beautiful stranger." A sketch of her face and the circumstances of her death were telegraphed to police agencies and newspapers around the country in hopes of learning who she was. Eventually an anonymous letter identified her as Kate Morgan.

Rumors and scandal spread like wildfire. Kate and her mysterious suicide captivated the nation. Why would any woman be traveling alone? It was speculated that she might have been having an affair with someone at the hotel, or that she was pregnant and had nowhere to go. According to one eyewitness, Kate and her husband Tom had been traveling together on the train. After a quarrel, Tom got off the train. Kate continued on to San Diego and the Hotel del Coronado. There, she waited for her husband. He never showed up. Five days later she was dead.

The Del sits like a multifaceted jewel at the ocean's edge of California's Coronado Island. It's easy to imagine why this Victorian rococo fortress was rumored to be the inspiration for Frank Baum's Emerald City when he wrote his Wizard of Oz series. The Del was the idyllic beachside playland of the rich and famous. The guest register is speckled with a who's who of Hollywood: Garbo, Chaplin, Bette Davis, Marilyn, Sinatra, and Madonna are but a few of the celebrities who have checked into the del Coronado. Princes and presidents have been wined and dined in the majestic Crown Room. Charles Lindbergh was honored at the Del after his historic 1927 solo transatlantic flight. The Del provided a magical setting for a long list of films, including the Marilyn Monroe / Tony Curtis / Jack Lemmon classic *Some Like It Hot*.

When the Hotel del Coronado announced the creation of a new Del historian position, Christine Donovan jumped at the opportunity. It's her job, as historian, to ensure that all the recorded history about the hotel is correct, including information about the resident ghost. Because the story was so sensational in its day, and there was so much speculation, sorting out the truth was no small task. There were many conflicting stories, not only about sightings of the "beautiful stranger," but about her actual tragic life and death. Through meticulous research of legal documents, recorded interviews with eyewitnesses, court transcripts, and newspaper accounts from as far away as Los Angeles, San Francisco, and Iowa, Christine was able to piece together the intimate details of this beautiful stranger whose life was tragically cut short by her own hands.

Christine has also collected a large number of eyewitness accounts from guests who encountered Kate's spirit. Many of these stunning accounts are from guests who had no idea that the hotel had a ghost, let alone that they were staying in the haunted room. One of these reports comes from Jennifer and Richard Rodriguez. Here is their story.

Sightings

It all started out innocently enough. Richard Rodriguez, a graphic designer from Lake Elsinore, California, wanted to surprise his wife Jennifer, a schoolteacher, by taking her to a quiet romantic getaway on Valentine's Day weekend. Surfing the Web, he stumbled across the Hotel del Coronado and was immediately struck by the magnificent architecture, with all its fairy-tale angles and turrets. He called to book a room but was told the hotel was full. Undaunted, he called back, and his diligence was rewarded with a reservation. "We have one room," he was told. Elated, he couldn't wait to tell his wife. He also made reservations to catch a play at the Globe Theater in nearby San Diego.

Richard and Jennifer were even more excited as they arrived at the magnificent structure. They were happy to learn that they had a room in the historic wing of the hotel. Shortly after they checked in, there was a knock at the door. It was the hotel manager, asking if he could look in the bathroom. He told Jennifer that there had been workmen in that wing, and he wanted to be sure the bathroom was in order and that no tools had been left. There was also a maid with the manager, but she waited outside the door, barely peeking in. Richard and Jennifer didn't think much about her at the time. The manager left quickly, and the Rodriguezes got ready and left for the theater and a late dinner.

When they returned, the room felt chilly, so they bundled up. Before long, Richard felt a tug on the blanket, so he tugged it back, figuring it was Jennifer. "Who ELSE would it be?" he commented later.

When "she" tugged it again, I ripped it back harder. The next time the blanket jerked down past my knees. I rolled over to tell Jennifer to quit it, but she was sound asleep. My eyes glanced up, and I could not believe what I saw. There was someone there at the foot of the bed, holding the blanket up in the air, so I couldn't see his or her head.

I'm a big guy. This thing was strong. I yanked back, as hard as I possibly could. It was holding on tight, but I managed to get the blanket back and over my head. I lay there frozen for a minute. I thought, Whatever is standing there by the bed is now uncovered. Do I really want to look? Like a kid watching a scary movie, with the blanket over my head, I slowly, painstakingly shifted the blanket and peeked out with one eye. "It" was gone.

I couldn't move. I couldn't scream. I couldn't even squeak out any sound at all to wake up my wife. All I could do was lie there under the blanket.

Then the voice started calling my name. The voice was sweet, enticing, luring me to the door. "Richard . . . Riiiichaaaaard. Come to the keyhole . . . come to the keyhole, Richaaaard."

This about scared me to death. Then I saw the doorknob turn. This can't be happening, I screamed silently. The doorknob was turning, faster and faster; then the entire door started shaking and rattling. I was beyond fear. All I could do was lie there, barely breathing, freezing cold, waiting for the daylight to end this living nightmare.

"Didn't you hear it, didn't you see it?" I gasped, wondering if I could get my breath even now.

Jennifer calmly told me that she had experienced the best night's sleep of her life. She slept through the entire ordeal!

Jennifer says a feeling of warmth and coziness enveloped her, and she was lured immediately into a deep sleep, dreaming of the Del the entire night. In her dreams she was at the beach in front of the hotel. There were lots of children, and lots of laughter. She woke up with an overwhelming feeling of joy and happiness—unlike Richard, who was beside himself.

After rehashing the night's events, Jennifer did remember that she, too, had seen the ceiling fan chain spin earlier in the evening, while Richard was changing. She hadn't thought much about it at the time, but looking back, it was odd, because there was no wind in the room, and nothing to make the chain circle like that. She says it was as if someone was batting or twirling it.

They had reservations to stay another night in that room, but Richard adamantly refused. They packed their bags to leave. When the bellboy arrived, he asked how they liked staying in the "haunted" room. Richard got upset with that, and demanded to speak to the manager.

Once they were a few feet away from the door to their room, they noticed that the air changed abruptly from icy to warm.

The manager didn't bat an eye when he heard Richard's account of his night in the haunted room. "You really should warn people," Richard advised.

"Some people experience strange things, some people don't," was the reply.

Now extremely curious about what had happened, and why, Richard and Jennifer stopped by the gift shop and bought two books about the ghost at the Del, and Jennifer read as Richard drove. She learned that some of the maids at the Del will not go into certain rooms by themselves. So that explained the maid that stood planted outside the door while the manager checked the bathroom.

Jennifer continued reading aloud. It was reported in the book that another guest, also in that room, heard a woman calling his name, beckoning him to the keyhole. That guest actually got out of the bed and went to the door. Peeking through the keyhole, he could see a beautiful lady, dressed in black, crouched outside in the hall.

"Help me, help me . . . I've just been murdered," she pleaded.

As he flung open the door to help, she vanished.

"In a way, it made me feel relieved, to know that someone else on Earth had this same experience," says Richard. "But still, I wanted to know why it happened to me."

Just a few days after their ordeal, the couple was bombarded with phone messages from the Globe Theater. "I thought they were trying to sell tickets, so I never called them back," says Richard. Finally, after a week of calls, he decided to put an end to it and tell the salesperson to bug off.

"But sir, you are our grand prize winner," the Globe manager told Richard.

"Grand prize of what? We didn't enter anything."

"We drew your ticket number. You won the grand prize!"

"Oh, yeah? What did we win?"

"A weekend at the Hotel del Coronado!"

"Oh, my God, IT WANTS ME BACK!" Richard groaned.

Six months later, the Rodriguezes did return to the scene of the crime, finally ready to face their questions and fears. This time, however, they asked for a room in the new building. Richard says his first night at the Del changed him forever. "It ripped open my beliefs, and opened a door. I can't ever go back," he claims. "But it's a good thing. I know there is something more out there. I used to be an atheist; now I believe in something greater than us."

Jennifer and Richard are now frequent guests at the Del. As a matter of fact, they request Kate's room. "We are drawn to the hotel. We can't stay away."

Best Rooms/Times

Although the room numbers have been reassigned throughout the history of the Del, through guest registers and architectural drawings it was determined that Kate was registered in what is now Room 3327. Room 3519, once very tiny and thought to be a handmaid's room, is also a flurry of activity. Several of the rooms seem to have poltergeist activity, including lights and televisions that go on and off by themselves and toilets that flush. Many of these rooms are on the same hall as 3327.

The Del Galleria, over twenty boutiques, gourmet shops, and curious specialty stores, is also haunted.

Several different shops carry a book about the ghost at the Del. The book flies across the room or drops off the shelves. It's always the same book every time, in each shop, no matter where it is moved on the shelves.

The Hotel

When the Hotel del Coronado first opened its doors in 1888, California was still a remote destination. With the discovery of gold in 1848, prospectors flocked to the state in hopes of striking it rich. With the invention of the railroad, travel to the West opened up. Grand luxury resorts were built to accommodate America's rich and famous, who traveled by train, many by private rail cars that could be hitched to the trains.

The Del soon became known for its exquisite architecture and innovative technology. At that time the hotel was one of the largest buildings in the country to have electric lights, telephones (though not in the guest rooms), and elevators.

Today, the world-famous Grand Lady by the Sea has been restored to her original grandeur. From the Grand Lobby, with its rich woods and textures, to the exquisite Crown Room, a fantasy ballroom fit for a prince, to the Windsor Lawn, which provides a seaside leisure setting with landscaped walkways and seasonal gardens, every inch of the Del has been meticulously researched and restored.

The Victorian building, a National Historic Landmark, gracefully combines historic ambience with contemporary amenities and features. All 381 rooms in the original building were restored with traditional Victorian decor. Every effort has been made to make the rooms as close to their original look as possible, including antique gold mirrors, ornate armoires and ceiling fans, and floor lamps with large fringed shades. Each room has a different, unique size and shape, many with nooks, crannies, or curved sides.

In the adjacent seven-story ocean towers and cabanas are another 318 rooms. These oceanfront rooms and suites boast every contemporary amenity. A spectacular private oceanfront villa is where Marilyn resided during the filming of *Some Like It Hot*.

Dining

The Del offers a variety of world-class and casual dining options.

The world-famous Crown Room defies the imagination. Whimsical crown-shaped chandeliers, designed by Wizard of Oz author Frank Baum, dangle from the glowing sugar-pine ceiling. Through the huge windows encircling the room are some of California's most exquisite views.

Inspired by the 1920 romance at the Del, Prince of Wales, the resort's fine dining restaurant, offers intimate indoor and spectacular outdoor terraced dining with romantic candlelight and breathtaking sunset views of the Pacific.

Sheerwater is the Hotel del Coronado's oceanfront

three-meal restaurant, featuring expansive outdoor dining terraces and giant fireplaces. Signature entrees are prepared in the exhibition oven.

The Palm Court overlooks the garden patio. Victorian high tea is served here daily by period-costumed staff.

Famous for its elegant surroundings and lavish service, the Del is also known for its festive holiday traditions. In 1904 the Del awed the world by presenting the first Christmas tree with electric lights. This Christmas tradition continues today at the annual Lighting of the Del Ceremony, including a visit from Santa. The entire hotel is transformed into a winter fairyland with thousands of tiny lights.

Don't Miss

For more information about the ghost of Kate Morgan, read Christine Donovan's book *The Beautiful Stranger: The Ghost of Kate and the Hotel del Coronado*.

The Hotel del Coronado
1500 Orange Avenue
Coronado, CA 92118
619-435-6611 or 800-HOTELDEL
e-mail: delreservations@hoteldel.com or
deldining@hoteldel.com

Don Cesar Beach Resort and Spa

St. Petes Beach, Florida

This famous Florida fairy-tale castle, known as the Pink Palace, was built by Thomas Rowe in 1928 and stands as a tribute to his long-lost love. Though her love was forbidden in life, through death they are once again reunited, and walk together through the halls and gardens of the Don Cesar.

Their love is the kind of tragic romance that inspired operas. In fact, the name of the hotel, as well as all the surrounding streets, are taken from *Maritana,* an American opera written by composer William Vincent Wallace.

Wallace had an equally tortured affair, which became the inspiration for his famous opera. Born in Dublin, he married and moved to Tasmania. A restless spirit, he left his wife and son with a two-thousand-pound debt and traveled through South America and Mexico, finally settling in New York City. There he met Helene Stoepel and fell deeply in love. Though they could never marry, she became his lifelong companion. His love for Helene inspired *Maritana,* his only successful opera, which premiered in London in 1845. The libretto weaves a tale of Don Cesar, a swashbuckling soldier of fortune, and Maritana, the beautiful gypsy girl he is in love with. Don José, minister of King Charles II, also has his eye on Maritana, and conspires with the king to win her. Don Cesar exposes the wicked minister, weds Maritana, becomes governor, and lives happily ever after, an odd outcome for an opera.

It was during a performance of *Maritana* that Thomas Rowe first spotted Lucinda, a dark Spanish beauty cast in the lead role. Smitten, he went to every performance. They fell deeply in love, but her parents forbade her to see him. As if imitating the plot of an opera, the couple was forced to meet illicitly in a secret garden. After each performance, she would race to meet him by the fountain, still in her gypsy costume. Here they planned their escape.

It was Thomas's last night in England before sailing to America, and the last performance in London before the troupe moved on to another city. The lovers were to meet by the fountain one last time, and Lucinda would leave with Thomas for America.

Thomas waited by the fountain, but his lover did not show. He raced into the theater, but it was dark and empty. His beloved Lucinda had left. Devastated, he moved to America without her, and eventually married someone else. Desperately unhappy, he left his wife and moved to Florida. There he made a fortune in real estate. He found a desolate strip of land on an isolated barrier island off St. Petes Beach, and claimed he would build a luxury palace resort as a tribute to his beloved Lucinda.

People told Rowe that he must be crazy. They told him he could never build such a large structure on that beach. The only access to the small, marshy isle was a frail, wooden toll bridge, opened at whim by its crotchety caretaker. But Rowe was unstoppable. He invented a floating concrete base and brought all the construction materials over by barge. The foundation has not sunk an inch in more than seventy-five years.

Rowe's dream was taking real shape. He had grandiose plans to crown his beach retreat with a castle. He subdivided the eighty acres into lots, and named the streets after the people and places in his favorite opera.

Rowe built his towering Pink Palace, with its six stately towers, to resemble an ancient Moorish castle. Inside, in the center of the hotel, he erected a fountain identical to the one in the secret garden where he had met Lucinda years before. Carrara marble and Italian tiles adorned the floors and walls of this veritable castle.

The fifth floor of this six-floor monument was the dining floor, which held the hotel's only kitchen. Food for the ballroom or beach cabana was prepared here, then sent down by elevator. Elegant white linen, sparkling crystal, formal Black Knight china, and gleaming silver were illuminated by brass chandeliers and sconces.

Opening night at the Don Cesar was January 16, 1928. Nearly 1,500 people attended the extravagant gala, dressed in their finest flapper-era evening attire. The Don received accolades from all over the country. The social elite of the Gatsby era, including movie producers, department store magnates, including the Gimbels and Bloomingdales, the Mayos of the Mayo Clinic fame, Franklin D. Roosevelt, Joe and Marilyn, and even F. Scott Fitzgerald himself wintered at the Pink Palace.

When the banks failed in 1931, the hotel hit hard times but was saved when Colonel Jacob Ruppert signed a three-year contract to house his New York Yankees there during spring training. All Yankees, with the exception of Babe Ruth, were quartered in the hotel. With the accompanying entourage of sports writers, fans, and team staff, the hotel survived the depression and thrived once again.

Rowe's beloved Lucinda never got to see the opulent castle erected in her honor. Upon her death, Lucinda's family finally relented and sent Thomas a note, written years before: "Time is infinite. I wait for you by our fountain ... to share our timeless love, our destiny is time."

Rowe passed away too, dropping to his knees in 1941 in the lobby of his beloved hotel, and was carried upstairs, where he died. He loved his employees so much, he tried to bequeath the hotel to them. On his deathbed, he tried to execute this will, but the two attending nurses refused to witness his signature, and the hotel passed to his ex-wife. Shortly after his death, stories of sightings of Rowe were whispered among the staff.

Though the famous fountain in the lobby no longer exists, the timeless love that Lucinda and Thomas share is felt at the hotel, as guests and staff observe a glowing couple, dressed in Gatsby-style attire, walking hand in hand through the halls, staring into each other's eyes and smiling, very much in love.

Sightings

Sightings of Mr. Rowe, dressed in his signature light-colored suit and Panama hat, began immediately after his death. He smoked medicated menthol cigarettes for "health reasons," and the pungent aroma would waft through the halls. Often a Don employee would smell his distinctive cigarettes and turn, expecting to see him. Even today you might catch a whiff of his cigarettes. Most often, he is seen with a beautiful, dark-haired beauty; the pair gaze deeply into each other's eyes.

When the hotel was being renovated in 1973, the manager was introduced to the construction crew. "If you are the manager, who is the man in the white suit who oversees us?" the men wanted to know. Once a photographer inadvertently captured Rowe; a man wearing a white suit and Panama hat was clearly visible in the print.

A newly hired reservations manager was walking along the beach near the hotel with her husband when they passed a man in a pastel suit. It was summer, and very warm, so she commented, "How hot and uncomfortable that man must be in a suit." Her husband replied, "What man?" Only later at her new employee orientation did she learn about the history of the hotel and the ghost of Mr. Rowe.

Scott, previously a disbeliever, has been a bellman at the hotel for eight years. One day, he was really busy. "Come on, Thomas, help me out here," he teased as he pushed the button for the elevator. It usually takes a very long time to get there, but this time the door opened right away. At the top floor, Scott asked for help again: "Thomas, hold the door for me." The elevator, which always remains closed, stayed open until Scott returned. By that time, Scott was getting really scared. He got into the elevator and said, "Lobby." It went to the lobby. "I was really scared," said Scott. "I will not get on the elevator alone again!" Susan Owen, who has been with the hotel for sixteen years, agrees. "Those older elevators can be very slow. But whenever I am racing around, I never have to push any buttons, the elevator just takes me where I need to be. It's very weird. I always say thank you to Mr. Rowe."

Michael Chagnon, director of sales, nearly walked in on the ghosts. He considers his experience to be "extremely bizarre." "I was never a believer in that, I never have been. I came in very early one morning. Nobody has a key to my office but me. I inserted my key into my door, and as I turned the knob I heard people inside. They were having a conversation. I could feel terror in every molecule of my body. As soon as the key turned, it was like someone said, 'Hush, someone's coming.' Then I actually heard them leave. I could hear every step she made. I could even hear the crinoline of her skirt rustling. Every pore on my body had the goose bumps. It was bizarre. I must have been pale, because everyone asked me was I okay. I don't understand what happened. I was stuttering in trying to relate it, because it was so foreign to me.

"We have literally had guests call down and complain about someone knocking on their door," Michael added. "When the guest opens the door, there is a gentleman and a woman standing there, not saying anything. They call down and tell us there is a weirdo at their door. We send security up to investigate. When asked to describe them, they always say the man is wearing a white suit."

Thomas and Lucinda are not the only spirits to wander the Don Cesar. In 1942 the impending war brought major changes at the Don. Purchased by the army, the hotel struggled for three decades as a World War II hospital and veteran's convalescent home. The once-luxurious penthouse became the operating room. The lobby housed the morgue, examining rooms, and lab. The Red Cross sponsored dances in the ballroom, featuring local girls who called themselves the "Bomb-a-Dears." Many men passed through the hotel, injured and wounded. Some came to recuperate. Some never left. Every morning the men who were able were brought out to the beach. Occasionally in the early morning someone will see a man in a wheelchair sitting on the beach, but he disappears when he is approached.

During this time, the hotel's extravagant interior was stripped to the bare walls and painted "government green." The fountain, a loving monument to a lovers' tryst, was ripped from the hotel. Original bronze fixtures, expensive oriental rugs, and rooms full of rich cherry and oak furniture were loaded into government trucks and hauled away. A note titled "The Passing of the Fish Pool, July 28, 1948," was tossed into the hole that was once the fountain and covered with flooring. This note lay undiscovered for twenty-five years before it was found during the 1973 restoration and published in the *St. Petersburg Times*.

The most prominent ghost from this era of the hotel is a nurse. She scared the wits out of the hotel's night chef. Frank is about six-foot-two and 250 pounds, so not much scares him. One night, he received an order for a hamburger and a salad. As he approached the walk-in cooler, he saw a woman in a nursing cap looking out the window from the inside! Scared silly, he called security and demanded that they check out the kitchen. It took so long, when the chef was finally able to prepare the hamburger, the hotel had to give it to the diner free. Another time, six employees were working in the kitchen when they all heard loud noises coming from inside the cooler. When they opened it, food was smashed up against the door, as if someone had thrown it. Guests at the Chef's Table, an exclusive kitchen-side table, have also witnessed food flying through the air with no apparent cause.

Recently a masseur was working on a client in Treatment Room 4. He glanced up and saw a woman standing in the doorway. She had wavy hair and an old-fashioned nurse's uniform and cap. The nurse's expression was as startled as his. Suddenly his client sat up, very upset. "Did you see something in the mirror?" she asked. They looked each other in the eye, and both gasped, "A nurse!"

Best Rooms/Times

Mr. Rowe wanders throughout the hotel and may greet you when he passes. He is most often seen in the lobby and hallways. The kitchen is another hot spot. The spa is where the World War II nurse is most frequently sighted.

The Hotel

The legendary flamingo-pink Mediterranean castle, with its Moorish bell towers and imperial turrets, sits proudly on the white Florida sands overlooking the Gulf of Mexico. Listed on the National Register of Historic Places, the St. Petes Beach resort features 277 newly renovated guest rooms, including 2 penthouses and 50 suites.

Surrounded by a tropical paradise of flowers and palms, guests enjoy a plunge in one of two Gulf-front pools, with underwater sound systems, or shape up with aqua aerobics while serenaded by a steel-drum band. The spa offers soothing sea salt body scrubs and surfside massages, or yoga on the beach to calm body and spirit.

Dining

Three outstanding restaurants are all named after characters from Wallace's famous opera. The Maritana Grille, named after both the opera and the heroine, is the resort's signature Four Diamond restaurant and is famous for its award-winning "Floribbean" cuisine. The restaurant is surrounded by 1,500 gallons of saltwater aquariums, containing hundreds of brightly colored indigenous Florida fish.

A recent offering at the Maritana is the Chef's Table. By reserving this table, guests are invited into the kitchen, where they dine with award-winning executive chef Eric Neri and his gourmet staff. The culinary adventure begins once inside the swinging doors leading to the kitchen. As a heavenly aroma foretells what awaits the taste buds, four to eight patrons are seated at a triangular table in a corner of the Maritana Grille kitchen, separated from the grill and preparation areas by a glass window enabling guests to preview the evening fare.

Sunday brunch is served in the highly acclaimed King Charles Ballroom, and combines gourmet delights and spectacular Gulf views with more than 180 scrumptious brunch selections. On the boardwalk on moonlit nights, the gardenlike setting, with wicker furniture and oversize wooden swings, enhances the dining experience at the Sea Porch Café. Or guests can enjoy a tropical Mai Tai or piña colada in the lobby bar or Sunset Lounge.

Don't Miss

A fun, fact-filled history tour takes guests throughout the colorful hotel and its entertaining past. Tours begin Wednesday and Saturday at 2:00 P.M. in the lobby. In October, the hotel adds a spooky nighttime ghost tour.

Don Cesar Beach Resort and Spa
3400 Gulf Boulevard
St. Petes Beach, FL 33706
727-360-1881 or 800-282-1116
e-mail: info@doncesar.com
www.doncesar.com

Eliza Thompson House

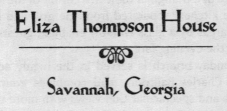

Savannah, Georgia

I was sitting at a small table near the back in one of America's most haunted bars. Hannah's East is the legendary hangout located above the haunted Pirate's House Restaurant in Savannah. Immortalized in the pages of *Midnight in the Garden of Good and Evil,* a frail but feisty Emma Kelly was at the piano, taking requests.

Beside me was Greg Profitt, tour operator and well-known authority on Savannah's hauntings. After a stint in the merchant marines, Profitt landed in Savannah, taking a job as a carriage driver. He did not believe in ghosts. "I didn't even consider such things," Profitt admits. "The only ghost I believed in was the Holy Ghost."

That was soon to change. Greg was asked to take a group of Girl Scouts on a night outing.

I had just hired on with the carriage company. I had to take a group of nine or ten Girl Scouts on a night tour. We were just passing the Kehoe House, which used to belong to Joe Namath. Years ago it was a funeral parlor. I was supposed to tell these girls about a supposed ghost, but I hadn't said a word because I was a new driver. Suddenly all the girls started screaming, and Clyde, my horse, took off running. I just lost control. By now, the girls were screaming louder. So was I, but for a different reason. I hadn't seen what they saw. Finally I got Clyde under control. The girls were still looking back toward the Kehoe House, screaming. Some of them were crying. They said they saw a woman with no feet in a flowing gown, hovering above the balcony, and that she was glowing. They were so terrified, I had to turn around and take them home without even finishing the tour. Some of the mothers were mad at me. They thought I overdid the ghost part a bit, but I hadn't even mentioned ghosts.

Two weeks later, Profitt had an encounter of his own. As he drove a carriage packed with tourists past the Colonial Cemetery, two specters floated out of the cemetery and toward them. "The horse reared, and I started screaming. Everybody started screaming."

So frightened was he by what he had encountered, Profitt ended the tour then and there. In fact, he took a few weeks off to "recuperate."

"It took me a few days to get used to the fact that I had seen what I had seen. If no one else had seen it, I would have thought I was having a flashback, but twelve other people saw it too."

After that, Greg developed a real fascination with the macabre. He also realized there was an audience of people out there with the same curiosity. Once he conquered his fears, he founded Savannah by Foot (no need to spook the horses anymore) and started the Haunted Pub Crawl. "I always wanted to find a way to make drinking pay," he laughs.

Greg had heard a lot of strange stories whispered late at night in the bars that he frequented. He checked out these tales with a number of sources, including personal witnesses and even the Savannah Historical Society. He will not tell a story he cannot substantiate. Drink in hand, Greg leads his group on a tour down the cobblestone streets of Savannah, from one haunted pub to another. He may stop at a popular nightspot, and then lead the group up a rickety back staircase to an eerie hidden room frequented by the ghost of a young woman who was locked in the room for many years, and then down the street to a dimly lit eighteenth-century tavern where the air somehow feels heavier, and a chilling electricity immediately makes your hair stand on end and your senses become alert. Even if you didn't know for sure, you can feel "them" there.

Don't let Profitt's Bostonian twang throw you off—this guy knows his stuff. A self-proclaimed born-again southerner, Greg has finally become an accepted part of Savannah's tradition, even by blue-blooded, blue-haired society ladies. "I don't consider myself a Yankee," Profitt protests. "I learned how to say y'all and fixin', but I ain't eatin' no grits."

I was frantically typing away on my laptop as Greg talked, trying to keep up with his sensational stories, when I glanced down at the screen. The words on the screen were not what I had typed. It read, "wome broughher fel i lov wit s\ale bo\adin i thn ehnous epromise t com eodngrhenle a0

\ackb." I realized something was really wrong with my computer.

"Wait." I panicked. "My computer is goofing up."

"What?"

"My computer stopped working. It's a brand-new laptop, and look what happens when I type."

Greg leaned in to look as I carefully pronounced, and typed, "My computer is goofing up."

The computer screen displayed, "m compute i gboffung up."

"Maybe it's because of where we are," Greg cautioned.

To test my computer, I typed his words, concentrating on each letter to make sure I hit the right keys: m a y b e_i t_ i s_b e c a u s e_o f_w h e r e_w e_ are.

"m be becaseo wherew aeae f a bsry" printed on my screen.

"Maybe it is the ghost," he said. "Better get your tablet." I reluctantly grabbed a pen and took notes by the light of a candle in the dark, smoke-filled room.

It was getting late, and Greg still hadn't told me about the Eliza Thompson House, where I was staying that night.

"Oh, it's haunted all right," Greg assured me. "There is the ghost of a woman, probably Miss Eliza, dressed in period clothing. People see her all the time, and then she just disappears. They also hear a baby cry. It's your typical haunting, nothing really complicated or terrifying there."

Easy for him to say. He wasn't about to spend the night in a haunted inn, all alone.

"Sorry about your computer," he added as we parted. "I hope you can get it fixed."

"Yeah, me too."

When I returned to the inn, I turned on my computer to

attempt to troubleshoot the problem. Then I raced for the phone to call Greg. "You won't believe this," I cried. "My computer works fine!"

Sightings

At one place, I was going to get a pint of beer when a couple approached and asked me in hushed tones, "Is any of this real, or is it just made-up stories?" Before I could answer, about thirty cocktail-sized glasses, hanging in a pyramid rack above the bar, shattered. They didn't fall down, they all shattered at the same instant. The bartender didn't say anything; he just cleaned it up. I think some of the people who work at these places get used to working with a ghost.

I had one group of two couples that was very obnoxious. They weren't listening to a word I said. I took them to the Pink House, hoping they would order a drink. I wanted a double. They ordered a soda, so I got a soda, too. I was sitting there wondering why they were there, when suddenly one of the ladies grabs this guy's arm, hanging on for dear life. Now I know this is crazy sounding, but I swear it's true. There is a wine rack above the bar. A wine bottle was spinning. It actually came out of the wine holder and levitated in the air. The guy said to the girl, "It's a special effect, they're pushing the wine." I thought that was ludicrous. Then the lights started going down. I looked at the switch itself, and it was moving . . . at least in my mind it was moving. They are looking at the wine bottle floating, and the lights going up and down. The people in the restaurant were screaming. The bartender turned to me in a gruff voice and ordered, "Take your people and get out of here."

I went back later. The gal behind the bar told me that as soon as we left, everything went back to normal. I don't know if these things latch on because you're talking about it. I'm afraid if I started trying to figure it out, I'd become a little obsessive about it. I've experienced some pretty scary things that are hard to explain. People ask, "How could this happen?" I don't have a clue.

I have another one about Pink House. I love it, but it's kind of unsettling. It was a rainy night. Only two people showed up, and there were supposed to be nine. The husband had been a Navy Seal. He didn't believe in ghosts. I can understand that. I respect these folks. The training is more dangerous than the coast guard. I appreciate people willing to put themselves in danger for their country. He admits that he's not going to believe any of the stories. I think he is enjoying the stories more than he expected. We were sitting there, when all of a sudden the guy freaks out. He looks real strange. He looks away from us, then runs out of the place. Now keep in mind, this guy was a rock.

Something got to him bad. It must have been pretty scary to make a guy like that run in terror. We ran out to find him. He was trembling when he told us that a little girl walked up to him with a tray of pastries. She was about seven years old, not dressed for this time period. "I ran right through her," he gasped. "I felt her as I walked through her."

Then there's O'Donnels. It used to be a place where indentured Irish servants would meet on the sly—legally, they weren't allowed to drink or congregate together. They were hard workers, and they rightfully wanted their ale. They had their own still in the back. The women would cook. Somehow, the word got out, and one day, someone set the place on fire. The man who started it was the only one to die. After that, strange things would happen. People see a sailor's hat moving on its own, as if someone were wearing it. At other times, it swings furiously, like someone is batting at flames. On one of my tours, three or four people saw something whitish and opaque hovering like a cloud. I can read people's faces. They looked very, very uncomfortable. It came toward them, then moved back to the back of the room.

Now, once a year, at Halloween, Profitt confronts his fears and spends the night in a haunted pub. The event has generated a lot of publicity and created quite a following. Today beer trucks and vendors line up outside while onlookers place bets on how long Greg will last. All proceeds go to charity.

It started out when this Englishman bet me two hundred dollars that I wouldn't spend the night alone at Hannah's East above the Pirate's House, haunted by the ghost of Captain Flint. Workers will not go near that place after dark. However, never one to refuse a bet, I accepted the challenge. We got to be great buddies. We thought rather than keep the money, we would donate it for leukemia research.

This is all absolutely true, no bullshit. Since Flint's last words were, "Darby, bring aft the rum," I brought some dark rum and three glasses, one for me, one for the Englishman, and one for Flint. I also brought a Bible and a crucifix. There was no doubt in my mind there was true activity in this place. When we went in, there were all kinds of weird noises, and banging on the walls, even though we were the only [living] ones inside. We were nervous. We sat on the floor to make our toast. I said, with emphasis, "Darby, bring aft the rum." I would swear on the Bible that the shot glass we poured for Flint vanished! The glass itself actually vanished! We would have bolted, but all of a sudden, at the same time, we went from being acutely alert to really exhausted. The next thing we knew, it was morning.

I don't believe that ghost can hurt me. If I

did, I wouldn't have gone up there. We never found the third shot glass. I don't know why I was so confident. When I think of everything that has happened to me, it boggles my mind.

Best Rooms/Times

Rooms 4, 5, and 6 in the main house are the most active rooms at the Eliza Thompson House.

The Inn/Hotel

In 1847, when the striking auburn-haired widow Eliza Thompson built her stately Federal-style town home, Savannah was enjoying prosperous times. Cotton was king, and the wealthy planters built extravagant winter homes in the city, returning to their plantations in the spring. Miss Eliza entertained often, hosting fabulous soirées for Savannah's finest.

When war struck our nation, the South was ravaged. Many of the South's most magnificent mansions were destroyed during Sherman's infamous "March to the Sea." But Eliza Thompson's home, like the rest of Savannah, was spared from this fate by General Sherman's "generosity." Historians differ on just why General Sherman chose not to burn Savannah, but legend has it that General Sherman felt a special fondness for the lovely city, and one of its equally attractive young ladies.

Today you will find the Eliza Thompson House, restored to its original elegance, nestled on a quaint cobblestone street on one of Savannah's most picturesque squares, in the very heart of the town's famous National Landmark Historic District.

There are twenty-five guest rooms, each one a magnificent representation of what it may have looked like if you had been attending one of Miss Liza's balls in the 1850s. The furnishings in the house are magnificent. The grand Chippendale dining table and chairs, Louis XV sofas, marble-top Empire china cabinets, and Federal bureaus, set amid richly designed fabrics and reproduction wallpaper, whoosh you back to a glorious era in the Old South. In the guest rooms, a tiny stepping stool sits, waiting to boost you up into the romantic canopy tester bed.

In the main house are twelve stately guest rooms. The courtyard wing, which was once Miss Eliza's carriage house, contains another thirteen guest rooms overlooking a magnificent fountain in the lush courtyard. All of the lovely rooms have fireplaces and private baths, and are furnished with period antiques.

The southern hospitality at this inn is never-ending. Capture the romance of a bygone era during the afternoon high tea, served in the formal parlor. During the cocktail hour, wine and cheese are served in the parlor, or out in the garden by the fountain. Coffee and dessert are offered from 8:30 P.M. to 10:00 P.M. nightly. In the morning, awake to the aroma of freshly brewed coffee, and enjoy a scrumptious breakfast made with fresh local products.

On Wednesday afternoons, Miss Eliza appears in

period costume and takes you on a delightful tour of the surrounding area. Her stories center on the history of the charming neighborhood and its colorful residents, both present and past.

Dining

A visit to Savannah is not complete without a visit to the Pirates' House. Since the early 1750s, this famous haunted pirates' den has been a source of delicious food, sturdy drink, and rousing good times. The original building, which now adjoins the Pirates' House, was erected in 1734 and is said to be the oldest house in the state of Georgia. As Savannah grew into a thriving seaport town, an inn was erected for visiting seamen. Situated a scant block from the Savannah River, the inn became a rendezvous of bloodthirsty pirates and sailors from the Seven Seas. Here seamen drank their stout ale and boasted about their outlandish adventures.

In the chamber known as the Captain's Room, with its hand-hewn ceiling beams, ship's masters negotiated to shanghai unwary seamen to complete their crews. Stories persist of a tunnel extending from the old rum cellar beneath the Captain's Room all the way to the river, through which unsuspecting sailors were carried, drugged and unconscious, to waiting ships. Indeed, many a drunken sailor awoke to find himself on a strange ship, bound for some foreign port halfway around the world.

Today, the thrill and romance of those exciting

days of pirate ships and buried treasure has been carefully preserved. Each of the fifteen unique dining rooms is filled with fascinating pirate memorabilia and shipping lore.

Hanging on the walls in the Captain's Room and the Treasure Room are framed pages from an early, very rare edition of the book *Treasure Island*. Savannah is mentioned numerous times in this Robert Louis Stevenson classic. In fact, some of the action is supposed to have taken place in the Pirates' House. 'Tis said that old Captain Flint died in an upstairs room. In the legend, his faithful mate, Billy Bones, was at his side when he breathed his last breath, muttering the famous words, "Darby, bring aft the rum." Even now many, including Profitt, swear that the ghost of Captain Flint still haunts the Pirates' House.

The food at the Pirates' House is fabulous. The famous okra gumbo is served by the kettle or the cup. Honey-pecan fried chicken, low-country shrimp boil, hearty black bean soup with red onions and sour cream, baby back ribs, and a delectable selection of seafood is offered.

Upstairs at the Pirates' House is Hannah's East, a noted jazz club where Ben Tucker plucked a mean string bass, and beloved pianist Emma Kelly belted out a tune like you wouldn't believe. The duo was world famous well before they were immortalized in the pages of *Midnight in the Garden of Good and Evil*. Hannah's is known for its ghosts as much as for its jazz.

Don't Miss

Try the Creepy Crawl Haunted Pub Tour (912-238-3843); robust spirits in these bars does not refer to alcohol. Waiting till darkness descends over the mystical city and the cobblestone streets become dark and shadowy, Greg Profitt leads you on a tour you will not soon forget, relating both personal encounters and local legends. You can tell from his expression and the excitement in his voice that he is seriously rattled, and that his ghostly experiences have shaken him to his very core. He is constantly updating his tour with the latest ghost sightings.

Eliza Thompson House
5 West Jones Street
Savannah, GA 31401
912-236-3620 or 800-348-9378
e-mail: innkeeper@elizathompsonhouse.com
www.elizathompsonhouse.com

The Fargo Mansion

✦

Lake Mills, Wisconsin

Enoch J. Fargo, descendant of the wealthy Wells Fargo stagecoach and banking family, brutally murdered his second wife, Addie, so that he could marry her young cousin, Maddie. His first wife, Mary, also died under questionable circumstances. These two vengeful wives, along with a mischievous pair of bears, haunt the Fargo Mansion.

E. J. Fargo and his first wife, Mary Rutherford, bought the mansion in 1888 from its builder, Elijah Harvey. They added a third floor ballroom and a wraparound porch. The Fargo Mansion became the social hub of the town, hosting the weddings, funerals, and coming-out balls for everyone who was anyone in Lake Mills.

Two years later, Mary and her daughter were taken ill with a mysterious ailment, and shortly thereafter they died. E. J. sent his surviving daughter off to live with relatives and married Addie Hoyt. Before long, Addie, too, became mysteriously ill. Fargo moved in her beautiful young cousin, Maddie, to be her nurse. But Maddie shared more than

Addie's home. It wasn't long before E. J. and Maddie were having an affair right under Addie's nose. Every night, E. J. would tiptoe down the long halls into the guest room in the wee hours when he thought Addie was asleep.

No one knows why Addie suddenly made a complete recovery, but E. J. was not happy. His hopes of marrying Maddie were dashed, so he took matters into his own hands. In spite of her continuing good health, Addie's "condition" suddenly "took a turn for the worse," or so the facts were reported, and she passed away unexpectedly one night. An hour later, a Dr. Oatway—not only E. J.'s personal physician, but one of his closest friends and most trusted confidants—arrived to examine the corpse and sign the death certificate. Together they conspired to keep Addie's murder a secret. There was no customary visitation. If there had been, people would have known that Addie had been shot in the head. Instead, she was buried before the break of dawn, "to avoid the spread of her very contagious condition." E. J. married Maddie before Addie's body was cold.

The events of that fateful night were kept secret for decades, until twelfth-hour fear and remorse prompted Dr. Oatway to a deathbed confession. He confessed that Addie had not died of illness, as he attested on the death certificate, but of a gunshot wound to the head. She was the victim of a cold-blooded murder, shot by E. J. as she lay innocently sleeping in her bed.

The scene of the crime, now called the Addie Hoyt Room, and its adjacent landing are the site of the inn's present-day sightings. Innkeeper Tom Boycks recalls that guests and an assistant innkeeper have often reported the presence of a female entity in that area.

Two bear ghosts also haunt the garden outside the mansion. Maddie loved animals, so for her amusement, E. J. built a bear pit in the north garden, complete with a twisting underground cave. Sally, a brown bear, and Jack, a black bear, resided in the pit for many years until they were "liberated" on Halloween night in 1913. Two jokesters from town lowered a ladder into the pit, and the mischievous duo escaped. With the bears on the loose, the townsfolk panicked, and spent a few sleepless nights until the fugitives were captured and sentenced to life in the Milwaukee zoo. The bear pit and underground tunnels still remain today.

Sightings

Both Tom and his partner, Barry Luck, frequently experience the distinct feeling they are being watched. Tom reports occasionally catching a glimpse of a female figure on the landing upstairs.

Linda Fisher was one of Fargo's early assistant innkeepers. One day she came downstairs, very upset. She had been vacuuming the foyer staircase when something, or someone, brushed up against her. As she turned, she thought she saw the shadow of a woman. This has happened many times since, always near the Addie Hoyt Room.

The curator for a major Chicago art museum stayed for two nights. "She was very delightful," recalls Tom. "When she came down for breakfast in the morning, she reported that she had the most wonderful night. She went on to tell us that something went on, and that she felt a presence at the top of the steps. She had the same experience the second night."

Many others since then have reported the presence, always in the same area, even though they had no previous knowledge of Addie's murder, or where she died.

Best Rooms/Times

Ask for the Addie Hoyt Room, and drift off to sleep in the room where Addie lay sleeping on that fateful night a century ago. But don't worry if it's booked. Her spirit is more often encountered on the landing outside. Look for her on a cold, dreary night in the dead of winter.

If you walk through the gardens at night, that shadow lurking behind you is likely to be the bear ghosts, Sally and Jack.

The Hotel

This place just looks like the stereotypical haunted house, with its porticos and turrets. Built in 1881, the Fargo Mansion is a classic example of Queen Anne architecture. Guests are encouraged to roam free through the immaculately restored Victorian showplace. The house is decorated in pastels, with delicately painted original artwork on the ceilings. Polished oak panels frame rooms full of the owners' extensive antique collections, each nook and cranny filled with delightful treasures. Upstairs, eight impeccably decorated guest rooms, each with a private bath, are laid out in a maze off the curved halls.

Rooms are named after the people who lived and died here, and are furnished with rich Victorian antiques. The Enoch J. Fargo Suite is my favorite. Like something straight out of a James Bond movie, a "secret" passageway leads through the wall. The focal point of the room is the original tile fireplace, flanked by identical built-in bookcases—identical, that is, until you push the "secret" spot, and the bookcase swings open. Inside is an exquisite Italian marble haven, the center of which is a step-down Jacuzzi tub for two.

Dining

Tom confides that guests who check in to the suite are often not seen again until checkout, though it's a shame to miss breakfast at Fargo Mansion, which consists of freshly baked homemade muffins, a delicious hot entrée, which may be quiche, omelets, or baked pancakes, fruit garnish, coffee, juice, and tea. A typical breakfast could consist of raspberry muffins, broccoli cheese casserole, fresh fruit, and beverage.

Don't Miss

The picturesque downtown of Lake Mills is filled with lovely architecture, restaurants, and gift and antique shops. When you walk down Main Street, you feel as if you have stepped right into a Norman Rockwell print. In the heart of the town lies the Commons Park, where you can enjoy seasonal events, farmer's markets, Friday-night band concerts under a Victorian gazebo, and an old-fashioned community ice-skating rink.

The Fargo Mansion
211 Main Street
Lake Mills, WI 53551
414-648-3654
e-mail: frontdsk@fargomansion.com
www.fargomansion.com

Historic Farnsworth House
Restaurant and Inn

❦

Gettysburg, Pennsylvania

A stately brick farmhouse sits just outside town, her thick walls protecting the desperate Confederate soldiers standing guard within. Bullet fire rings from the attic, as shots are fired at the battlefield below. Shots that still ring out today. "I was ordered to stay put," one young soldier told a startled guest. And like any good soldier, he did, even after his death.

"Do you still hear the ghost soldiers?" passersby would stop and whisper to the family members who moved into the home three decades ago.

Long known for its ghosts, the Farnsworth House, a Civil War monument, stood witness to the horrors and bloodshed of the final battles of Gettysburg. Some historians believe that Jenny Lind, the only civilian mortally wounded during the war, died of a rifle shot from the Farnsworth attic. More than a hundred random bullets intended to maim and kill struck the structure and remain lodged in the old walls. Ghostly soldiers still keep sentinel from the attic above.

Ghosts are an accepted vision in the town of Gettysburg, and on her sprawling battlefields. Maybe it's because there are so many men who lost their lives, or because passions were so high. The emotions of the dead are so heavy in Gettysburg that I am overcome with a deep sadness. Thousands of men lost their lives. It's hard to imagine that many men and animals lying dead and wounded in the fields. It took months and months just to bury all the bodies. Local floorboards are still stained from the oozing, crimson blood of painfully wounded and dying young men, a reminder of the horrific events of 1865. At the old college dorms, converted into a makeshift hospital, blood was so deep that holes were drilled in the floors to let the seeping scarlet serum drain to the floors below. Textbooks were crusted and sealed with dried blood.

Patty O'Day grew up at the Farnsworth House. "I'm part of the family," she told me.

We restored the place in 1972. I knew it had a reputation for being haunted, but back then you didn't really say much about it. People would stop and say, "Do you still hear the soldiers in the attic?"

I always felt like someone was following me. One time I saw a woman in the hall. My grandmother, who lived with us, had experiences too. We just had our own secret sessions where we talked about it. She told me about her experiences as a child. One night, her father sat at the foot of her bed and told her that he loved her. He said that he had come to say good-bye, and that he would always be with her. In the morning, she learned he had died in the middle of the night. After that, she was very open to the spirit world.

She warned me not to tell the other children what I had seen. She knew the kids would make fun of me. Nowadays, if you haven't had a ghost experience, there is something wrong with you.

My grandmother used to see a woman standing beside the fireplace in her room. She would always smell heavy gardenias before the woman appeared. Grandmother would say, "Those are funeral flowers." They used to have wakes right in the house, and the smell of gardenias would remind her of those times. Sometimes she would hear footsteps. She has had so many experiences.

Everybody always had a haunted house in their town. In Gettysburg, I learned, there were many. I would always feel like there was someone behind me. It got to the point where I stopped being so afraid, and I would just say hello. Finally I opened up, and started telling the stories when I waited on tables. In 1987, a lady said I should tell my ghost stories in public. So I started the ghost tours, almost by accident.

It wasn't until 1991 that I learned who the ghosts were. The local television station brought in a psychic, Carol Kirkpatrick, whom I had never met before. Carol was looking behind me. I thought, She sees whoever is behind me. She told me it is a girl named Mary, who came to visit her brother John and care for the wounded. She is still watching out for the people in the house, like a caretaker or sentinel. If someone is sick, or sad, that is usually when she appears.

I took Carol up in the attic, where she could sense the presence of three soldiers. Only one actually appeared, a Confederate lieutenant. He was firing at Union soldiers on Cemetery Hill, about 600 feet away. Carol didn't know anything about Gettysburg, or the house. She didn't know that at night we would hear pacing upstairs in the attic, along with the sounds of a Jew's harp, and heavy trunks being dragged across the floor.

We get a lot of people coming through, searching for their ancestors who died here. Also a lot of reenactors stay here. I believe the reenactors are drawn to the field where so many people died. It's interesting to talk to people and share in that journey they are on. Just as long as I don't have to come back and haunt the Farnsworth.

Patty now probes timid guests to learn about their encounters in her home. "It's scary if you've never had an experience like that. We are not really going to know for sure what is going on until we cross over ourselves. I like to ask guests, 'How did you sleep . . . did anything happen?' They probably think I'm crazy. I ask people to fill out papers when they have an experience. It's very interesting how similar these stories are."

Sightings

"For a short while, the attic was open as a bed-and-breakfast room," Patty says, but some people became disturbed by the soldiers who haunted it. Several couples who stayed in that room left in the middle of the night. One man had his wife call back the next day. She said he was really upset, after seeing a soldier standing next to his bed. The man had just retired, so he knew he was wide awake and not dreaming. He bolted up and said to the soldier, "Who are you, and why are you here?"

A tired voice answered him, "This is my post. I am ordered to stay at my post." The man felt overwhelmed with emotions for the lone soldier.

We opened the Sweeney Room after my grandmother died. In that room people would feel extremely sad, like they wanted to cry—even grown men. A couple of women told us they felt like they were in labor in that room. They couldn't sleep, and felt cramps. They sometimes saw a presence by the fireplace, or someone standing over the bed watching them. Sometimes it is absolutely overwhelming in that room, and you just feel like you want to sit on the edge of the bed and cry.

When Carol, the psychic, came, she smelled the gardenias that my grandmother used to smell, and she felt the presence of a woman named Nan. Carol said Nan was a midwife, and she was there to help a young woman Florence who had just had a stillborn birth. That explains all those feelings.

I hadn't even told my mom what Carol said

about the dead child. Less than a week later, a woman and her daughter stayed in that room. The girl was around five. They were trying to decide between the Sweeney and the Sarah Black Rooms. There is a Victorian comb case on the dresser. I got it down to let the little girl play, while her mother and I stepped out into the next room. Nothing was ever said about ghosts or hauntings. We noticed that it was awfully quiet in the next room. When we went to the Sweeney Room, we noticed that the case was on the floor. I looked into the alcove. A green velvet chair that sits in that corner was pushed out. The little girl was behind the chair, crouched in a ball, hiding. She said, "Mommy, the baby's dead!"

I call that my skeptic story. The little girl had seen this baby's death. There was no way she could have known anything about the room. I had just found out myself.

We had another lady who claims she dreamed about the Farnsworth House for twenty years, although she never knew it was a real place. She remembers running down the hill to this house, and being scared to death. She came to Gettysburg with some friends. When they started walking down the hill, she saw the house and remembered. She became very excited, and insisted on going in. The people with her didn't believe, so here she was reliving this entire trauma on her own. Mom said, "There is something going on with this woman." I took her upstairs to the attic. We had to stop a couple of times because she was very nervous and anxious, but didn't know why. When I opened the attic door, she turned to the right, toward the window, where the sharpshooters took aim, and then fainted.

The basement is also very active. It's where we have the Mourning Theater. There is the spirit of a woman named Mary. I've actually seen her in the hallway, and once during a performance. She was standing at the bottom of the stairs in the back of the theater. I knew other people had seen her. I wanted to stop and say, "Did you guys see her?" but I went on with the show. Afterward I found out that four other people saw her too, but they all thought she was a special effect. She is often accompanied by the scent of roses. Sometimes people watching the theater feel her hand on the back of their hand.

Best Rooms/Times

Of the ten rooms at this inn, half are known to be haunted. These include the McFarland Room, the Catherine Sweeney Room, the Sarah Black Room, the Jennie Wade Room, and the Shultz Room. The haunted third-floor attic room, the Garrett, is no longer rented out, though footsteps and voices can still be heard below, even when no one is in the room.

Some of Gettysburg's troubled ghosts also roam the dining room, staircase, and basement of this poignant Civil War shrine. The theater is a hotbed of activity.

The Hotel/Inn

The rooms in this inn are spectacular. Some of these idyllic grown-up playrooms are labeled "Adults Only." Each room is individually decorated with nineteenth-century antiques, fine draperies, private baths, and air conditioning. Some have fireplaces and exquisite two-person whirlpools. Rooms are named after noted Civil War heroes and owners of the inn.

In the Lincoln Room are a four-poster antique bed, original newspaper photos of Lincoln's funeral procession, and a reproduction of the rocking chair in which Lincoln was assassinated at Ford's Theatre. The Belle Boyd Room, named for the notorious Confederate Spy, is labeled "Adults Only." It has a working gas fireplace, a Victorian couch, and a large reclining nude oil painting. In the large tiled "Roman-style" bathroom is a two-person Jacuzzi under an exotic dolphin mural. Other rooms have unique period pieces, Civil War memorabilia, stained-glass windows, and other antebellum accoutrements. Many have antique claw-foot tubs and Victorian high-tank pull-chain toilets.

Dining

Gettysburg's only Civil War dining room is presided over by oil portraits of the two commanding officers at Gettysburg, General Robert E. Lee and General George G. Meade. Period furnishings and candlelight add to the authentic feel. Delicious period fare includes game pie, peanut soup, spoon bread, sweet potato pudding, and pumpkin fritters.

You may opt to dine in an open-air garden alongside a beautiful spring-fed stream. This stone-lined stream provided a water source for both the Confederate and Union armies.

The Killer Angel Tavern, located behind the Farnsworth House, was created to look as it might have during the war. Tavern keepers do not respond to modern-day questions, and speak only "Civil War." They are well versed on the subject and have spent many hours conversing with historians and local folks to give patrons an authentic experience. Three glass cases display an assortment of props, costumes, and memorabilia from the movie *Gettysburg*.

Don't Miss

The Mourning Theater offers guests the opportunity to experience slices of life from Civil War days. Actors portray soldiers and read real letters written to loved ones before their untimely deaths. You never know what might happen during one of these performances. Look closely. Is that an actor, or a ghost? Theater guests have felt a hand on their shoulder, and one visitor was grabbed by the pants leg.

Candlelight Ghost Walks are led by a period-dressed guide down the very streets the soldiers walked. Tales and legends blend with bits of human interest and historical fact. There is also a historic ghost tour on six blocks of Baltimore Street between the Jenny Wade House and Farnsworth.

Historic Farnsworth House Restaurant and Inn
401 Baltimore Street
Gettysburg, PA 17235
717-334-8838
e-mail: farnhaus@cvn.net
www.farnsworthhousedining.com

General Lewis Inn
and Restaurant

❦

Lewisburg, West Virginia

The General Lewis Inn sits in the center of a community that is a hotbed of paranormal activity and Civil War ghosts. Built in 1834 by General Lewis, the property is just a stone's throw from both Revolutionary and Civil War battlefields, and from the old Civil War Cemetery. The entire historic town is laden with the ghosts of soldiers slaughtered in battle.

In 1929 Randolf K. Hock and his wife, Mary Noel, purchased the estate. They added a new wing and opened the home as an inn. Today's owner is a third-generation descendant. The walnut and pine front desk, added by Mr. Hock, is the same desk used by Patrick Henry and Thomas Jefferson when they signed into the neighboring Sweet Chalybeate Springs Hotel.

One ghost is that of a lady wearing antebellum attire. She apparently lives in the old section of the house, and never goes into the 1920s addition.

Another ghost is a little girl, who died in the 1850s. She looks to be about eight years old. The maid has encountered her in one of the rooms, and the night watchman has seen her coming down the stairs. Often she is seen playing outside, only to vanish into thin air. Sometimes guests see the rocking chairs rocking by themselves.

Footsteps in the dining room and lobby are common, especially at night. Elizabeth, a waitress at the inn, reports seeing a figure in black enter the dining room. When she approached to take an order, the figure vanished. She says sometimes they see someone walk past in the dining room or kitchen, and there's no one there. Other times, crashing and banging is heard coming from the empty kitchen. Heavy pots have been thrown across the room. "Sometimes you feel something pulling at your skirt. You turn around to smack someone, but there's no one there and no one has walked by. It's happened a couple of times."

Assistant manager Jeanne Anderson never believed in ghosts until she came to work at the inn. She was upstairs in one of the bedrooms when she heard someone come to the door. "Is anyone in here?" a man's voice asked. She looked up and saw a ghostly image outside the door, but when she ran toward it, the ghost had vanished. The maid working in the next room also heard the voice, but thought that Jeanne was speaking with someone.

The most disconcerting sound is a deep, guttural moaning. It seems to come from Room 206; however, if you open the door to investigate, the sound moves. Sometimes it goes on for hours. Even owner Jim Morgan, a skeptic by nature, has heard what he terms "strange sounds" on a couple of occasions.

Sightings

One of the ghosts seems to reside in a painting. Gloria Edwards and her family stopped at the inn one stormy night in 1968 when travel conditions became unbearable. With her were her physician husband, two daughters, ten and two years old, and an eight-year-old son. The following excerpts are taken from a long, emotional letter she later sent to the staff.

We stopped at a warm, welcoming inn, the General Lewis. We knew nothing of its history. We fell in love with the lovely large room with fireplace, spinning wheel, two four-poster beds with stepping stools to climb up on them—and a portrait of a pretty woman and a two-to-three-year-old child hanging over an antique settee. My husband said the little settee was the perfect spot for our youngest daughter to sleep, but for some reason that I could not explain, I said, "No, she MUST sleep with me!"

I am a restless sleeper. I opened my eyes, and found myself staring at a mist forming around the portrait, then slowly but definitely coming in a circular motion directly over the bed, settling directly over my two-year-old. I threw my arm instinctively around my sleeping child and called out for my husband. When he turned on the light, there was nothing.

In the morning, I shared my experience with the innkeeper. He told me there had been other reported ghost stories from the room where we had stayed, Room 208.

Twenty-three years later, we revisited the inn for the first time. As I walked through Room 208 and carefully studied the portrait, I felt a feeling of something very special. I was amazed at the resemblance of the young woman in the portrait to our now twenty-five-year-old daughter, the one the mist seemed most interested in. No one on the staff knew anything about the painting, except that it has been hanging in that room since the inn first opened.

Best Rooms/Times

Rooms 206 and 208 are the most haunted rooms. Sightings seem to pick up in the winter.

Hotel/Inn

Built in 1834, the house survived the ravages of two American wars. In 1929 an additional wing was added, and the home was converted into an inn. Two rooms and two suites were part of the original 1834 home. Twenty-one more rooms are in the new wing. Every room is furnished with local historic antiques.

Just beyond the lobby is Memory Hall, a rich collection of historic pioneer memorabilia, including tools, guns, household utensils, covered wagon parts, and musical instruments. Many are handmade relics. Throughout the inn are numerous old cupboards filled with early glass pottery, china, and curios.

Antique rockers line the veranda. In the center of the lush gardens, amid century-old statuary, is a life-size three-room dollhouse, converted from an eighteenth-century "necessary," where the present owner played as a child. A primitive but ornate stagecoach from the early 1800s sits outside. It was used to transport passengers to the popular springs resorts that lined the James River when presidents Adams and Monroe, and many other revolutionary celebrities, spent their summers at the famed Allegheny Mountains resorts.

Dining

The dining room is on the first floor of the original 1834 home. The large hand-hewn beams in the dining room and lobby were part of the slave quarters. Many of the furnishings came from the dining room of the original owner. Old-fashioned southern specialties, including peanut soup, country-fried chicken, pan-fried trout, homemade breads fresh from the oven, and of course pecan pie, reflect the period dining theme.

Don't Miss

Down the highway a bit, near a small cemetery, a highway historical marker commemorates Zona Shue and her famous court case. It reads: "Interred in a nearby cemetery is Zona Heaster Shue. Her death in 1897 was presumed natural until her spirit appeared to her mother to describe how she was killed by her husband Edward. Autopsy on the exhumed body verified the apparition's account. Edward, found guilty of murder, was sentenced to the state prison. Only known case in which testimony from ghost helped convict a murderer."

The famous case is documented in the annals of the American justice system. Zona finally rests in peace a few steps from the highway marker.

Seven miles away, in White Sulphur Springs, the famous Greenbrier Hotel is also rumored to be haunted. Built in 1780, the exclusive resort was the playground of wealthy elite of old southern society. During the Civil War, the resort doubled as a hospital.

In 1960, deep beneath the Greenbrier, a top-secret relocation center for the president and U.S. Congress was built into the mountain, accessible through a false wall in the Exhibit Hall. Hotel guests, employees, and even the townspeople who helped build the new wing had no knowledge of the top-secret government bunker below until Ted Cup broke the story in the *Washington Post*. Since then, the 112,000-square-foot facility has been featured on national television, radio, and newspapers worldwide. Scheduled tours of this former Cold War congressional fallout shelter are offered daily (800-453-4858; www.greenbrier.com). "The bunker is also available for unique theme parties," the hotel advertises.

General Lewis Inn and Restaurant
301 East Washington Street
Lewisburg, WV 24901
304-645-2600 or 800-628-4454
e-mail: info@generallewisinn.com
www.generallewisinn.com

The Grove Park Inn Resort and Spa

❧

Asheville, North Carolina

The famous "Pink Lady," who met her death around 1920 when she fell from a third-floor balcony onto the floor of the Palm Court atrium, has walked the halls of the Grove Park Inn Resort and Spa for nearly a century. Over the decades, employees, guests, and workmen have heard, seen, and felt her presence, and have made strikingly similar reports about encounters with the feminine ghost. The hotel has taken these reports seriously, and has joined a handful of world-class resorts in America and around the world that have engaged the services of a legitimate scientific research team to investigate the ghostly sightings. Top-notch scientists and parapsychologists were hired to research and document the paranormal phenomena.

The Grove Park Inn Resort and Spa is one of the American South's oldest, finest, and most famous grand resorts. When Edwin W. Grove stood atop a magnificent mountaintop vista known as Sunset Mountain, overlooking the unparalleled beauty of the Blue Ridge mountain range, he knew he had found the perfect site for the grand resort hotel he had dreamed of. Owner of Grove's Pharmacy and Paris Medical Company of St. Louis, Missouri, Grove had been spending his summers in the quaint town of Asheville after a doctor suggested the soothing mountain climate as therapy for his occasional bouts with bronchitis.

Workers from all over the South converged to be part of this extraordinary project. Using the latest technology— hundreds of mules, wagons, pulleys, and ropes—workers built the giant complex out of massive granite stones, some of them weighing as much as 10,000 pounds each.

When Grove Park was completed, it was nothing short of a masterpiece. Since it opened, eight presidents have stayed. Politicians, movie stars, and entertainers have spent time at the resort, including Will Rogers, Thomas Edison, and F. Scott Fitzgerald. And, of course, the Pink Lady.

Until recently, most of what was known about the Pink Lady came from the memories of senior staff members and ex-employees of the hotel, from legend, and from a continual string of eyewitnesses. Far too many credible people, including one chief of police, had encountered her to deny her existence. But many questions about her life and afterlife had been left unanswered.

Wanting to learn more about who she was, and why she haunted the hotel, Grove Park management hired Joshua Warren, a local expert and author on paranormal activity. For six months in 1996, Warren conducted in-depth research of the Pink Lady phenomenon, using a combination of scientific field research, investigative reporting, and interviews with those who had seen her. He spent dozens of late-night hours in the hotel collecting scientific data. He searched old newspapers and public records for clues to the historical basis for the Pink Lady. And he interviewed nearly fifty people, some twenty of whom had firsthand experiences with the Pink Lady in one form or another.

Knowing nothing about the ghost in advance, Warren determined that although she's been seen and experienced in a number of places in the historic Main Inn, scientific evidence concludes that she favors Room 545, two stories above the Palm Court atrium floor. Her activity in that room has barred the entry of various contractors and employees. Her activity is not limited to that room, however. She has been encountered in other fifth-floor guest rooms, in the lobby, and even in Elaine's, the Grove Park nightclub. One young son of a Florida college professor asked, "Who was that nice lady?" and "Where did the nice lady go?" after napping in his Main Inn guest room.

The Pink Lady has been described in great detail, or as a "pinkish pastel smoke." Many have mistaken her for a living person until she vanished into thin air.

During World War II the inn served as a confinement center and later as a rest and rehabilitation facility for wounded American naval personnel. This may have contributed to the phenomena at the hotel. War hospitals seem to have more than their fair share of ghostly activities, possibly stemming from the number of deaths, or the strong passions of war.

Sightings

Guests, many of whom were not aware when they checked in that the hotel was haunted, have learned firsthand about the famous Pink Lady. Some have written letters to the hotel relating their sightings. Many of these are written months or even years later, as it may take that long to fully comprehend the magnitude of the encounter.

The following is an excerpt from one of these letters, written by Kathy J. Urbin of Tennessee (reprinted with permission):

I am finally writing you a description of an event that transpired when I spent the night at the Grove Park Inn 3½ years ago.

I had never heard any stories about supernatural events involving the Inn. Therefore, what occurred was a great surprise to me, as I am a Christian and was a ghost doubter!

I arrived with my husband and our two teenage daughters. We stayed in a room on the upper floor in the old part of the Inn with two tiny windows facing the front drive. Inside, the room opened over the Palm Court. When we checked into our room, I found the door between our room and an adjoining guest room unlocked. I called the front desk, and they sent someone up who locked it. He stated that he was sure it had been locked earlier in the day. I quickly dismissed this comment at the time.

The room we stayed in had two double beds. Our daughters slept together in the bed near the window, while my husband and I shared the other, closer to the room's entry door and located adjacent to the door adjoining the neighboring guest room.

After falling asleep, I was fully awakened about midnight by the sound of what I presumed was the noisy entrance of someone checking in to the adjoining guest room. As I lay in bed on my back, listening for more sounds of the new guest arrival unpacking, I was content holding my husband's hand. Implausibly, I realized that the hand I was holding was on my left side and that my husband was lying on my right side.

Thinking that one of our daughters must have also been startled awake by the guest checking in next door, I turned my head to my left, expecting to find one of our girls standing there holding my hand. To my complete surprise, no one was there, and instantly the experience of holding a warm hand was gone. I was left feeling confused by this unexplained experience.

The next morning I mentioned this strange occurrence to a front desk clerk. He informed me that no one had checked into the guest room adjoining our room that night.

Best Rooms/Times

The famous Pink Lady is sighted in the original part of the hotel. Though she has been seen in many different rooms, she is most frequently encountered on the fifth floor, and specifically in Room 545, two stories above the Palm Court atrium floor, where she met her early demise.

The Inn/Hotel

Located nearly 2,500 feet above sea level, the Grove Park Inn Resort and Spa offers panoramic views of the Blue Ridge Mountains and the legendary mountain city of Asheville, North Carolina. With its distinctive granite boulder construction and undulating red clay tile roof, the inn captures the essence of the Arts and Crafts movement.

Today there are a total of 510 rooms at this luxurious mountaintop resort. Charming guest rooms in the historic Main Inn have been restored, and still have the original solid oak Arts and Crafts–era furnishings, with hand-hammered copper Roycroft drawer pulls. Two newer wings, the Sammons Wing and the Vanderbilt Wing, were added in the 1980s. These rooms are larger and more modern than those in the historic Main Inn, and are furnished with Arts and Crafts reproduction furnishings.

Built to become the "finest spa in America," the Spa at The Grove Park Inn Resort is extraordinary. Natural waterfalls, lush gardens, high stone walls, and refreshing crystal blue ponds at this magnificent place of revitalization are built right into the hillside. In the spa's pool area, sunlight streams in from a glass skylight above, while the chamber's high stone walls and torch lighting recall the grandeur of another place and time. Dual waterfalls plunge into an exquisite soaking pool, offering a unique "waterfall massage."

With enticing names like "Fire, Rock, Water, and Light," "Sanctuary of the Senses," and "Color and Light Therapy with Aura Imaging," the spa offers a unique variety of services. A romantic treat for two starts with a candlelit couples massage, followed by an aromatic bath sprinkled with fresh rose petals, surrounded by more candles, while the bathers sip champagne and feast on decadent chocolate-covered strawberries.

A full juice bar offers smoothies and tropical alcoholic drinks, while the Spa Café serves fresh vegetarian fare and daily quiche.

An eighteen-hole championship golf course is set among tree-lined fairways and winding streams. At the golf pro shop, guests can take private lessons or attend clinics. A huge sports complex features six tennis courts (three indoor and three outdoor), racquetball, indoor and outdoor swimming pools, a cardio workout area, a weight room, aerobic and yoga classes, and a children's center with an outdoor playground.

E. W. Grove was not the only dreamer to become captivated by the natural beauty of the Blue Ridge Mountains; George Vanderbilt also built his magnificent 250-room mansion nearby. Completed in 1895, the Biltmore Estate, the largest private home in America, is a 255-room French Renaissance chateau. Daily tours showcase the upstairs and downstairs of the main house, the estate winery, and the exquisitely manicured gardens and grounds.

Dining

Several outstanding restaurants reside within the hotel. The premiere restaurant, Horizons, offers spectacular views along with award-winning, innovative classic cuisine served in a formal setting. One of the South's most famous and popular outdoor dining verandas, the Sunset Terrace offers majestic views and sunsets over the city skyline and mountains beyond. Chops serves prime beef and seafood. The Blue Ridge Grill boasts its original Roycroft lighting fixtures and sideboards, combined with incredible views of the Blue Ridge Mountains, and serves continental cuisine and southwestern fare. Or you may choose to dine outdoors at the Pool Cabana.

The Great Hall Bar in the Main Inn is reminiscent of the days when the inn opened in 1913, with its massive fireplaces and original antique furnishings. Early-evening piano entertainment provides just the right ambience.

Don't Miss

In January the hotel is host to a special "Paranormal Weekend," hosted by the LEMUR Paranormal Research Team, original investigators of the hotel, and its founder, Joshua P. Warren, noted parapsychologist and award-winning author. Students meet a panel of paranormal investigators and learn how to document ghostly activity using scientific methods. In the evenings, participants experience late-night ghost hunts using the methods they have learned, as well as a side trip to witness the eerie famed "Brown Mountain Lights," an unexplained phenomenon of the mountains nearby.

Additional paranormal activities include the services of a renowned psychic and a personal aura photo—a picture made with a special "aura camera" that displays the colors of one's aura.

The Grove Park Inn Resort and Spa
290 Macon Avenue
Asheville, NC 28804
828-252-2711 or 800-438-5800
e-mail: info@groveparkinn.com
www.groveparkinn.com

Historic Jameson Inn and Saloon

Wallace, Idaho

Maggie sits primping at the bureau in her room upstairs at the Jameson, idly running a comb through her long, curly locks. "Maybe today," she whispers as she applies her crimson red lipstick. "Maybe he will come today."

It's been torture, day after day, waiting for her true love to return on the train from back East, where he went after striking it rich. He promised to come back and marry her. That was nearly one hundred years ago!

You might see her reflection in the mirrors, or standing in a doorway, or you might hear her soft, desperate voice in the night. She leaves her hairbrush or other personal items (antiques by now) around—and these things may appear out of thin air. On bad days, she walks around the hotel, slamming doors. Whether intentional or not, she has locked guests into her room, where they are stranded until the staff arrives the next morning to free them.

"She's been here a long time," claims Rick Schaeffer, longtime manager of the Jameson. "She spent her life upstairs, waiting. She was here a long time, until finally she gave up and left. After she died, she came back."

Theodore Jameson built the "steak and billiard hall" in 1889 in the boisterous Idaho mining town of Wallace, purported to be the largest silver district in the world, and the "Red Light District of the Northwest." Mining and prostitution were the two biggest businesses. Colorful bordellos lined the streets; pretty young things dressed in skimpy lace lingerie would call from the doorways. Jameson's population consisted of miners, floozies, and women of the night. It was a time when men outnumbered women nearly 200 to 1, and ladies and children did not come to Wallace unescorted.

Today the rich, historic downtown Wallace stands frozen in a bawdier time. Prostitution and gambling were legal in this Old West town until 1989. Five brothels operated continuously until that time. Listen up, gals—with a population of just under 1,000, the town is still comprised of mostly men.

Sightings

"Wild parties go on downstairs in the old saloon," says Schaeffer.

> The men, woozy after a few rounds, get loud and boisterous. Sometimes they carry on all night, laughing and even arguing. It makes you want to join in. Trouble is, you can hear 'em, but you can't see 'em.
>
> Most of the staff, and even some of the

guests, have heard the ruckus. It goes on for hours at a time, even if you are standing right in there. Mike, once a chef at the hotel, was the only person in the hotel, working late with his ordering, when the voices started. He thought someone had come in, so he went to investigate. He said the lights were all out in the saloon, but he could hear voices from in there. It really shook him up. He grabbed his coat and ran out, without even turning out the kitchen lights. He quit shortly after that.

Occasionally, when some of 'em start arguing really loud, I get worried. I hope the ghostly customers don't get into a fistfight and start knocking things around, or even worse, pull out a gun and start shooting.

One night, I was up in Room 8, waiting for a late arrival. I dozed off to sleep, with the fan off. We have a buzzer at the front door that rings upstairs when the guests arrive. The buzzing woke me up. I looked at the clock, and it was two A.M. The next thing I knew, there were footsteps coming up the stairs! I wondered how they could have gotten in. I ran out to greet them, and no one was there. It was really weird.

Lots of times, guests tell us that they see a young woman in Victorian clothing, sitting in Room 3, or walking down the stairs. On occasion, guests have been locked into her room, or the "bathing room," and they have to wait until morning to get out.

Trica Anthis also worked at the hotel. One time she saw an image in the upstairs hall that "really freaked her out." It was a woman in a long, flowing dress. "I was always afraid to go on the third floor," admits Trica.

It always felt like I was being watched. I used to have to bribe my little brother to go up there with me. One time I had to paint the prep room, so I brought him. He had to use the bathroom. I told him to just use the woman's room, because no one else was around. Every time he went in, the light went out by itself. He screamed at me to quit it. I was standing on the ladder. He was completely freaked.

Another year, on Mother's Day, the hotel had a big brunch buffet. Every few minutes, the breakers would blow, and we had to keep going downstairs to reset them. We were giving carnations out to all the ladies. Someone said she was probably mad because she didn't get a carnation. We went downstairs and put a carnation by the breakers. The breakers didn't blow again after that.

She doesn't hurt anybody, but it just kind of freaks you out. Now I would probably just tell her to quit, but I was in high school and I didn't know how to deal with a ghost back then.

Another waitress, Twila Ives, was in the upstairs bathroom. A woman started talking to her. She thought it must be her mother Rosie, who worked there too. When she realized no one human was in the room, she was terrified, and ran screaming from the room. She refused to go back up there by herself, and she would actually pay the dishwashers to go up with her.

When I was there, I took no chances. I posted my sister to sit sentinel outside the door while I took my bath.

Best Rooms/Times

Maggie "lives" in the hotel. Although Room 3 upstairs is "her" room, during the day she moves about the hotel, retiring to Room 3 after dark.

The Hotel

When Theodore Jameson built his "steak and billiard hall" in 1889, the establishment quickly became noted as "a good bar, always stocked with fine liquors . . . embellished with valuable curios and collections of minerals." The Old West Victorian hotel, done in beautiful deep woods of cherry and mahogany, with a "triple wide" staircase, was once called "the finest hotel in Idaho."

The original restaurant, saloon, and billiard hall are on the main floor. Up the grand staircase to the second floor, the old poker room, where men would drink and gamble all night long, now houses the business office. The ballroom is still used for special events.

There is a common parlor with six guest rooms on

the third floor, furnished in turn-of-the-century Victorian style. The rooms overlook Jameson's main street and the old Depot Railroad Museum below. There are no bathrooms in the rooms; guests use one of two original "water closets" and two "bathing rooms." In the morning, if Maggie hasn't locked you in, a country breakfast is cooked to order.

Dining

Once a miner's cafeteria, the 1889 restaurant is adorned with the original stainless steel and rich cherry wood and offers specialties like "Molly B'Damn," the "Maggie Burger," or the "Reubenesque." Western steak dinners are the best in town, complete with spuds and salad bar. In the summer, guests enjoy Wild West dinner theater while they dine.

The saloon, with its mirrored back bar, ceiling fans, and polished brass, offers a full range of drinks.

Don't Miss

It seems the entire historic downtown Jameson is still alive with the spirits of the hardworking miners and ladies of the night who lived and toiled here.

A short walk from the Jameson is the Oasis Bordello Museum (605 Cedar Street; 208-753-0801), haunted by several floozies who once called the Oasis their home. The two-story brick building, opened in 1895, was one of five brothels operating on Wallace's main street all the way up until 1988 (the last recorded entry in the "hotel" registry). A federal ban on prostitution did not put a damper on these popular, prosperous bordellos until federal officers raided the famous street in January 1988 and customers fled, half-dressed or naked, through back doors and down dark alleys, some not even stopping to get dressed. Clothing, makeup, toiletries, food, and personal items were all left behind; they remain today, untouched. A tour of the upper rooms gives a glimpse into the town's bawdy past, with details that range from poignant to hilarious.

Another well-known haunting is the ghosts at the Sixth Street Melodrama, a theater occupying the old Lux Building. Built in 1891, it is the oldest remaining wood-frame building in Wallace's historic district. The upstairs was famous as a "ladies' boarding house." Actually, Lux Rooms was also one of the town's five celebrated brothels. Today, the unique eighty-seat theater presents vaudeville melodramas (212 Sixth Street; 208-752-8871).

The restless spirits of miners who lost their lives in the dark caverns deep beneath the earth still roam through the old Sierra Silver Mine, still a working silver, lead, and zinc mine. Tours offer a rare and exciting opportunity to personally experience the underground world of mining in the richest silver district on Earth. Hard hats are issued at the portal before you walk through the main drift of the mine (Sierra Silver Mine Tour, 420 Fifth Street, 208-752-5151).

Historic Jameson Inn and Saloon
204 King Street
Wallace, ID 83873
208-556-6000
e-mail: rshaffer@imbris.com
www.wallace-id.com/jameson

Jekyll Island Club Hotel

❧

St. Simons, Georgia

Jekyll Island, like many of Georgia's coastal islands, is rich in history, legend, and tradition. The island has been occupied at various times by Indian tribes, Spanish missionaries, English soldiers, French settlers, treasure-hunting pirates, and finally by the nation's elite, the wealthy Americans who shaped the country in which we live today.

Jekyll's first recorded inhabitants were the Guale Indians. They were living on the island, which they called Ospo, when Spanish missionaries began arriving in the late sixteenth century. Santiago de Ocone, the Spanish mission on Jekyll, and others along the Georgia coast vanished in the face of hostile Indians and pirates and increasing pressure from the English. By the time General James Edward Oglethorpe established the first permanent Georgia settlement at Savannah in 1733, the Guale Indians and the Spanish missions had long since disappeared from Jekyll.

In 1734, during an expedition southward, Oglethorpe passed by the island and renamed it for his friend Sir Joseph

Jekyll, who had contributed generously to his Georgia venture. William Horton, one of Oglethorpe's most trusted officers, established a thriving plantation on Jekyll. It was destroyed by the Spanish who crossed the island in retreat after their defeat at the Battle of Bloody Marsh on St. Simons Island in 1742. Undaunted, Horton rebuilt his home and by 1746 had restored the plantation to its previous state. The shell of this second house still stands on Jekyll Island.

Horton died in 1749, leaving the property to his son, who showed little interest in it. Subsequent owners experienced difficulties in developing Jekyll into a successful plantation. The island was sold at public auction for nonpayment of debt and taxes several times before Christophe Poulain du Bignon acquired ownership of the island around 1800.

Du Bignon, who immigrated to America as a result of the French Revolution, raised Sea Island cotton on Jekyll until his death in 1825. It was in 1858 under the ownership of his son, Henri Charles du Bignon, that the slave ship *Wanderer* arrived at Jekyll Island and unloaded the last major cargo of slaves ever to land in the United States.

The Jekyll Island Club opened in 1888 as a hunting retreat for America's wealthiest families. Nestled in the natural setting of a barrier island off the Georgia coast, the northern millionaires could winter in scenic southern seclusion. They would travel to the island on luxurious 300-foot yachts, miniature floating hotels for family, friends, servants, tutors, and nannies, boasting a crew that was nearly as large.

The elite club opened its doors in January 1888. From the outset, demand for membership was tremendous. Membership was originally limited to fifty members. These powerful families, which included the Rockefellers, Carnegies, Macys, Goodyears, Morgans, and Vanderbilts, controlled as much as 20 percent of the world's wealth. If you were accepted for membership into this exclusive club, you were able to make the contacts necessary for any project you could envision.

In 1896 a syndicate, including J. P. Morgan and William Rockefeller, built an adjoining six-unit apartment building they named Sans Souci. In a sense, those units became the first condominiums. In 1901, an attached annex was built to handle the expanding needs of members.

Between 1888 and 1928 several members built cottages on the island to have more expansive accommodations. Some of these bungalows were up to 8,000 square feet, large even by today's standards. The members who built the cottages also enjoyed mansions in major northern cities and huge summer residences in Newport.

Throughout the club's history, many recreational amenities were added. The first golf course was laid in 1898, with two more added in 1909. A marina was built to handle all the yachts. A swimming pool, tennis courts, and other facilities were added. Dinner was the highlight of the day, and members, being family oriented, ate with children, caregivers, and tutors. There were as many as three waiters per guest at the nightly dining event.

It's said that all good things must pass, and by 1942 this popular club had only eighteen members. This is partly attributed to the death of the beloved director Mr. Grove, who had managed the club operations with passion and proficiency for over forty-two years. The imminent threat of German submarines off the coast also contributed to the club's demise. With the threat of war so close to her shores, members departed, thinking they would one day return. They never did.

The island was sold to the state of Georgia, and all remaining furniture was auctioned off. The club sat vacant for many years until 1985, when work began to restore the clubhouse, the annex, and the Sans Souci into a world-class hotel and resort.

Sightings

The Jekyll Island Club was rumored to be haunted before it even opened. General Lloyd Aspinwall, the club's first president, died unexpectedly on September 4, 1886, more than a year before the club would officially open. Several members were shocked to see him, hands clasped behind him in a military manner, walking the Riverfront Veranda the day after his death.

There are also visitations by railroad magnate Samuel Spencer, who left this world quite suddenly when two trains—both owned by companies for which he was a board member—collided. Spencer continues to visit his suite in the annex, where he enjoys sipping coffee and reading the morning newspaper regardless of who is currently occupying the Presidential Suite. Many a guest has returned from the shower to find his paper in a mess and his coffee cup empty.

A bellman dressed in an antiquated uniform and cap walks around the hotel greeting guests, particularly bridegrooms. He has been seen, mostly on the second floor, delivering freshly pressed tuxes. More than one bridegroom, who had not ordered these services, has inquired about the mysterious bellman, who has even been sighted by the current—real—bellman.

One of the most bizarre encounters occurred during the time of the renovation of the club in the 1980s. The future manager of the hotel found himself lying, dazed and confused, on the lawn outside. His last memory was of being in the fourth-floor turret, which he had gone to inspect. He ascended the spiral staircase that is the only access to the tiny, fifth-floor tower. When he turned to come back down the stairs, the opening had vanished. He started feeling woozy and disoriented, and the next thing he knew, he was outside, sprawled on the lawn. To this day, he does not know how he got from the turret to the lawn. Everyone I have interviewed has told me that this man is "a very solid sort," and was legitimately distressed and disturbed by what he encountered.

Max Wohlfarth, who now manages the Windsor Hotel in Americus, was once the executive chef at Jekyll Island. He couldn't wait to tell me his experiences at the Jekyll. "That's a hotel with some cool ghost stories," he enthused.

So many things go on there. Sometimes there are things that guests think are part of the presentation, like voices and knocking on doors, but they weren't. On more than a few occasions, a woman would tell me that someone "cupped her rear end." I have even seen the ghost. That place is really haunted.

One night I was on the third floor, outside the Presidential Suite, by myself. As I turned to the right toward the opposite end of the hall, I saw a tall man, standing erect, wearing a black suit and top hat. As I stood there, he continued to walk toward me. When I took a step forward toward him, he would back up. He did this a few times. Obviously he saw me. Finally he turned and went to the stairwell. I ran to catch him, but he had disappeared.

Late one night, it sounded like a party was going on in the dining room. I opened the door, and it became completely silent.

The weirdest thing that happened was when I was training a young lady on the front desk at two or three in the morning. The phone rang, and a gentleman was screaming into the phone that someone was trying to break into his room. I ran to his room, and as I waited for him to answer, I examined the paint on the door to see if it was chipped. I didn't see any sign of forced entry. He was in his pajamas. I said, "Tell me what happened." The inconsolable man was shuddering as he told of his perpetrator. I assured him that he was safe, and suggested that he bolt his door and secure the chain.

Half an hour later, he called down to the desk again. This time, he was hysterical. "Someone got into my room," he panted. "Are you sure?" I questioned. "I saw him, he was at the end of my bed shaking it, trying to wake me up." The terrified man described a young man in his twenties, dressed in a uniform. I told the man to stay in his bed until I got there. I could hear him unlock the deadbolt and remove the chain before he opened the door. He described the intruder as having dark hair and a funny uniform with a striped cap that almost looked like a military uniform.

Two days later the general manager and I went to the opening of a local museum exhibit. They had an old bellman's uniform from Jekyll Island on display, with a striped cap. I had to excuse myself. I was pretty blown away.

Another [living] bellman was to deliver garments returned from the dry cleaners. He delivered garments in the first room, but found from his list that several items were missing. In the next room, another garment turned up missing. When he got to the last room, all of the missing garments were there in the closet, waiting for him. He checked with the other bellman to see if anyone had moved the clothes, but he couldn't find a solution. I think that's pretty interesting.

Another man who used to work in the kitchen with me told me that several times he heard glasses and silverware clinking in the dining room, "like the whole place was filled with people eating." Thinking there were people in there, he went into the dining room. The minute the door opened, there was no noise whatsoever. Uncertain, he turned on the lights and looked around. No one was there. Back in the kitchen, the tinkling started back up again, but this time he did not go back to investigate.

We would also see a tall woman with blond

hair, dressed in a long blue dress, going through the doors from the dining room into the Riverview Room. Her features were perfectly visible, but she was see-through.

Best Rooms/Times

The impressive Presidential Suite is the most haunted room in the hotel.

The Hotel

This Victorian fairyland underwent a meticulous restoration in 1986. The club was returned to its original elegance and features leaded art glass windows, ornate woodwork, and Rumford fireplaces. From the lofty tower to the wide verandas, Victorian charm still permeates this hotel once occupied by America's wealthiest. The original ninety-three fireplaces, heart pine floors, wainscoting, beamed ceilings, and window transoms remain from an era where money was no object. Even the original plush black velvet drapes of the turn of the century have been re-created to transport guests back in time.

The hotel encompasses three of the original club buildings, the main clubhouse, the annex, and Sans Souci. Many of the opulent cottages are still scattered around the hotel, and one of these has been turned into a museum.

Each guest room is unique. Original turn-of-the-century appointments like the Victorian fireplace mantels and custom-made mahogany furnishings blend with modern conveniences.

As a Victorian aficionado, I found my room to be one of the finest I have ever seen. It also contained the largest bathtub by far that I have ever bathed in. Lined with countless tiny jets, this spa tub took up the space of a normal-sized bathroom and was about three feet deep. It was a wonderful experience.

Dining

The Jekyll Island Club Hotel features several dining options. The Grand Dining Room, restored to its historic splendor, features gourmet continental cuisine specializing in fresh seafood from the coast of Georgia, and a scrumptious Sunday brunch. The Café Solterra is a bakery and New York–style deli where guests can purchase specially prepared picnic baskets to take to the beach, biking, or boating. The outdoor Courtyard at Crane is open for lunch, weather permitting, boasting "a Northern California wine country flair." The Surfside Beach Club offers light snacks, while the Poolside Bar and Grill serves grilled chicken and burgers, salads and chips.

J. P.'s Pub is an intimate Victorian pub with antique armchairs and an impressive original oak bar.

Don't Miss

Jekyll Island also has its dark tales. One stormy night in 1858, half a century after the importing of slaves had been banned, the slave ship *Wanderer* smashed into the island's shores, carrying the last cargo of slaves ever brought from Africa. To this day, when the night is dark and the thunder rolls, people claim to see the glimmer of ghostly fires amid the sheltering trees.

At nearby St. Simon's Island, many slaves were brought ashore along Dunbar Creek. Legend has it that a group of chained slaves had just arrived on the *Wanderer*. Rather than live their lives in slavery, bound by iron chains, the slaves made a suicide pact. Chained side by side to one another, they boldly marched into the water, chanting, "The sea brought me, and the sea will take me home," in their native African tongue.

It is said that this part of the beach, near Ebo's Landing, is haunted by these brave kindred spirits, and sometimes, after darkness falls on the island shore, you can hear the unsettling sounds of chains rattling and voices chanting as these noble souls march to their deaths in the ocean.

Jekyll Island Club Hotel
371 Riverview Drive
Jekyll Island, GA 31527
912-635-2600
e-mail: info@jekyllclub.com
www.jekyllclub.com

Lafitte Guest House
❧

New Orleans, Louisiana

In the center of the French Quarter, the most haunted part of America's most haunted city, sits one of her most haunted houses, the Lafitte Guest House. Lafitte's is one of the oldest mansions in town, set amid streetcars, jazz musicians, and voodoo queens on famed Bourbon Street. This eighteenth-century French manor, with lacy iron balconies, original *garçonnières,* carriage house, and courtyard, is a landmark in the Vieux Carré.

The haunted property was formerly owned by Dr. Robert Guyton, a retired physician, who says, "All my life I have dealt with scientific facts, and am by and large a very realistic type individual. However, since owning the Guest House, I have come to believe there is indeed a departed spirit among us, and I believe it to be Madam Gleises, who owned the home for many years. I would assume that a spirit that inhabits a dwelling century after century has enough unsettled business to prevent them from departing to the place of eternity.

"I am not the only one who has felt the presence of our resident ghosts," he continues.

On many occasions my guests have asked me if I was aware there was a ghost in the house. Recently one young lady told me she had been awakened by profound sobbing in the corridor outside her room. She got up and looked out into the hallway. The noise ceased, but the minute she closed the door and got back into the bed, the sobbing continued. She said that after a while the sobbing drifted down the hall into the distance and seemed to go up the stairs to the next level. That was outside Room 23.

On another occasion a guest in Room 3 insisted a ghost had been in her room, and that things actually moved about the room without anyone visibly moving them. To prove it, she took a photo. Later, she sent us a snapshot of what she said was a reflection of the ghost in the mirror. A wave of energy appears on the lower left corner, which could not have been caused by a camera leak.

Dr. Guyton says that the elevator will go up and down on its own, in a rhythm similar to its real use. "The double doors will close and lock. The elevator creeps up to the third floor, where the doors open, and it remains for quite a while. Then the doors close again, and it travels to the second floor, where the doors open again and remain for a while, before returning back to the first floor. Back on the first floor, the doors open, and it stays there."

He also reports getting up from his desk, only to return minutes later to find everything rearranged, even though no one else was around. "I do not believe that Mrs. Gleises has completely departed this earth, and I think that she is still roaming the halls of the house at 1003 Bourbon. She probably will continue here until someone who has the ability to reach across this line that separates the living from the dead can communicate with her more completely, can help her resolve whatever problems she continues to deal with and release her to her place in eternity."

In life the Gleiseses, owners of the home in the early 1800s, suffered tragedy upon tragedy with the loss of four of their eight children. They owned the mansion for several decades. Shortly before the Civil War, the house was deeded to Mrs. Gleises. The family then moved to Philadelphia and later to New York, never to return to New Orleans, though Mrs. Gleises did retain ownership of the house until the conclusion of the war in 1866, when she finally sold the home.

Even before the Gleiseses owned the house, it was the scene of suffering and pain. The land was originally donated to the church by the king of Spain in 1793 to be used as the site of a charity hospital. Those too poor to pay for medical services came to the hospital, often too late to be helped. In 1809 the hospital burned to the ground, and everyone inside died.

A psychic was called in to investigate the occurrences at Lafitte Guest House. Dr. Guyton purposely did not tell the psychic any of the history of the home; he wanted to see what she would pick up on her own.

Plans were made, and a séance was held in Room 21, believed to be Mrs. Gleises's bedroom. Eight people were present. As they sat around the table and turned out the lights, the psychic went into a trance and started scribbling furiously on a tablet of paper. Dr. Guyton confirms, "Although portions of the document are very difficult to read, and it appears that part of the conversation with the spirit was in French, it would appear from the transcripts she wrote by hand that she did indeed contact Mrs. Gleises."

The writing Dr. Guyton describes is automatic writing, created by the psychic in a trance state. I saw a copy of the session. It's the ramblings of a woman who writes about being tormented over the loss of her children—recalling the death of four of the Gleiseses' eight children.

Sightings

Most of the sightings center around Room 21, Mrs. Gleises's room, but she is not the only spirit that remains at Lafitte's. There have been sightings in all rooms. Mrs. Gleises is most often encountered as a smoky mist that takes the form of a woman. Occasionally, she is heard crying.

Nolan Abshirethe, the night clerk at the hotel for many years, described his experiences: "The guy who trained me told me a few things that had happened. I wasn't scared, I was fascinated by it. Then the maids started telling me stories about the spirit that frequents Room 40. They call her Christine. One of them wouldn't even go up there.

One day a guest in Room 5 came down around eleven P.M. and told me that there was someone in his room. 'What do you mean?' I asked. He said there was someone standing at the foot of his bed. Room 5, off the courtyard outside, is where the original carriage house was, and the driver lived out there.

Nolan says gratefully that the only thing he has experienced is a "whoosh of cold air coming down the hall" when he is working alone late at night.

Another employee, Burlon, worked the night desk once a week. He would hear the front door rattle and feel the breeze. Not seeing anyone enter through the front, he would turn to see if the door to the courtyard was creating a draft. That's when he would see a man standing there in a long black coat with a big top hat. When he spoke to the man, he vanished. There is no access to the courtyard except past the desk, and the only room off the courtyard is Room 5, the old carriage house.

One lady, staying in Room 3, the same room that purportedly has a female ghost, claimed that a lamp slid across the desk and fell into her arms. When she and her husband returned from dinner, a satin cloth on the lavatory was soaking wet. Neither she nor her husband had seen the cloth before. Later, the couple was mystified by the smell of burning candle wax. Minutes later, the bed collapsed.

Guests frequently leave comments in the guest register concerning their ghostly encounters.

Best Rooms/Times

The dead of night in winter seems to be the most likely time to encounter the spirits at Lafitte's. Most reports come from Rooms 3, 5, and 21, the third and fourth floors, the entry hall, and the courtyard. In other words, just about all the rooms of this Victorian mansion are haunted.

The Hotel

The opulent Victorian antebellum complex originally consisted of a main house three stories high, with a full attic, and an attached wing of outbuildings at the rear of the house. The second and third floors of the outbuilding were used to accommodate the slaves, and later the home's servants. There was one bath on the second floor. The first floor housed the kitchen, carriage house, stable, and coal house.

The parlors, dining room, bedrooms, attic, and the original kitchen and servant's quarters outside on the courtyard have all been converted into guest rooms. Typical of the bedrooms found on the second and third floors of homes in that day, these rooms have high windows that open out onto the balconies, cooling the rooms in the humid summers.

Each of the elegant rooms is decorated with period furnishings and is uniquely different in detail. Some rooms offer private wrought-iron balconies overlooking Bourbon Street. Modern conveniences, such as television and telephone, are hidden so that they do not detract from the graciousness of the building.

Dining

Continental breakfast of coffee and delicate local pastries is served in your room, in the traditional New Orleans courtyard, or on your own private balcony overlooking the whimsical architecture of the Vieux Carré.

Every evening, guests gather in the luxurious Victorian Parlor, done in red velvet and rich burgundy wallpaper, for wine and cheese.

Across the street is the famous Lafitte's Blacksmith piano bar, also haunted. This dark landmark tavern, once part of the Lafitte complex, is also known for the spunky little old lady at the piano belting out tunes.

Don't Miss

Haunted History Tours (504-861-2727; www.haunted-historytours.com) offers a choice of four ghostly tours through the famed French Quarter, widely accepted as America's most haunted city. Choose from the Ghosts of New Orleans Tour, the Witchcraft and Voodoo Tour, the Voodoo / Cemetery Tour, or the Vampire Tour, which includes a visit to a noted vampire bar. Tours depart from Rev. Zombies Voodoo Shop on St. Peter, across the street from legendary Pat O'Brien's and the Great American Music Hall.

Lafitte Guest House
1003 Bourbon Street
New Orleans, LA 70116
800-331-7971 or 504-581-2678
e-mail: lafitteguesthouse@travelbase.com
www.lafitteguesthouse.com

Linden House Plantation

Champlain, Virginia

"Have you ever felt like you're losing your mind?" she whispered. "You know, like you're out of your gourd."

Sandra sat on the couch, shoulders hunched, head bowed, unconsciously twisting strands of her golden blond hair, talking about how she felt after she bought the 250-year-old Colonial plantation and started "seeing and hearing things."

"I didn't know what was happening, if I was going crazy. You try to explain all these things away. At first, I thought maybe I was physically ill. Maybe the fumes from the paint, or the paint thinner we were using to restore the inn. So I kept all the windows open. But that didn't help," Sandra confided. "The visions continued."

So she went to see her doctor. She asked him about all the medications she was taking, even aspirin, and demanded to know what side effects or interactions they might have, or if any of them might be the cause of her hallucinations. When he could provide no comfort, she went to her pharmacist and grilled him. But no medical condition or drug interaction could explain away the things that she was seeing, or the voices that she heard.

So she took the next logical step: she called her priest.

Her husband, Ken, a tough ex-cop with over twenty years' service, was fighting his own battles in coping with the strange goings-on. Ken's years on the police force in Maryland had done nothing to prepare him for this. In those years, he had faced real danger. How could he admit he was afraid? Ken, too, was doubting his own sanity. Ironically, neither one admitted to the other what was going on—until they started experiencing what they both called "the light beams."

Sandra was the first to encounter the beams. She always went to bed before Ken. One night, after she turned out the light and said her prayers (she had been saying them a lot lately), she saw "a really, really bright light beaming through the keyhole from the dark hall outside. It was blinding.

"All of a sudden, the light just disappeared." Then it appeared again, and disappeared, she said. "I rolled over, but then I couldn't resist looking back. The beam was there again!"

Determined not to freak out, she forced herself to sleep. The next morning, she asked Ken to put tissue in the keyhole.

The next night, as she said her prayers, "the light rays came over the top of the door frame and reflected on the ceiling, like a sun ray going in different directions." Frightened out of her wits, Sandra turned away from the light, and she could see from the shadows in the room that the beam had disappeared. When she was brave enough to look back at the door, to her horror, "the light came back on even stronger and bolder, then shrank back again." She lay there wide awake, waiting for her husband to come to bed. As much as she wanted to tell him, she knew he was going to be all alone the next night, and she didn't want to scare him.

"My experience was a little different," the ex-cop confides. "With mine, you kind of turn your head, like someone is right there with you. I didn't think much of it. When Sandra left town, I took the tissue out of the door. She had said something about the light coming through, but I thought she was crazy . . . until I saw the same thing. I looked up, and I could see the ray over the door, spreading out onto the ceiling. I knew there had to be some logical explanation, though I couldn't think of any. When I would look, it would go back out into the hallway. I just wanted to forget the whole thing, especially being there alone. I didn't sleep that night. It wasn't a ray, it was kind of floaty. The color was like skin, pale skin, and it waved. It looked like it had fingers, long fingers." Ken was speaking faster and faster. "I was scared," he admitted. "When it finally got light outside, I didn't see it anymore. But it really made me think!"

The Pounsberrys often hear voices. Once, Sandra heard a couple talking upstairs. Afraid it was guests who might miss their dinner reservations, she ran upstairs to remind them. No one was there.

"Sometimes, it sounds like someone is leaving a message on the answering machine, going over and over like it's stuck. But we go upstairs, and no one has called. This can be annoying, especially when you come into the house with an armful of groceries, you hear the voice, and you rush to pick up the phone, thinking someone is speaking, only to realize no one is there," Sandra complained. "That has happened dozens of times.

"Three times in a row I heard footsteps that would start

at the top floor and come down the staircase, never going back up," Sandra continues. "Sometimes that hall reeks with a real pungent odor. There is also another smell, like the smell of sweet tobacco."

Even their story about finding the Linden House sounds like the stereotypical Hollywood movie cliché of a haunted house: a young couple, driving around, comes upon an eerie vacant mansion, which they are somehow compelled to buy. In town, they notice that the townspeople treat them with curiosity. Shortly thereafter they begin to experience supernatural phenomena. They go to the historical society, where blue-blooded, gray-haired ladies fill them in on the "strange happenings out at the old homesite." Finally, they seek out their priest to exorcise the house.

"We were looking for a house for two and a half years," Ken explained.

We were driving one day and just happened to spot the Linden House, a run-down white brick four-story colonial estate sitting vacant off the road. We decided to just stop and look. From the moment we walked into the wide center hall, we KNEW it was where we belonged.

What struck us was the condition of the estate, after sitting vacant for so many years. A structure like this where we came from would have been burned or vandalized. Of course here, we later learned, it was the reputation of the ghosts that kept the place standing.

As soon as we moved in, we noticed that when people from town came to visit, they always left before dusk. Even the man who took care of the yard left before sunset. After people got to know us better, they started asking us how we were getting along with the ghosts. We were known to them as the couple who bought the ghost house.

While they were restoring Linden, the activity seemed to increase. Even the contractor, a burly nonbeliever who stayed in the home while he was working on it, would wake the family up at least three times a week because he heard noises in the middle of the night. The men would grab the guns and meticulously search the house, floor by floor. Of course, nothing was there—or at least nothing human. The Pounsberrys were glad when he was finally finished and they could get some rest at night.

Sightings

Early one morning, Ken and Sandra's daughter Kimberly saw an old woman sitting alone in the dining room. She thought the woman must be a guest, waiting for breakfast. Kimberly ran to find her mother. Confused, Sandra told Kimberly there were no guests. When Kimberly went back down, no one was there. She described the woman as grandmotherly, with gray hair, wearing a thin purple sweater, just sitting there waiting.

Bess Hale, a longtime resident of Champlain, worked at the library. She showed the Pounsberrys a composition written by her grandmother about the ghosts of Fredericksburg. In it, she claimed that the night she spent at the Linden House was "the worst night of her life."

Bess also spent the night at Linden, many years after her grandmother. She says that she heard footsteps all night long, going down the stairs but never coming back up. Apparently, at one time, a very nervous widow owned the home. She could not sleep, so she paced all night.

A bouncing ball kept one couple up all night. When they came down in the morning, they told Sandra that a ball lying on the floor had bounced all around the room by itself.

Best Rooms/Times

The Robert E. Lee Room is where the Pounsberrys were sleeping when they saw the light beams. It seems to be the most active, though the entire house is haunted.

The Inn

Built around 1750 by Nicholas Faulkner, Linden House sits on over 200 acres that include a carriage house, pastureland, a horse farm, a formal English garden, and a graveyard. Nearby are the birthplaces of both George Washington and Thomas Jefferson. "It's the peacefulness of it, the rolling landscape, the grazing cattle, the wildlife, that helps you relax," Sandra remarks.

Guest rooms are located on the third and fourth floor of the colonial estate, as well as in the restored carriage house outside. Each guest room has its own private bath, TV, fluffy robes, and refrigerator. The Jefferson Davis Room boasts a steam room and a Jacuzzi spa for two.

In the morning, guests congregate in the English basement to order breakfast from mouthwatering selections posted on the chalkboard. Homemade muffins, juices, and coffee await while you make up your mind.

Dining

A very special event is the planter's dinners, scheduled throughout the year. These prix fixe dinners may include stuffed shrimp, Maryland crab cakes, stuffed tenderloins, Cornish hen, seafood, greens, soup, salad, homemade breads, and a tantalizing dessert. Also, if you are lucky enough to arrive when the Pounsberrys are catering, they will make additional portions available to their guests.

Don't Miss

A short drive away are Strafford Hall, the birthplace of Robert E. Lee, George Washington's plantation and birthplace, and several Civil War battlefields.

Linden House Plantation
P.O. Box 23
Tidewater Trail (Route 17)
Champlain, VA 22438
804-443-1170 or 866-877-0286
www.lindenplantation.com

Little A'le'Inn

❧

Rachel, Nevada

I kept one eye glued to my rearview mirror, watching for cars, as I made the left turn onto the long, deserted road known as Extraterrestrial Highway. No one was behind me. As a female traveler, you can't be too careful. The desolate desert terrain enveloped me, extending for miles in all directions. I was alone.

As dusk approached, my eye was pierced by a glare in the mirror. I looked up. A big green light was behind me. There was nothing else there, just the gigantic glowing green fluorescent beam. I hit the gas. The light sped up as well, staying about twenty feet behind my car and about ten feet off the ground. I sped up even faster. It followed. By then it was pitch dark. I approached some low, winding hills, blindly traveling at about sixty miles an hour through the twists and turns. It stayed with me. I sped up to seventy miles an hour, knowing I was risking my life. I heard a sickening thud, and prayed that I had run over a tree limb and not an innocent creature startled by the blinding headlights.

The light was right behind. It was still another ten miles to Rachel. I knew that was my only hope of escape. With my jaw clenched I tightened my already aching grip on the wheel and sped on, frantically making deals with God.

Suddenly, it was gone.

I didn't tell the people at Little A'le'Inn about this incident. Maybe I should have, but at the time I had no explanation for what was pursuing me. I still don't. Maybe I would rather not know.

"Earthlings Welcome," the sign outside the Little A'Le'Inn Motel, Bar and Café beckons to passersby on State Route 375, officially renamed the Extraterrestrial Highway by the state of Nevada. On the doormat you will find a similar greeting: "Aliens Welcome."

This quirky motel, a haven for UFO enthusiasts, is included in this book because although it is not haunted by ghosts, per se, there are numerous reports of "an energy or intelligence" that witnesses claim manifests as beams of light or implanted knowledge. Whether this energy comes from outer space or inner space (i.e., the other side) remains a mystery.

Little A'le'Inn sits in the middle of a cow pasture in Rachel, Nevada, just a few miles from Area 51, a top-secret military facility about ninety miles north of Las Vegas. The site for Area 51 was selected in the mid-1950s due to its remoteness for testing of the U-2 spy plane. Documentation of alien spacecraft began twenty years ago when several former government officials claimed they had actually worked with the aliens at Papoose Lake, just south of Area 51. Locals, however, had been encountering alien activity here for decades.

The only respite amid miles and miles of cow pastures, Little A'le'Inn started out as a truck stop, with just a bar and café. A few trailers were added to accommodate the occasional weary truck driver, and as time went on and the area became more noted for UFOs, more trailers were added.

Pat and Joe Travis own the place. They claim they have daily communications with alien beings. Shortly after they moved into their trailer, they had their first encounter. "We were sitting in the living room when an eerie ray of light beamed right through the center of the back door, as if someone had bored a hole through the door and was shining a giant flashlight. At the same time, we both felt a weird presence, as if someone were looking at us. We just looked at the beam, and then looked at each other. Then Joe spoke to the light. 'Go ahead, make yourself at home. If you can come through a steel-clad door, you can definitely make yourself at home.' "

The couple had a rough time getting their business off the ground. When Joe's battery-operated flying saucer went out of control and smashed their bright blinking sign in front of the bar, the Travises were ready to give up, and they even talked about selling.

Later that night, they saw flashing lights in their bedroom. "It looked exactly like it does when the sign is on, with the room lighting up, then going dark. Only the sign was broken." Joe thought someone must be outside with a pulsating light. He ran out, but no one was there, yet the shadows inside kept blinking. Pat knew it was a sign from the aliens, telling them not to give up on the place. When the UFO craze hit, their motel became a booming business.

Sightings

Many of the employees have had encounters, especially Alice Fallen (name changed), who has worked as a waitress at Little A'Le'Inn for twenty years. Alice is convinced that the U.S. government makes communications with the aliens at top-secret Area 51. She has seen strange lights and flying objects on several occasions—once in broad daylight, as she was driving through the desert. "It was long and silver, hovering in the sky not far from my car. I just kept driving. After about a half an hour, it just took off."

Another lady in town, who wishes to remain anonymous, claimed she was actually abducted. She says she was spared from a lot of experimentation only because she was "beyond childbearing age." "I was driving down the highway near the hills," she relates, "and when I rounded a corner, I could see the spacecraft in front of me. I was under some kind of trance. I pulled over, and they came and got me, and took me into their craft. They were very pale, and had round heads and big eyes. I don't remember much about what happened. The next thing I knew, I woke up back in my car."

One guest came to Little A'le'Inn hoping to work out her anger at the aliens for her own alleged abduction. "She was very upset when she arrived," says Pat, "but during her visit, she realized the aliens are not here to harm people but to offer love and understanding. When she left, she was finally at peace.

"We get airline pilots who come in and tell me they've seen UFO's," Pat says. "Most of them don't report it. But they want to talk about it. So that's what we do here. We allow people to come and talk freely, and listen."

Have the Travises actually seen a UFO? "One time, Joe and I were driving back from Vegas, and I saw this round object, like a ball of translucent light, moving along the side of the highway. I said 'Joe! Do you see that?' He replied, 'Yeah, but I thought I was imagining it.'"

Best Rooms/Times

Most, though not all, of the UFO sightings in Rachel occur at night. Joe says they have been spotted every day of the year, including Christmas. Pat's "burst of energy" comes every day at 4:00 P.M. A psychic explained to her that that's the time that the aliens arrive, in a group, "like a flight squadron that swoops in every afternoon."

On different occasions, guests staying in Rooms 2 and 3 have reported visitations, always described as a presence that seemed to talk to them through "mind transference." Sometimes the thin image of a white being was reported.

The Motel

"The rooms aren't fancy, but they are neat and clean," Pat boasts. The units are actually mobile home trailers scattered around the property, each trailer divided into two small motel units with one bedroom and a shared bath. There are no phones or TV, but videos are available should you become bored with your UFO watch. The Travises are planning to add several more trailers over the next few years.

Dining

The restaurant and bar are the focal point of the property. The walls are plastered with UFO paraphernalia and articles about sightings. The cooking claims to be "out of this world," the specialty being the "alien burger," a giant patty on a saucer-shaped bun. An old-fashioned wooden bar runs across the entire east wall. The restaurant is a small-time family operation. Joe tends bar, and Pat does the cooking.

Don't Miss

Twice a year, Little A'Le'Inn hosts a UFO seminar, featuring a noted UFO expert. Enthusiasts come from all over the world to attend these events, and the property is littered with people sitting on car hoods or tarps on the ground, waiting and watching. One year, a sighting reportedly occurred.

Don't try to enter Area 51. The entire perimeter is heavily protected by armed guards, sensor devices, and helicopter surveillance.

Little A'Le'Inn
P.O. Box 45
Highway 375
Rachel, NV 89001
702-729-2515

The Lodge at Cloudcroft

❧

Cloudcroft, New Mexico

In the 1930s at the Cloudcroft Lodge, a stunning, seductive beauty with flaming red hair and striking blue eyes was brutally slain in a fit of rage by her jealous lumberjack boyfriend. He dragged her lifeless body into the woods behind the lodge and buried her in an unmarked grave. The next morning, concerned coworkers searched the hotel and the brushy woods beyond. Her body was never found. Her boyfriend had hastily checked out of the hotel in the middle of the night and was never heard from again.

Rebecca has been sighted often at the hotel since her murder. Some say she desperately seeks revenge for a life that was cut short. Others say she is perfectly content, playfully living in a place where she was once happy. The lodge has become her shrine. Images of Rebecca are scattered throughout the property. Her portrait, composed from details provided by those who have sighted her, hangs in the lobby. A massive stained-glass image of Rebecca dominates the restaurant, named Rebecca's in her honor.

The lodge originally catered to timber cutters working for the Alamogordo and Sacramento Railroad. It opened in 1899 as a rooming house for lumberjacks. Several years later, the lodge was expanded, and opened to the public as a mountain retreat. Over the years, hundreds of politicians, entertainers, authors, and artists have enjoyed the privacy at the scenic mountain getaway, including Pancho Villa, Judy Garland, and Clark Gable. Both U.S. and Mexican government officials have long visited the historic retreat. And—what better recommendation for a hotel?—world-famous hotelier Conrad Hilton managed it in the 1930s.

Back in those days, the staff lived at the hotel, in dorm rooms in the basement. When Rebecca accepted employment as a chambermaid, she moved her trunks and personal belongings into the dorm. Exquisitely beautiful, she soon became a favorite, not only at the lodge but also around town. She quickly learned that her beauty enabled her to pick up a few extra dollars from generous guests.

For years guests and staff have recounted tales of Rebecca's appearances and claim she is still residing at the hotel. Rebecca has been called a flirtatious, mischievous spirit, who likes to have fun and play tricks on the living.

One startled male guest walked in on a beautiful, stark-naked, redheaded lady bathing in his tub! Embarrassed, he called the front desk and insisted they send someone up to inform this woman that she was in the wrong room. When the clerk arrived, the exposed young lady had mysteriously vanished.

Another man heard a strange scraping sound coming from the hallway late one night. Cautiously, he cracked open his door wide enough to peek out, and saw a woman with long red hair, in a 1930s-style floor-length nightgown. She was busy rearranging the flowers in a vase on top of the antique chest sitting in the hallway outside his door.

Rebecca delights in frightening new employees, and most new hires encounter her before they have worked at the hotel a month. One employee, who had been living in an upstairs room for a couple weeks, was getting ready to come down to work when she saw in her vanity mirror the toilet handle move by itself, flushing the toilet. Rebecca was mischievously welcoming her to the lodge.

The Governor's Suite has a chronic telephone problem. The line will ring downstairs, but when the operator answers, no one is there. The phone rings from that room even when no one is staying there. The operators keep hoping that one day Rebecca will actually talk to them. Housekeepers make up the bed in that room, only to come back later and find an indentation on the spread as if someone had sat or reclined on the bed. Occasionally a guest in that room will discover his or her shoes missing. The shoes later turn up in another guest room, to the surprise of the guest who finds them.

The basement is also a favorite spot for Rebecca. When Mr. and Mrs. Sanders purchased the lodge in 1982, they kept their spare clothes in suitcases in a small storage room off the basement. One night as they descended the basement stairs, they saw an eerie light glowing from the back of the room. The light was moving! When they turned on the overhead lights, they found that their trunks had been moved, and that an old, dusty door inside the storage room, which was always locked, was now wide open. It led to another tiny room. By now, the strange light had moved into that tiny room. They followed the light into an old, sealed bathroom. When they entered, water suddenly burst from the old faucets at a furious rate. After turning off the water, Mr. Sanders inspected the basement but found no signs of forced entry, no broken windows, and nothing missing. Other employees told him it was just Rebecca, up to her old tricks, welcoming them to her inn.

Other times, doors open and slam shut, lights go on and off, and appliances start up by themselves, scaring people out of their wits. Now, employees who must go down to the basement, especially late at night, always announce their presence to Rebecca.

Sightings

"They say she was very pretty, very flirtatious. Mischievous. You know . . . loose. What they would call a 'full-service maid,'" explained Nosi Crosby, who has been a bartender at the hotel for nearly twenty years. "She was a chambermaid in the late 1930s. They didn't have that many maids back then like we have today. There were a lot of lumberjacks staying here, and she was very popular with the men."

Nosi had an encounter that just about scared her to death, and made her reconsider her employment at the hotel:

I was very busy one day, and I had to use the bathroom. I ran downstairs to the bathroom in the basement. I looked under both stalls to see which one was available, and they were both free. When I got through, there was no toilet paper. I lost it. I said, 'Oh, s***, there is no toilet paper!' Just then, a ghostly white hand reached under the stall and handed me a roll of paper. I just freaked! I ran out without even using it!

I have very dark olive skin, but I was pale as a ghost. My manager asked me what was wrong. It was the scariest thing. For the longest time I wouldn't go down to the basement. All I can say is, if you ever run out of toilet paper, don't ask!

There is a big beautiful black piano in the dining room area. When the pianist leaves, he locks the piano and puts the key in a drawer so the guests won't play it. One time, I heard the piano playing. I said, 'Oh, no,' and I ran to the dining room. I thought a guest was playing. When I got there, there was a lady sitting at the piano in a long white gown. When I went up to her, she disappeared!

A lot of things happen in here. A waitress named Kathy worked for the restaurant. Every time she opened a bottle of wine for table 6, the entire bottle would shatter all over the table-cloth and guests. The first time they told her it's the ghost. She said, "Oh, no, there is no ghost." But after it happened so many times, she quit.

A lady was staying in Room 104. She woke up because a man was singing "Won't You Be My True Love?" right in her ear. Then she felt an icy-cold hand clamp down on her shoulder. She lay there petrified for quite some time, afraid to move. When she finally got the nerve to turn and look at who was there, she felt a whooshing movement, and "it" was gone. She grabbed her husband, a sound sleeper, shaking him frantically. When he finally woke up, he said he hadn't heard a thing.

Best Rooms/Times

Room 101, the Governor's Suite, is the most haunted. The theory is that the Governor's Suite was the place where Rebecca most frequently offered her services, visiting the room late at night and pleasuring wealthy male guests. She also likes to hang out in the Red Dog Saloon.

The Inn/Hotel

Perched high atop the mystical Sacramento Mountains, the mountaintop lodge is situated near the southernmost ski area in the country, Sunset. Surrounded by towering pine trees and spectacular mountain scenery, the elegant three-story Victorian structure is reminiscent of an old European-style mountain resort. A massive, four-story lookout tower dominates the historic structure. Outside, a picturesque pond and waterfall reflect the tranquillity of this peaceful setting.

Inside, the two-story lobby is decorated in French country style, with rich leather sofas and armchairs and deep mahogany tables. The sixty-one tasteful guest rooms are all individually appointed with period antiques. Each room has high ceilings, down comforters and French eyelet linens, and clinking steam radiators.

The lodge offers delightful activities for all seasons. In the summer, guests can relax by the pool, play a round at the lodge's historic golf course, or take a hike in the woods, where Rebecca's grave lies undiscovered. Horseback riding, fishing, and tennis are available nearby. In the winter, guests can relax by the fire after a day of skiing or tubing. In any season one can savor the services at the spa: sauna, massage, and an outdoor hot tub.

The Lodge Golf Course was added in 1899. Governed by the Scottish tradition of playing different tees and separate flags on each hole, this exquisite nine-hole course, when played twice, becomes a challenging eighteen-hole round. At 9,000 feet above sea level, the Lodge Golf Course is one of the highest courses in North America.

Dining

The restaurant is named after the lodge's resident ghost, Rebecca. A colorful stained-glass window bearing her likeness is its focal point. A number of signature dishes are dedicated to Rebecca. The award-winning chef prepares scrumptious southwestern and continental cuisine.

The restaurant caters to lovers, and has created special "dinners for two," tempestuous delights like flambéed lobster tails, rack of lamb, or chateaubriand, served by candlelight to the romantic melodies of the grand piano.

Don't Miss

The Red Dog Saloon is located downstairs. With its plank floors, rough wood walls, and Victorian decor, the saloon has the feel of an Old West saloon. The hotel provides live entertainment and dancing on weekends.

The Red Dog Saloon, built in the space once used as a shower area for inn employees, is one of Rebecca's favorite haunts. Rebecca likes an occasional drink, and she has been known to help herself. Customers have seen the reflection of a beautiful young woman in the mirror. When they turn to look, she is gone. More than one guest has approached a beautiful redheaded lady sitting at the bar and watched as she vanished into thin air.

Rebecca loves to dance. Workers cleaning up after the saloon has closed have observed her twirling on the dance floor. Overnight guests have called in the middle of the night and complained about the loud music coming from the Red Dog—even when it was closed and dark. Even stranger things have been witnessed in the saloon: ashtrays move across the table by themselves, and flames suddenly burst out of the fireplace . . . with no logs or other source of fuel.

During the Prohibition era, gambling was popular in the saloon. One evening, a stack of old 1930s poker chips were found lying in the middle of the floor—which had just been swept.

The Lodge at Cloudcroft
1 Corona Place
P.O. Box 497
Cloudcroft, NM 88317
505-682-2566 or 800-395-6343
e-mail: info@thelodgeresort.com
www.thelodgeresort.com

The Martha Washington Inn

❧

Abingdon, Virginia

The faint strains of violin music waft down the halls, the chilling resonance of a melody that has been echoing the halls of the third floor of this inn for over a century. But the haunting melody is not the only sound of times past. A Civil War soldier, a frightened young girl, and a proud stallion also walk the halls of the Martha Washington Inn in Abingdon, Virginia.

During the War of Northern Aggression, a Yankee officer, Captain John Stoves, was badly wounded and taken to the mansion's third floor, a private school for girls that had become a makeshift hospital. He was tenderly cared for by a young student, known today only as Beth. To comfort the wounded and dying, she played her violin, often taking final requests. Late one evening, his strength ebbing, Captain Stoves called out, "Play something, Beth, I'm going." With trembling fingers, she played the sweet southern refrain that had comforted him so often during his illness, the melody that haunts the inn today.

Several other Civil War–era spirits also haunt the inn, including a riderless ghost horse, an angry young soldier trapped deep in the underground tunnels below the hotel, and a bloody stain on the spot where a Confederate soldier was mortally wounded, which will not go away, no matter how often the spot is scrubbed or bleached.

"We don't have ghosts at the Martha Washington Inn, we have spirits," explains Adrian Chew, who oversees the operations at the historic property. "All of our spirits can be traced back to real people who lived and died here." The inn is notable for many things, but the most intriguing of them is its spirits.

The inn, built in 1832, began life as a magnificent southern mansion, the private residence of General Francis Preston and his family. Two years later, upon his death, the house passed to the local Methodist church, which transformed it into a finishing school for young ladies. The school was named Martha Washington College, and was referred to simply as the Martha. Elaborate balls and receptions were an integral part of the college life. At the annual George Washington Ball, the girls donned colonial costumes, descended the winding staircase, and "flitted to and fro" in the stately parlors, dancing to the strains of the Virginia reel and the minuet. The gaieties concluded with songs alluding to soldier lovers, scandalous in that day, but quite tame by today's standards.

During the Civil War, the grounds of the Martha were converted into barracks for Confederate officers, and the school was designated as a hospital—a common practice, as it ensured that the building would not be attacked by Union troops. All the girls became "nurses." Bloody battles were waged in the quaint town of Abingdon, Virginia, and the injured were carried to the Martha Washington, where the girls nursed both Union and Confederate soldiers. The inn's spirits, for the most part, originated during this turbulent period.

Young and impressionable, many of the girls fell deeply in love with the stricken soldiers they nursed. Beth is probably the most famous of these. She fell in love with Captain Stoves, and upon his death, she was stricken with typhoid fever and died. The two are now united in Abingdon's Green Springs Cemetery, and today Beth's haunting violin serenades are a testament to her love.

Beth was not the only student to watch in horror as life was sucked from her beloved. One Martha student fell deeply in love with a young Confederate soldier. Camped not far from the college, he was given documents describing the strength and positions of the Union forces and ordered to take them posthaste to General Lee. Before he left, the young man crept up a secret stairway to bid good-bye to his sweetheart. Unfortunately, Union troops appeared unexpectedly. The frightened soldier drew his pistol in defense but was shot dead in front of his beloved, staining the floor at her feet with his blood. Attempts through the years to remove the stain have been futile; it persisted and stubbornly reappeared. Eventually, the unrelenting stain had to be covered over with carpet.

The Martha is host not only to human but equine spirits as well. One evening in December 1864, Union forces rode into Abingdon around sunset to raid the town. Nearby Confederates had been alerted, but as they approached, several of the Union soldiers escaped. One Union soldier rode west and, as he turned into the alley east of the school, was struck by a Confederate bullet. The wounded soldier was carried inside and died there about midnight. For hours, his horse roamed the campus grounds, waiting in vain for his master. Many claim that they have witnessed a ghostly, riderless horse galloping on the inn's south lawn.

Yet another spirit, described as "angry," haunts the underground tunnel that connects the Martha Washington with the Barter Theater across the street. During the Civil War, during the era of the Underground Railroad, slaves were smuggled into the Martha or the Barter Theater and down into the secret tunnel. At one time over thirty miles of caverns ran underneath the streets of Abingdon.

Ammunition was hidden in the basement of the Martha and smuggled out through the tunnel, up through the Barter Theater, and out into the fields. A young Confederate soldier, killed in the dark tunnel after the Union discovered this ammunition, might be the spirit who protects the tunnel to this day.

Despite the war, the college survived. However, the Great Depression, typhoid fever, and a declining enrollment eventually took their toll, and the Martha closed in 1932, standing idle for several years. For a time in 1934, the facility housed aspiring actors who appeared at the renowned Barter Theater, until, in 1935, the Martha was opened again as a hotel. Throughout the years it has entertained many famous political and Hollywood figures, including Eleanor Roosevelt, President Harry Truman, Lady Bird Johnson, Jimmy Carter, Elizabeth Taylor, and Gregory Peck.

Barter Theater

The histories of the Barter Theater and the Martha Washington Inn are permanently and inexorably linked. The Barter Theater is a cultural Virginian landmark. Created by Robert Porterfield in 1933 on the site of the Abingdon Opera House, it is the longest-running professional resident theater in America. At the time of its founding, with the economy in a depression, few people were attending the theater. Porterfield conceived the idea that the audience could literally barter food or services in exchange for entertainment and so provided depression-era actors with both food and work. He convinced the town to allow him to bring his acting troupe to the abandoned Abingdon Opera House, which became known as Barter Theater.

When the theater opened in June 1933, the advertised admission was "35 cents or the equivalent in produce." The first ticket was bought with a small pig! The little porker squealed so loudly, the actors tied him out front to serve as the theater's barker. People bartered everything from produce to haircuts for entrance fees.

The actors weren't the only ones to receive payment in edibles. Playwrights including Noel Coward, Tennessee Williams, and Thornton Wilder, received their royalty fees in Virginia hams. One exception was George Bernard Shaw, a vegetarian, who exchanged the rights to his plays for fresh spinach.

Barter's heritage is rich and colorful and includes many famous thespians: Gregory Peck, Ernest Borgnine, Patricia Neal, John Spencer, Stacy Keach, Steve Martin, Kevin Spacey, and Ned Beatty have all appeared on its historic stage.

Sightings

Rick Rose, producing artistic director at the famed
Barter Theater for ten years, has seen and heard a lot
of stories during his artistic tenure.

The main ghost here is Robert Porterfield, of
course. Many people walking down Main Street
look up and see him looking out the window
upstairs. I've heard that from dozens of people.
The alumni see him on opening night. It's always good luck if you spot him in the audience
on opening night. He usually sits right in the
front row, or up in the balcony. Sometimes
ushers would go to seat people, and there
would be a man in a white suit sitting there. The
ushers would turn around to check the tickets,
to see if they had the wrong seat number. When
the ushers turned back, he would be gone.

Since we renovated the theater, we've seen
him in the stage manager's booth. Many of the
actors have seen him in the reflection off the
window. This is another symbol of good luck.

A group of us got together and did an interesting thing after the renovation. There is a life-
size portrait of Bob that hangs in the theater. A
group of Barter Company members took his
portrait throughout the entire building. We
made a procession, taking him to every closet,
every bathroom. We wanted him to know the
new space and be comfortable. Hazel Young,

the production manager, was the ringleader. We want to be sure he stays happy.

Personally, I've never had the ability to see ghosts. I have come up through several theaters that were haunted. Bob pulls little pranks on the stage crew. He moves things around during a performance. People have seen things backstage—props move across a table, a broom moves from one place to another. People can actually watch it being moved and say, "What's going on here!"

There is another ghost that haunts the basement of Barter Theater, in the old tunnel that connected the Barter to the hotel. We use that tunnel now to run electrical cables. In 1890, the tunnel collapsed. A man was killed. It's always been our belief that that's who haunts the tunnel. They filled in the rest of the tunnel when they were working on the streets, and the Martha closed their end about five or six years ago. On our end, you can still see the tunnel.

I've heard from actors who were here in the 1930s and '40s, all the way through to today, about the ghost in the tunnel. You never see this guy, you just kind of feel him, and when you do, you run like hell. He never goes past the original door that runs outside. That's why we think it was either the soldier that smuggled ammunition to his allies or the man who died when it collapsed. It's definitely an evil force. You can feel the evil. You just bolt as quickly as you can.

Fascinatingly enough, when we were doing

the renovation, there was a group of four carpenters downstairs in the middle of the night. All four of them were eating their lunch at four A.M. Suddenly, all four of them got up and bolted. They never said a word to each other . . . they didn't even look at each other. The first guy grabbed his lunch and left, and the rest followed. They refused to go back down there at night.

I asked one of the alumni if the apparition appeared just to northerners. He said no, the ghost has scared a good many southern boys out of there as well.

The first year I was here, a funny thing happened at the rehearsal hall. I had just arrived, and two of our staff, the musical director and an actor, came running out, as pale as they could be. I asked them what the hell was going on. They told me they had just experienced a ghost. They said this ghost came walking across the rehearsal hall. They couldn't see her, but they could hear her steps one by one. Suddenly she hollered, "Get out!" I have heard that story a lot; especially if people were rehearsing late, or stayed too late, she would chase them from the building.

One of the beliefs is that there was a woman who was the housekeeper at the inn where we house our actors. Every night she would hold a séance in the pyramid room. The ghost started appearing after she died. She would cast evil spirits out of people and lock them in the pyramid room. A lot of people today say they can't stay in there, so we keep that room locked.

We have a horrible ghost at the Barter Inn, where the actors stay. This ghost is nasty. He cusses and swears, slinging really gross epithets from underneath the bed. At least one hundred of my people have told me this story. Many of them, understandably, won't stay in the room. Even dogs, who normally follow their owners everywhere, will not go anywhere near that room. It's a very mean ghost.

It usually starts in the middle of the night. It stands at the foot of the bed, staring at you until you wake up. Then it starts berating you. It howls, going on and on. It's really disturbing. You can't see it clearly, but you can see the image.

We know that an intern hung himself in that room under somewhat suspicious circumstances. It was never proved that someone else did it. The body was found dressed in women's clothes. The family never came to claim the body. It was a fairly prominent family, in the 1960s. The vast majority of people, when they walk into that room, they won't stay there.

Best Rooms/Times

Although the spirits at the Martha wander through every room, even in the new wing, the Camberley Suite seems to be the most haunted room. The soft ripples of violin music echo through the halls of the third floor.

Stepping outside the Martha onto Main Street, you might catch a glimpse of Robert Porterfield in the window of the Barter Theater. On opening night, look for him in the control booth, in the front row, or up in the balcony.

The Inn

You will find more than ghost stories in this elegant hotel. The original rooms and parlors are extravagantly decorated in a style in keeping with the inn's southern plantation heritage.

The Martha is an elegant testimony to a colorful past. Through the years, the mansion was filled with priceless gifts and furnishings. Fortunately, much of the inn's historic charm, antiques, and architectural detail were preserved. A rare and elaborate Dutch Baroque grandfather clock, measuring over nine feet tall, was shipped from England by one of the Preston daughters. It now resides in the East Parlor and still works today. An original eighteen-foot art deco table made of silver by Oscar Bock had been stored for many years at the hotel. It now presides again over the dining room. Original pieces are still showing up, donated by gracious benefactors.

The sixty-four rooms are all unique and different. All are furnished in keeping with the history of the hotel, with antebellum furnishings and decor.

The exquisite murals in the entry hall colorfully depict historical dates in American history: West Point cadets drilling on the Hudson, the Natural Bridge in Lewisburg, which Jefferson and Washington loved, Niagara Falls, and Charleston, created by Mr. White of Atlanta.

Dining

Martha's dining room presents traditional Virginia Appalachian fare. Rich regional flavors of bourbon, whiskey, or molasses are a reflection of these tastes. Specialties include Martha's she-crab soup, Virginia crab cakes, fried chicken livers with grilled toast points and sweet Virginia tomato jam, and rib-eye steak marinated in bourbon chipotle molasses. An extensive wine list, with an exclusive "library" of rare vintages, is offered.

Down the street is the Tavern, Abingdon's oldest building. Built in 1779 as an inn for stagecoach travelers, with such guests as Henry Clay, King Louis-Philippe of France, and President Andrew Jackson, the Tavern has a ghost or two of its own.

Don't Miss

Chartered in 1778, Abingdon is a Virginia Historic Landmark, the oldest town west of the Blue Ridge Mountains. As you stroll down the shaded brick sidewalks of the twenty-block historic district, featuring outstanding examples of Federal and Victorian architecture and lined with historic buildings and quaint stores that showcase regional arts and crafts, you feel as if you have stepped back in time. It's easy to imagine the frightful night spent by Daniel Boone, the girlish laughter echoing from the Martha Washington Inn, and the applause of an audience of poor farmers at the Barter Theater.

Another one of the many hauntings in this town rich in history, legends, and ghosts is the Virginia Creeper Trail. Originally a Native American footpath and later a railway, this historic path is now a National Recreation Trail, where you can walk alongside the spirits of the Indians and soldiers who traveled this momentous trail throughout its captivating history.

The Martha Washington Inn
150 West Main Street
Abingdon, VA 24210
540-628-3161
e-mail: reservations@camberleyhotels.com
www.camberlyhotels.com

Barter Theater
Abingdon, VA 24210
www.bartertheatre.com

The Mason House Inn

◈

Bentonsport, Iowa

While it may be easy for some people to discount personal accounts of ghost encounters as boasting, sensationalism, or just plain lies, how do you dismiss the ghostly encounters when the person recounting the experience is a Baptist preacher?

Bill McDermott, Doctor of Religion, pastor of the United Methodist Baptist Church, talks candidly about his conversations with Mary Mason, onetime owner of the Mason House, who has been dead since 1911. He talks about her as if she is a personal friend. To him, I'm sure she is.

"She looks solid, very natural. She's in her sixties, with short black hair," says Bill. "She dresses in long full dresses in an older style. She always sits in the same chair, upstairs in the study, where I would go to do my writing or accounting. She seems to know when I am there. She is never there when I first go up. She only appears after I am already in the room. We chat for a few minutes, and then she disappears. Usually she says she is happy with what we are doing here, but one time, just after we tore out a wall, she left pretty abruptly."

McDermott says he was not scared by her presence, because the event seemed so natural and real. His wife, Sheral, also a graduate of religious studies, is relieved that Mary has never appeared to her. The McDermotts look as if they could have been the models for Grant Wood's classic painting *American Gothic*. As former owners of the Mason House, they ran the charming brick inn on the banks of the Iowa River for over ten years.

Bill isn't the only one who has seen Mary. Apparently, she frequently visits her old friend George across the street. Rubye Dowell, a retired schoolteacher, lived across the street from the Mason House in the house of George Greef, who died in 1894 and was a good friend and confidant of Mary Mason. Rubye swears not only that George is still in the house, but that Mary comes over to visit him there. Rubye hears footsteps and bits of conversations between a man and a woman, punctuated with the deep belly laugh that George was known for.

But Mary is not the only spirit to inhabit the inn.

The names in this story have been changed, because "Jane," a sweet, unpretentious old lady, lives in town to this day. When she was a teen, her own father sold her to a local lecher, "John," for four hundred dollars. Even though he was fifty years her senior, John married the girl and then became her pimp. Men would go in and out of that house at all hours of the night or day. Jane was terrorized, victimized, and desperate, but possessed neither the foresight, nor the funds, to get out of the situation.

Fanny Redhead [real name] was the owner of the Mason House at the time. Her heart bled for the poor child, and she took her in and hid her. When Jane didn't come home, old John was livid. Through town gossip, he eventually learned that she was hiding out at the Mason House. Toting his shotgun, he went to the inn, climbed the big maple tree in the backyard, tied himself to the tree, and waited for his wife to show up. He didn't realize that both Fanny and the girl were already inside, laughing at him. Hours later, when he saw them through the window, he became so enraged that he fell out of the tree and hung himself. Today, John is occasionally spotted in the old maple tree, watching for Jane.

There have been several other deaths at the Mason House, though none quite so dramatic. The Masons' granddaughter Fannye froze to death as she sat in her rocker in front of the fireplace, the embers long extinguished. Some guests, unaware of the inn's history, report seeing a woman sitting in a rocker by the fireplace.

Sightings

The inn has long had a reputation with the locals for being haunted. For several years, when the building was vacant, passersby observed lights going on and off inside, though no one was there and the electricity was off.

In 1992 an attorney and his family from Cedar Rapids came to stay. They rented two adjacent rooms, 3 and 9, on the second floor. In the middle of the night, when everyone was asleep, the occupants of both rooms were awakened by loud knocking, as if someone were frantically trying to get in. The family members all ran out to the hall, both groups going to see what the other wanted. When they realized it was not a family member, they thought that the innkeepers must have been playing a joke on them. In the morning, they complained, in spite of assurances from Bill that neither he nor Sheral got up that night. "It's just not something we would do," he adds.

Best Rooms/Times

Encounters at the Mason House can happen any time, day or night. Bill's conversations with Mary all took place in the middle of the day. People see Fannye in the Keeping Room; she is mostly likely to appear when there is a warm, cozy fire in the fireplace. For that reason, fall and winter seem to bring more reports.

Guest rooms near the second-floor landing seem to have more activity, especially rooms 3 and 9. The entire hallway gives Bill a funny feeling most of the time.

The Inn

Mason House, the oldest steamboat hotel on the Iowa River, was built in 1846 as a river inn by Mormons making their way to Salt Lake City. Shortly thereafter, it was sold to the Mason family, and remained in their family for ninety-nine years. Mary Mason, their daughter, inherited the inn from her parents, and is the same Mary who visits Bill.

The river was the only form of transportation before the railroads, and Bentonsport, now practically a ghost town, was a bustling city. People who could afford to would stay in the private rooms on the second floor, while the rest would stay in a third-floor dorm room that spanned the entire length of the inn. Abe Lincoln stayed twice; Mark Twain, a friend of the family, stayed several times; and Robert Waller, author of *The Bridges of Madison County,* stayed a week before he wrote his best-seller.

The Mason family brought many fine antique furnishings from New York in 1857, and today more than half of the original appointments remain. The original bedroom set of Mr. and Mrs. Mason is in the Mason Room. You will not find any closets, since they were taxed as regular rooms in the 1840s, so instead there are coat hooks on the walls.

The "shared bath," an old copper-lined "Murphy" tub that unfolds from a wall cabinet, is in the Keeping Room by the fireplace to keep it warm. At one time, everyone in the inn bathed there in the same bathwater, one at a time. But don't worry, today all the rooms have private baths.

Inside the house are five guest rooms. Country comfort describes these rooms, filled with antiques, and stenciled walls. An old railroad station from the next town was moved next to the inn and for years was an old country store, carrying everything from clothing to candy. It has been converted into four more bedrooms, each with a different theme, taken from items left from the store. One room is filled with ladies' corsets, garters, and pantaloons from the turn of the century.

The Keeping Room contains a wonderful library, including a collection of books written by authors who have stayed at the inn. The entire downstairs is open to guests, and on a Saturday night, guests can be found lounging in the front parlor, engaged in a card game in the Keeping Room, or sitting by the fire.

According to Bill, Mary Mason approves of the changes to her old inn.

Dining

A full breakfast is served in the Keeping Room beside the 1880 Buck's cook stove.

Don't Miss

Today, Bentonsport has a population of thirty-one people and nine dogs. The town has a lot of character and is surrounded by gorgeous Iowa scenery dotted with bridges and gazebos. You can explore the ruins of old mills along the river, stroll across a century-old iron bridge, or just sit on the riverbank and imagine the sight of a steamboat comin' round the bend. Treasures await you in the specialty shops, where you can watch shopkeepers as they work at their crafts. There's even a potter's shop and a blacksmith's shop. It's like stepping back in time.

The Mason House Inn
100 East First Street
Bentonsport, IA 52565
319-592-3133 or 800-592-3133
e-mail: mhibprt@netins.net
www.showcase.netins.net/web/bentonsport/

Hotel Monte Vista

❦

Flagstaff, Arizona

This Hollywood hot spot in the center of Flagstaff, Arizona, is haunted by a host of very unusual and eccentric spirits as varied and sordid as the hotel's own intriguing past. Located just one block north of the famous Route 66, the hotel was a popular spot for Hollywood stars and starlets during the 1940s and 1950s, while more than 100 Westerns were filmed nearby. Since its grand opening festivities on New Year's Day in 1927, many celebrities have made the Monte Vista their "home away from home," including Bing Crosby, Jane Russell, Gary Cooper, Spencer Tracy, Cary Grant, Clark Gable, Carole Lombard, and many others.

Today, many rooms are named after famous guests who occupied those rooms. If you're a fan of classic romantic movies, you can request to spend the night in the room where a scene from *Casablanca* was filmed.

The hotel was notorious for its Wild West parties, gunfights, drunken brawls, and ladies of the night. It's rumored that many a cowboy rode his horse into the lobby and bar, and more than one sheepherder kept a sheep or two in his room. The well-trodden red-light district was right around the corner from the Hotel Monte Vista. In fact, two of the hotel's more popular ghosts, both prostitutes, were said to have been murdered in the hotel, though another version of the story is that they died when they hit the pavement outside after they were thrown out the window.

Always on the edge of notoriety, the hotel has been host to a number of suspicious operations. In 1931 the Monte Vista Lounge, host of a well-known speakeasy, was nearly closed down when local officials put a major Flagstaff bootlegging operation to an end. Between 1935 and 1940 two industrial Flagstaff residents, Fred Nackard and Rex Gobel, ran slot machines out of the hotel lounge and lobby—the only slot machines ever to be used in Flagstaff.

In 1970 three bank robbers decided to stop at the hotel lounge for a drink after a nearby heist. One of the men had been shot during the robbery. As he sat toasting with his buddies, he suddenly slumped over and died on the bar. Apparently he is still enjoying his liquor in the Monte Vista bar.

Many noteworthy historic events have also occurred at the hotel. In 1927, Mary Costigan became the first American woman to be granted a radio broadcasting license, and her three-hour radio show aired daily from her second-floor studio at the Hotel Monte Vista, Room 105.

Though numerous ghosts allegedly haunt the hotel, some of the most famous include a "phantom bellboy" who knocks on the door of the Zane Grey Room (210) announcing "room service," a ghostly woman who wanders the halls, an annoying old-man ghost in Room 220 who perpetually awakens guests in adjoining rooms with his coughing and hacking, and eerie band music coming from the second-floor balcony. An unknown woman was murdered in her room in the late 1930s. Hotel clerks are very careful never to put guests with pets in that room, because dogs go crazy with fear and tear up everything in the room.

A rocking chair sits at the window in Room 305. No matter where in the room the cleaning staff moves the chair, the next morning it is back in its original spot next to the window, as if someone were sitting there watching out the window to the street below.

Sightings

John Wayne is probably the most famous person to experience a ghostly encounter at the Hotel Monte Vista, or at least the most famous person to admit to a sighting. In the early 1950s, Wayne reported seeing a ghost in his hotel room.

After a fight broke out in Room 220 and repairs had to be made, a maintenance man was sent up to survey the damage. When he left, he turned off the lights and locked the door. When he returned to the room just a few minutes later, he found the lights back on, the television blaring full blast, and the bed linens on the previously made bed stripped and lying in a pile on the floor. A strange long-term boarder, known for his bizarre behavior and outlandish dealings (he was known to hang raw meat from the chandelier) died in that room in the early 1980s. His body wasn't found for two or three days. Employees believe this eccentric character may still be residing in Room 220.

Jerry Underwood managed the hotel for many years. Every morning when he unlocked the bar, he heard the same male voice greet him with a cheerful "good morning." The first time, Jerry answered the voice before he realized that no one was around.

"I felt pretty foolish," he confessed. "But I felt better, I think, when I learned that many of the other employees responded to the voice their first time as well."

Common at the hotel, says Jerry, are televisions that go on by themselves when no one is occupying the room, phone calls from empty rooms, and piano music. On Jerry's first night, he claims his hair stood on end when he was downstairs alone and he heard the downstairs commode flush. Another time, Jerry and a female bartender were talking after hours, long after the place had closed. Suddenly something stumbled through the bar, knocking chairs over, and crashed through the doors. Jerry and the bartender watched in disbelief, as there was nothing visible to cause the commotion.

Voices and loud music emanate from the bar late at night, long after it has been closed and locked up. For a change of pace, 1950s music seems to come from the mezzanine, though its exact source has never been found.

"There have always been strange things here," says W. W. "Johnny" Johnson, who owned the hotel for many years. "There are so many ghosts here, we can't figure out who all of them are."

Best Rooms/Times

Ghostly activity seems to pick up in the late afternoon, and again after midnight. Rooms 210, 220, and 305 are the most haunted, as well as the second-floor mezzanine and bar.

The Hotel

Occupying nearly an entire city block, this five-story hotel was once the grand dame of Flagstaff, and was host to a long string of celebrities. Many rooms are named after those who once slept in them, including the Carole Lombard Room, the Humphrey Bogart Room, the Bob Hope Room, the Theodore Roosevelt Room, the Jane Russell Room, and more.

The original sixty-four rooms have been updated and remodeled into twenty-eight rooms, each with a private bath.

As it expanded, the Hotel Monte Vista incorporated part of the old post office, built in 1917 by famous local citizens. The historic post office is still an important hub of the hotel and today serves as the Old Post Office Day Spa, owned and operated by Jim Craven.

Dining

The Monte Vista restaurant, with its tin ceilings, plush red velvet wallpaper and red carpets, and rich oak bar and tables, has maintained its Old West atmosphere. The restaurant serves a variety of steaks, burgers, and seafood.

The haunted Hotel Monte Vista Cocktail Lounge is located on the lower level of the building. The bilevel lounge offers live music in the lower level of the bar in the evenings and billiards upstairs.

Don't Miss

Dotted along old Route 66 were all sorts of unique mom-and-pop restaurants, cafés, gas stations, and trading posts. These wonderful places gave the historic highway a unique flavor. This is also much of what gave travelers of the 1940s and '50s such fond and vivid memories of "America's Main Street." Unfortunately, most of these places closed as bigger and faster highways were built, and people no longer traveled the romantic road. The advent of I-40 signaled the demise of an American icon. In 1968 Flagstaff was bypassed, and in 1984 the last bypass at Williams, Arizona, was completed. It seemed as if the love affair with the open road had ended for good.

The Museum Club (3404 East Route 66; 520-526-9434) is one of those few, unusual spots that remains today as a piece of Americana, and a monument to Route 66. Today, as one of the most unusual bars in the nation, this campy club made *Car and Driver* magazine's top ten roadhouses. The bar began as a taxidermy showcase. Dean Eldredge began his taxidermy business in 1918, and by 1931 opened a museum to display his unique collections of Native American artifacts, rare rifles, and wild animals that he gutted and stuffed, adding dark, beady glass eyes. Thousands of tourists and hunting buffs would stop by the Dean Eldredge Museum on Route 66 to see this impressive collection of critters and artifacts.

Doc Williams, a Flagstaff-based saddle maker, turned Eldredge's museum into a nightclub when Prohibition ended in 1936. Constructed around five huge ponderosa pine trees, it soon thereafter began to lay claim to being the largest log cabin in Arizona. The peculiar entrance to this club is none other than a huge inverted ponderosa pine tree trunk that has branched off into two separate treelike formations. Ponderosa pines appear to grow right out of the huge dance floor. An impressive 1890s bar lends an Old West feel. The glass eyes of bobcats, bears, owls, peacocks, mountain lions, and various other animals, hanging on the walls or perched in tree branches above the dance floor, glare down at visitors, giving the place its local name, "the Zoo."

During the 1960s and 1970s almost everyone who was or became somebody musically played at the Museum Club, due to its high level of visibility on Route 66 and its nationwide reputation as one of the hottest roadhouses in the country. Willie Nelson, Waylon Jennings, Bob Wills and the Texas Playboys, Wynn Stewart, Wanda Jackson, and Asleep at the Wheel are just a few of the many famous acts that have appeared at the Museum Club since its inception in the 1930s.

Don and Thelma Scott owned the Museum Club in the 1960s and '70s and lived in an apartment above the bar. A big-time promoter, Don is credited with bringing so many legends to the club and putting the place on the map again. Both met untimely deaths—

Thelma tripped and fell down the stairs and broke her neck, while Don, broken up over her death, shot himself in front of the fireplace—but neither left.

The fireplace upstairs where Don took his life suddenly bursts into flame, even when there is no kindling. Footsteps go up and down the stairs and into the rooms above the Zoo that used to belong to the Scotts. Lights in the bar turn on by themselves when no one is there.

Thelma has been sighted on the staircase, and actually pinned down an employee who dared to enter her old apartment. When he walked in, he saw Thelma coming toward him, knocking him down, and holding him captive. She finally released him, and he ran screaming from the room.

A customer ordered a drink from the female bartender at the back bar. When she ignored him, he complained to management, but was told that not only was there not a bartender at the back bar, the area was closed. Another customer was pretty distressed when he bought a drink for a lady sitting alone at a back table. When he approached with the drink, she vanished.

Hotel Monte Vista
100 North San Francisco Street
Flagstaff, AZ 86001
520-779-6971 or 800-545-3068
e-mail: montev@infomagic.net
www.hotelmontevista.com

The Oatman Hotel

Oatman, Arizona

Route 66 is notorious for its stretches of haunted highway: the ghosts of long-dead gunslingers and robbers, a lone ghost girl hitching a ride, the phantom engines gunning and wheels screeching in an invisible drag race, or the ghostly convertible passing you, its occupants waving.

One of the most famous hauntings on Old Route 66 is in Oatman, Arizona. The lonesome highway twists and winds through miles of rusted red rock, until you suddenly come upon a ghost town smack dab in the middle of nowhere. It's a place where time stood still seventy years ago.

Oatman began almost a hundred years ago as a mining tent camp and quickly became a flourishing gold-mining center. In 1915 two miners struck a $10 million gold find, and within a year the town's population had grown to more than 3,500. Oatman was named in honor of Olive Oatman, who was kidnapped by Mojave Indians as a child and later rescued in 1857, near the current site of the town.

A fire in 1921 burned down most of the town. Three

years later the mining company United Eastern Mines shut down operations for good. Oatman's population plummeted from a peak of nearly 10,000 to a low of 15 residents.

But today Oatman, long ago abandoned, has taken on a new life. The entire town, about four blocks long, looks much as it did in its heyday, when Clark Gable used to hang out with the boys. Main Street, a portion of Route 66, is the only street in town. Wild burros, descendants of the gold rush burros, wander aimlessly down the street, causing a traffic jam, if that's possible in a town of population 45. Many claim they have seen ghost burros as well, ambling down Main Street. Oatman is a fun place to visit—an authentic old western town with gunfights staged on weekends. Because of its Old West feel, the town was chosen as the location for several movies, including *How the West Was Won*, *Foxfire*, and *Edge of Eternity*.

The old Oatman Hotel is the center of town, both physically and socially. This is the hotel where in 1939 Clark Gable and Carole Lombard spent their wedding night. They were married in Bull City, Arizona, and were driving back to Los Angeles via Route 66. After driving thirty miles, they arrived in Oatman and checked into Room 6 at the Oatman Hotel. Clark returned often to spend hours playing cards with the locals. Clark loved the anonymity, and the locals loved him—he usually lost. It's rumored that Gable and Lombard return from time to time to relive their honeymoon. Even though it is now blocked off as a museum, guests and staff frequently hear giggles and passionate moans coming from their old room.

The most notorious ghost in Oatman is "Oatie." Because of his antics, poor Oatie now gets the blame for everything. According to the staff, Oatie hides things, moves them around, and even breaks them. If his favorite song is not playing, the jukebox won't work.

When Oatie isn't down in the bar, he is often upstairs in his room, where he sits in the chair by the window, rocking. You can see the chair rocking all by itself. He also likes to lounge on the bed, and the impression of his body appears solidly on the covers, even after it has just been made up. Once a window was left open, and dust covered the room except for the bed, where the outline of Oatie's body was clearly visible.

I was referred to Reverend Uncle Charlie, Oatman's self-proclaimed "preacher, bartender, silversmith, gunfighter, and gold miner." I met up with him at Cactus Joe's. Uncle Charlie has regular conversations with Oatie. Once a nonbeliever, Uncle Charlie first attributed Oatie's visitations more to the spirits in the bar than to a living spirit.

Uncle Charlie used to live at the hotel. One night Oatie awoke him from a deep sleep and started talking to him. Uncle Charlie was spellbound as the spirit told his tale of woe.

Many years ago, Oatie told Uncle Charlie, he had checked into the Oatman Hotel, eagerly awaiting the arrival of his fiancée from Ireland. But she never showed up. Never knowing what happened to his beloved, if she was even alive or if she had abandoned him, Oatie became depressed, and literally wasted away. He died, lonely and despondent, outside in the cold behind the hotel. His body sat for days until it was discovered, and then was hastily shoved into a shallow grave just a few yards behind the hotel.

In subsequent visits, Oatie begged Uncle Charlie to free him from his plight. He pleaded with the preacher to dig him up and give him a proper send-off. Figuring Oatie wouldn't leave him alone until he complied, Uncle Charlie went to investigate the spot behind the hotel where Oatie claimed to be buried. Sure enough, there was a sinkhole in the shape of a body. To this day, Uncle Charlie has not yet dug Oatie up, but he has promised that when this book comes out, he will do so, and Oatie will finally have an Irish wake and burial like the town has never seen.

Sightings

The Oatman Hotel is another place where I personally encountered the paranormal while researching this book. I was told that I was the only guest, except for a couple of hotel employees who lived there. In the middle of the night I woke up and heard what sounded like something heavy, maybe a trunk (or body?), being dragged down the hall, right outside my door. I really wanted to investigate to be sure it wasn't someone playing a trick on me, but hard as I tried, I couldn't bring myself to open the door.

Most of the employees of the Oatman Hotel have encountered Oatie, in one way or another. The most common sightings are of things flying through the air without being broken, or glasses that shatter as they sit untouched.

One lady staying in Oatie's room watched in disbelief as a quilt that had been on the bed floated across the room to Oatie's favorite rocking chair. Then she watched in horror as the chair started rocking all by itself, the quilt draped over it as if someone was snuggled up under it. She was so shaken up, she insisted on being moved to a different room.

For many years guests and employees have heard giggles and moans coming from the honeymoon suite. While all this playfulness is credited to Gable and Lombard, probably many couples have left their mark in that room.

A female apparition began to appear a decade ago, after the death of beloved resident hotel manager Mary Knight, known to everyone as "the Christmas lady" because to her, "every day was Christmas." Although she died in 1982, tourists still come to the hotel looking for the gaudy plastic Christmas tree that adorned the restaurant during her ten-year tenure. It remained for another ten years after she died to honor her. Residents and tourists alike claim to have seen her today, sitting in the front window, at what would have been her kitchen table, where she sat working when she was the manager.

Best Rooms/Times

Undoubtedly, Oatie's room is the best place to be if you are looking for an encounter. Guests have reported cold spots and items floating across the room. The imprint of a body appears on the bed when the room has been vacant.

As for best times, Uncle Charlie's communications with Oatie all occurred around 3:00 A.M., but Oatie's pranks are manifested at any time. He delights in moving things around and just generally letting people know he is present.

The Hotel

The Oatman Hotel, built in 1902, is the oldest two-story adobe structure in Mojave County and has housed miners, movie stars, politicians, and other scoundrels.

The hotel, like the town, looks pretty much the same as it did back then. Thick red carpet lines the lobby and ascends the massive oak staircase, bringing to mind a bygone bordello. The hotel is full of memorabilia from the gold miners who spent much of their time there. For many years the hotel was preserved as a museum, with only the bar and restaurant in operation. The current owners have recently opened the rooms upstairs, which are small and sparsely furnished, to overnight guests. All the rooms share one common bath in the hall. But the rooms are obviously not the main attraction—that's the bar, and the assortment of characters that you will find. With just over a hundred residents in Oatman, you are likely to meet the majority of them in any one day. It's best on a weekday, when you can really sit and absorb the colorful tales woven by the locals. They will be more than happy to tell you about Oatman and its ghosts.

Be sure to look up Reverend Uncle Charlie when you are in town. He can usually be found at the hotel, where he bartends three nights a week, or at Cactus Joe's, shooting the bull with Lance from the jail or Ginny, who has written a booklet about Oatman's ghosts. These characters alone make the trip to Oatman worthwhile.

Dining

The biggest attraction at the hotel, or in all of Oatman, is the bar at the hotel. The walls and the ceilings of the bar and restaurant are covered with signed and dated dollar bills. This tradition of Oatman's miners ensured that if they were ever out of money, they had at least one more beer coming at the bar. At any given hour, you will find half the residents of Oatman draped around the western-style saloon.

Don't Miss

The two-block Main Street is lined with unusual shops and shopkeepers. Many of the shopkeepers make their own products, including handmade leather goods, handmade Indian jewelry, and excellent knives sold right from the wooden sidewalks running the length of the town. Some of my favorites are Cactus Joe's, Classy Coyote, Silver Spur, and Fast Fannie's.

Nearby Hoover Dam sits on the Nevada-Arizona border. The dam harnessed the Colorado River, but this didn't come without a price. The work was extremely dangerous, and many men lost their lives while working on the dam. To this day rumors persist about the ghost in coveralls seen boarding the elevator for another day's work.

The Oatman Hotel
181 North Main Street
Route 66
Oatman, AZ 86433
602-768-4408

Palace Hotel and Casino

❦

Cripple Creek, Colorado

The old mining town of Cripple Creek, Colorado, has a rich, colorful history. In the late 1800s, when most of the state's silver mines were drying up and closing down, Cripple Creek was prospering. After gold was discovered in her scenic mountains, the town's population swelled to over 50,000 people. Once the most productive gold camp in North America, Cripple Creek was a hotbed not just of newly made millionaires but also of innovation.

A horrible fire ravaged the town in 1896, destroying many of the wooden buildings downtown. The Palace Building was rebuilt out of brick on the original corner site. The Palace Pharmacy, which was housed in the building, was one of the oldest businesses in Cripple Creek. The adjoining soda fountain was very popular among the children and young adults. The second floor of the building was used for doctor's offices, the third floor rented as furnished rooms.

Between 1908 and 1918 Dr. John Chambers and his wife

Katherine (Kitty for short) owned the Palace Pharmacy. Kitty's name noticeably disappeared from newspaper accounts about the pharmacy after 1913, leaving researchers to believe that she died—very possibly upstairs, in the hotel. When eyewitnesses to the beautiful, dark-haired ghost at the Palace are shown old photographs of Miss Kitty, they are convinced that her spirit roams the hotel. For many years locals have reported that they have seen Miss Kitty looking out from her second-floor window, even during the years when the hotel sat vacant.

By the late 1920s the Palace was allegedly a brothel. In 1932 the hotel was purchased by Gertrude Dial. From all reports, this feisty woman (who is the great-aunt of singer Stevie Nicks) was very charismatic. Gertrude renovated the restaurant, dubbing it "the Girl's Café." Under Gertrude's skillful direction and with the support of her partner, Maude, and her husband Speed (yes, Speed Dial), the Palace once again became a glorious showplace.

"Gertrude was really a character," former Cripple Creek mayor Chip Paige reminisces. "She could tell some wild stories about the residents of Cripple Creek. When she died, the town lost one of its greatest legacies."

By the late 1930s Gertrude owned both the Cripple Creek Hotel and the Palace Hotel, and hired a very gifted black man named Vidas to entertain her customers. Every night he pounded out lively tunes on the piano at the Cripple Creek Hotel, then walked home to his small room at the Palace. It was tough enough to survive in those days in a boisterous mining town; it was even harder if you were black. Vidas also happened to be blind. His family survived by selling butter to the locals.

It is believed that Vidas stayed in Room 16; as Mayor

Paige explains, "Room 16 has some strange things going on."

Vidas would sit in his room at night—with the lights out, of course. People would walk down the hall and hear voices coming from his room. They could hear two or more people engaged in conversation. When they knocked on the door, it would get quiet, so nobody really knew if Vidas was talking to dead people, or if he was using different voices.

One night he and a couple of his buddies drove to Victor. They were all quite drunk, and somehow they thought it would be funny to let Vidas drive home. By some miracle, he got them back safely. They say someone was watching over that guy. His buddies all claim they heard strange voices in the car, talking to Vidas. The voices taunted Vidas, admonishing him that he should not be out drinking and carousing, let alone driving a car. His buddies were convinced they were experiencing alcoholic hallucinations when the disembodied voices began arguing amongst themselves.

Vidas dropped his buddies off and walked the rest of the way back to his room at the Palace. He staggered down the dark alley behind the hotel, up to the wrought-iron staircase that led up to his room on the second floor. Because he was black, Vidas wasn't allowed to use the main staircase. The next morning, in the snow, Gertrude found Vidas frozen stiff at the base of the stairs. He never made it up to his room.

In the 1990s they added on the Palace Casino, right over the spot where Vidas died. It's the same spot that has had lots of ghostly reports. It stands to reason that the ghost in that spot must be Vidas.

The former mayor has his own theory about why mining towns seem to have more than their share of ghosts:

> Mining towns by nature are very volatile. There were very few women in mining camps. The men were like animals. Anything went. If a mining accident didn't kill you, disease would, or you got robbed in a back alley or got knifed in a drunken brawl. The average age of death back then was forty. Our cemeteries are loaded with people who met an untimely death and didn't want to. Their spirits may be unsettled.
>
> Add to that a very high electrical energy. Ionization is very high, from all the minerals. A lot of electricity is concentrated in this area. If you look in terms of electromagnetic fields and auras, that may give us a clue. Nikola Tesla, famous for inventing AC and remote control at the turn of the last century, came to Cripple Creek to test his methods because of the high ionization. They ran him out of Colorado Springs because under normal ionization, his tests blew out half the electricity in that town.

Sightings

By the 1940s, Cripple Creek was a mere ghost town. The once-booming population of 50,000 had dwindled to less than 500. The mines were closed, and many of the miners enlisted or were drafted. Houses were stripped or torn down, the copper roofs utilized in the war effort. By the 1960s many of the buildings sat vacant. Sidewalks were nonexistent, and residents had to pick their way through overgrown stone paths.

Bob Lays and his wife Mary bought the empty, run-down hotel in 1976. "I used to walk to the post office every day and peek through the windows into the boarded-up old hotel," says Bob. "One day, a real estate agent caught me looking. He told me he had a key, and asked if I wanted a tour. When I saw the theater inside, I became very excited. My wife used to be a performer, and my sons sang. So I bought the hotel before I even thought about it."

Once again the Palace Hotel offered dinner theater, melodrama, variety acts, cancan, and comedy. However, when gambling came to Cripple Creek, the restaurant and theater were converted into a casino.

Although Bob tells himself there is no such thing as ghosts, he encountered Kitty late one night. It was around 2:00 A.M. and Bob was in the dining room, shampooing the carpets. He admits that he had an uncanny feeling that he was being watched. Suddenly he heard a loud crash coming from the lobby. He spun around and yelled, "Who's there?" As he turned he saw a woman walk past the doorway. She had long, dark, flowing hair and was wearing a long white gown. She stopped, looked him the eye, and proceeded up the stairs. He ran to the lobby and looked up the stairs. She was not there. He searched the hotel up and down but did not find her.

"I don't believe in ghosts," Bob claims. "But . . . if there is one I've seen her."

Kitty loves to hide the key to her room. It would frequently disappear when Bob needed to use it, and then plink to the ground in front of him when he least expected it. Only the key to Room 103 would disappear. One night Bob and Chip searched everywhere for the key, finally giving up. The next morning they found it lying in the middle of the lobby floor. "We were both dumbfounded," admits Bob. "We were the last ones out, and the first ones in. We would have tripped over it had it been there before."

When Bob's son used to manage the hotel, he stayed in Room 1. Sometimes, he would get thirsty late at night and go down to the kitchen for a glass of milk. When he glanced in the dining room, he always found one of the candles still lit on one of the tables. He would unlock the dining room and blow it out. He repeatedly found lighted candles on that same table. He would jump on the waitresses for not checking the candles. The dining room had wrought-iron gates, and they were padlocked at night. No one else had the key. This went on the entire eight years that he lived there.

Chip and one of the bartenders watched aghast as the candle on that very same table lit right before their eyes.

We had been debating the existence of ghosts. There was no one else in the hotel, and we were embroiled in some pretty heavy con-

versation. I took the stand that they do exist—
I had seen too many of Kitty's antics at the
hotel. He was adamant that there is no such
things as ghosts.

As the night progressed, our arguments became more testy. "Okay, let's do an experi-
ment," I challenged.

"Sure," he smugly agreed. "I will prove to you
once and for all that ghosts don't exist."

So we went through the building and locked
all the doors to be sure we were alone. We
walked into the dining room, to the one table
where the candle would always be lit. I walked
over to the table and said, "Kitty, if you do exist,
will you please come over and relight the
candle." Nothing happened. We walked out into
the lobby, through the theater, the bar, into the
kitchen, through the waiter's station, and back
into the dining room. The candle, like all the
others, was not lit.

My friend the bartender started giving me all
this grief. He told me he was stupid to even fall
into this trap. He was really ragging on me. Suddenly a chill came over the dining room, and
there was this fine white mist that moved, not
past us, but right through us! It was really a
freaky thing. As it passed the table, that candle
lit right before our eyes. We were far too upset
to continue the argument. It freaked me out
too. I really wasn't expecting that.

Another time I was watching the front desk.
A couple wanted to know how to get to Victor.

We walked outside, and I pointed down the road. When I turned around and started walking back inside, I looked up and saw that the lights were on in Room 3. That's weird, I thought. Could the maids have forgotten to turn out the lights?

I went back in and got out the ledger. Sure enough, no one was in Room 3. I grabbed the key and walked up the stairs. I knocked on the door, just in case. When no one answered, I opened the door. The light fixtures had pull chains back then. When I opened the door, it was pitch black inside, but the light chain was swinging back and forth. Obviously, Ms. Kitty had something to do with it.

"There is also spirit activity on the third floor of the hotel," Chip adds. "Bob's sister-in-law was on the third floor, making up her room. Her husband and the kids were down in the theater watching movies. She heard kids running up and down the hall, cutting up. She yelled at them to go downstairs and watch the movie. As she continued making the bed, she felt a child tugging at her pants leg. She said, 'Gary, go downstairs!' The kids were driving her crazy. Finally, she lost it. She ran into the hall, but she couldn't find the kids. She stormed down to the theater room, where she irately instructed her husband that she didn't want the kids upstairs anymore.

"'What do you mean?' he responded. 'They have been down here the entire time.'"

One of the desk clerks had a spine-chilling encounter. She wore her street clothes to work but changed into a Victorian ball gown after her shift to attend an historic ball at the Elks Club. She left her street clothes in a second-story office. After the ball, she stopped by the hotel to get her clothes. She entered the Palace and started up the stairs. As she rounded the corner to go up the second flight, she saw a woman on the landing, coming down. As they passed, their eyes met. In that fleeting second, she realized that the woman was wearing the exact same Victorian ball gown, identical in every detail. She whirled around, but the woman had vanished. She had to get an escort before she would go back up those stairs. She described the woman as dark-haired, dark-eyed, and very pretty. She had just described Kitty to a tee.

Best Rooms/Times

Rooms 3 and 16 are the most haunted. If those rooms are not available, ask for a room on the third floor.

The Inn/Hotel

Bob Lays renovated the hotel to look as it did in the 1890s. From the lobby to the room decor, and even the casino, the Palace has a "Gay Nineties Victorian" look. Bob has received several restoration awards for his efforts.

Bob turned the twenty-two sparse rooms on the

second and third floor into fifteen larger rooms, maintaining the old-time feel but adding all the modern amenities. Although several of the rooms have a shared bath, most have private baths. A hearty miner's breakfast is served in the morning.

Dining

Mayor Paige recommends Maggie's Restaurant. "Maggie's got its name from their resident ghost," he says.

The building used to be a mortuary. A woman in her twenties died in that building around 1899. When new owners purchased the building and started changing things around, Maggie began to act up. The owners told her she could stay—as long as she behaved. Often it's children dining at the restaurant who ask, "Who is that lady?"

I had a friend who was care-taking the building. He had a little apartment above the restaurant where he could do his artwork. One night it was snowing outside. His heater was on, but he felt an unexpected cold draft. He cracked open his door, looked downstairs, and saw that the back door was wide open. Thinking it must have blown open from the wind, he went down, closed the door, and locked it. He was just starting to get comfortable again when he felt the same harsh chill. He opened his door, looked down the stairs, and lo and behold, the door was wide open. This time he brought some framing wire. He looped the wire over the knob and tied it shut. Problem solved.

He had just started reading again when he heard a woman's footsteps walking up the hall. He sat frozen in his chair, trying to reconcile what he was hearing. The footsteps came closer and closer, until they were right outside his door. All of a sudden the doorknob to his apartment started to turn, and the lights went dim, as if something were sucking out all of the energy in the room, even sucking his very breath out of that room.

Just as suddenly, the doorknob released and popped back to its original position. The lights in the room came back on. He heard the footsteps walk back down the hall and into the night.

When he finally got his nerve back again, he dashed out of that place. When he hit the bottom of the stairs, he tripped. Looking down, he found the framing wire wadded into a tight ball. The back door was wide open. There were no footsteps in the fresh snow.

Needless to say, when he finally went back to collect his things, he took several of his larger buddies with him. To this day, he vows never to set foot in the place again.

Don't Miss

I highly recommend the Cripple Creek Ghost Walk Tours. Did I mention that Mayor Paige also presides over these tours? Donning a vampiresque black cape and top hat, he weaves a tale of extraordinary ghostly encounters. Unbelievable, he claims, except for the fact that he actually experienced them. A die-hard believer, Chip is animated, entertaining, a storyteller extraordinaire. Tours leave nightly from the Palace Hotel, May through October. A haunted cemetery tour is offered by appointment (719-689-3234).

Another don't-miss is the Mollie Kathleen Gold Mine (719-689-2466). In the 1890s women were not "allowed" to file claims, but a woman named Mollie Kathleen Gortner insisted that her stake be recognized. She finally persuaded the powers-that-be to recognize her claim. Even so, the miners refused to work for a woman. Mollie technically turned the management over to her son, but actually ran the business herself.

Palace Hotel and Casino
172 East Bennett Avenue
Cripple Creek, CO 80813
719-689-2992 or 800-585-9329
www.palacehotelcasino.com

The Queen Mary

❧

Long Beach, California

The *Queen Mary* is one remaining icon of a Cinderella time, when high-society dames and glamorous celebrities traveled to Europe on magnificent luxury ocean liners—a way of life that no longer exists today. Along with the *Titanic* and a handful of other luxury liners of this bygone era, it was the only mode of transportation between the two continents. The term *jet-setter* had not yet been coined. Instead, the rich and famous enjoyed romantic, leisurely voyages between New York and London.

Christened in 1934, the *Queen Mary* soon became known as "the Queen of the Atlantic." Bedecked in art deco elegance, the ship was unlike anything the seas had ever known. Superb craftsmanship was found throughout her twelve decks, and some of the world's most renowned statesmen and stars made Atlantic crossings in her cabins and staterooms. The duke and duchess of Windsor were guests on a number of occasions. Winston Churchill was another regular, especially during the war. Film stars and celebrities lazed by the pool and dined in the first-class salons. Fred Astaire, Clark Gable, Marlene Dietrich, Gloria Swanson, and Liz Taylor all made the voyage.

This idyllic way of life was not to last. When jet travel was introduced in 1963, travelers gave up their leisurely week-long voyage for a quick, fifteen-hour flight. After 1001 transatlantic crossings, the *Queen Mary* was sold in 1967 to the city of Long Beach, where she proudly rests as a luxury hotel today.

Life was not always so easy on this magnificent ship. During World War II, the *Queen Mary* entered a new era as she was converted to a military ship. Painted gray and dubbed "the Grey Ghost," between March 1940 and September 1946 she carried a total of 765,429 military personnel and logged a staggering total of 569,429 wartime miles. At times, the 1,957-passenger ship transported over 16,000 soldiers at one time, many of them wounded and returning to the United States. She carried 12,886 GI brides and children to meet, or collect the remains of, their husbands and fathers.

The Grey Ghost proved herself as an important member of the Allied forces. Adolf Hitler offered a $250,000 reward and the Iron Cross to any submarine captain who could sink her. Many tried, but she was invincible.

Then tragedy struck. While performing a routine zigzag pattern to avoid detection, the Grey Ghost struck the British cruiser HMS *Curacao,* slicing her in half. Over 300 British soldiers went down with the *Curacao*. Forty years later a television crew left their audio recorder running overnight in the exact location where the two ships collided. As they played the tape the next day, incredible sounds of smashing and pounding could be heard. Others have claimed to hear voices and bloodcurdling noises from the same area.

Many other restless spirits haunt the ship. On July 10, 1966, during a routine drill, an eighteen-year-old man was violently crushed in Doorway 13 in the depths of the engine room. Numerous sightings have been reported by both visitors and crew members, who describe a young bearded man in blue overalls walking the length of Shaft Alley, often disappearing by Door 13. It is no coincidence that he was wearing a similar outfit that fateful day in 1966.

The first-class swimming pool, no longer in use, has been the location of many ghost sightings. There have been reports of women dressed in vintage bathing suits wandering the decks near the pool, the sound of splashing, and a trail of wet footprints leading from the deck to the changing rooms. Although no drownings in the pool have been documented, this location has been described by experts as the vortex for the paranormal activity aboard the ship, which allows ghosts from other realms an entrance to the *Queen Mary*.

The Queen's Salon, the former first-class lounge, has been the backdrop for many sightings, yet the details of the story rarely change. It seems that a beautiful young woman in an elegant white evening gown is often seen dancing alone in the shadows. One of the most chilling sightings occurred when a little girl on a tour pointed out a "woman in white." Looking around, the tour guide saw nothing. The little girl insisted, and kept pointing to a corner of the room, not knowing that she was just one of many to make the same report.

Many occurrences have taken place within the confines of a number of first-class staterooms. There have been reports of water running or lights suddenly turning on in the middle of the night, or the phone ringing at early hours of the morning. Passengers have reported hearing heavy breathing and people tugging on the bedcovers, only to realize that there was no one else in the room.

The ship had so many strange reports that noted parapsychologist Peter James was called to investigate the ship's ghosts. His research spanned a six-month period. "We found many many different spirits at the *Queen Mary*," reports James. "We used the most up-to-date scientific equipment. We were actually able to record images and voices. In the stem of the ship, site of the collision, our equipment picked up the sounds of wrenching steel, followed by screaming. We also picked up the voice of a young girl. The *Queen Mary* is a vortex to another dimension."

James's research has been integrated into a theatric on-board presentation called, appropriately, *Ghosts and Legends*.

Sightings

Ron Smith has been the *Queen Mary*'s historian since 1993. He has heard lots of stories, from guests and employees.

"There are so many sightings," reports Smith.

There is a woman in a bathing costume standing on a balcony above the pool, or around the pool edge like she is going to jump in, and then she disappears. Even though the pool is empty, there are wet footsteps around the pool.

A woman in a long white evening gown is seen in the Queen's Salon, sitting alone at a table, or on the stage area, dancing to herself, by herself, in another world. We had a little girl on the tour asking her mother who the lady was dancing. No one else could see her.

It's not possible to put a name to some of the apparitions. There were no records, no names to the ghosts. I think maybe many of the ghosts return trying to recapture some happiness in their life. It stands to reason if they have the freedom, they can go back wherever they want.

Many people are hesitant to talk about their encounters. I spoke to a woman several months after she stayed. She woke up in the middle of the night and saw someone sitting at the writing desk in the corner. At first she thought it was her boyfriend. She looked over at him, and he was sound asleep. She looked back at the desk, and the apparition was gone.

Engineers and security officers on the night shift, when everyone was gone, would hear laughter and splashing in the pool area. When they would go in, though, no one would be there. The pool is empty, yet even after the water was removed, splashing could be heard and wet footprints were found.

Some of the reports are just a feeling, a smell or sensation, or a feeling of coldness. People smell cigars or pipe tobacco, or sometimes perfume, when no one is in the area.

Elise Bova, a fifteen-year-old student, stayed at the *Queen Mary* with her family in Room 160. She woke up and saw a strange man in her room. She kept her eyes tightly shut as the man walked over and touched her face.

It was around three A.M. I felt kind of weird, so I rolled over and looked around the room. There was a guy standing in the corner. His face was just like a big blur. He was smaller, around five-two, but I felt like he was an adult.

I was like, "Maybe my mind is playing tricks on me." I tried to go back to sleep, but every time I looked, he was still there. Then he came over and touched me. It felt like a warm kind of pressure. It went up behind my ears, and down by my shoulders.

In the morning, I asked my mom if she saw anything, but she didn't. She said, "Well, that's interesting, you might have seen a ghost."

"Yeah," I thought. "Maybe I did, because it's like a haunted hotel."

Donny Crawford had a special reason to visit—his father came to America on the *Queen Mary*. To honor his father, Donny booked a room on Father's Day. Late that night Donny and his wife Dawn decided to take their own self-guided tour into the dark bowels of the ship.

"We were definitely going into places we shouldn't have," admits Dawn.

We ran into these two teenage boys, Jerry and Lawrence, who were doing the same thing, so we teamed up. First we went into the isolation ward . . . nothing weird there. Next was the engine room. When I walked through Door 13, I felt a sudden gush of cold air and I got a really creepy feeling, but I blew it off, thinking that my imagination was getting the best of me.

Next it was on to the B Deck, Room B-340, where a man was murdered. Suddenly, we heard Jerry screaming. He was behind us. I ran around the corner to look, and there was this vapor rising to the ceiling. Jerry said as he turned the corner, he ran into it. He said his whole upper body went through it, and he had actually breathed it in! He said it was like inhaling freon, that it felt really cold all the way down his throat. His heart was pounding so hard, I could see it beating through his shirt, and his pupils were dilated. I was just blown away. I couldn't believe it. I had seen it too, as it was leaving. We were afraid that whatever it was, it might still be inside him.

Finally, when Jerry was able to move, we left there and went to the first-class pool. That was really spooky. Next we found our way down the Grey Ghost passageway and into the room where you can see the boiler room from up above. Boy, is that place creepy. Finally we went to our cabin, but I couldn't sleep.

The next day, when we got home, I downloaded all my pictures. I have the most incredible photo from the engine room of what looks to be a fireball. Here is the spookiest part: it starts precisely at Door 13. We saw nothing while we were standing there, just had that eerie feeling.

Another photograph, of the boiler room, turned out pitch black. I brightened up the picture so that I might see into the darkness. All over the room there are orbs, like bubbles, everywhere. The only explanation that I have for this is the shipwreck with the HMS *Curacao*, and all those men who died. It really looks like wandering souls. You'd have to see these photos. They are incredible.

Dawn and Donny Crawford are now frequent guests at the *Queen Mary*. "We never forget to bring our camera," Dawn smiles.

Best Rooms/Times

The first-class pool, the boiler room, Door 13, the Grey Ghost passageway, the isolation ward, the officer's quarters, and the engine room report the most ghostly activity. The most haunted guest cabins include Room B-340, and all of the original first-class cabins.

The Hotel

The original deck plan of this magnificent ship spanned twelve decks and provided accommodations for 1,957 passengers and 1,174 crew members. Impeccably restored to preserve her historic charm and art deco ambiance, the ship is listed on the National Register of Historic Places. Much of the decor and rich wood paneling is original from the 1930s.

Today's guests also stay in the original cabins, though the ship does not leave port. There are 365 rooms and suites, and as with guests of yesteryear, you have a choice of a first-class or tourist-class stateroom, or inside staterooms. An historic tour is included with each stay.

Also onboard are a spa and fitness center, an art gallery, unique shops and boutiques, restaurants, a reading room, and daily tours and exhibits.

Dining

The four award-winning restaurants aboard the *Queen Mary* offer fabulous food and beautiful ocean views. Sir Winston's, the most elegant of these, features superb continental and California cuisine and an extensive wine list. Chelsea's specializes in fresh seafood. Check out the Promenade Café for casual dining or a quick snack.

Two of the most haunted places aboard ship are the original first-class dining room and the first-class lounge. Hotel guests or day-trip visitors can ghost hunt while dining or enjoying their favorite libation. Now the Grand Salon, the ship's original first-class dining room is an elegant setting for a spectacular Sunday champagne brunch. This elegant brunch features a harpist to set the mood, food from around the globe with more than fifty world-class entrees, and of course, champagne.

Another original hot spot, the stunning art deco Observation Bar is filled with some of the most beautiful historic artwork to grace the ship. Here they advertise "a wide variety of spirits, live music and dancing." Slowly sip your drink as you carefully study the other customers. You may notice that the lady in the corner, dressed in white, is wearing 1930s clothing. You turn away, and look again, only to discover that she has vanished.

Don't Miss

Serious ghost busters can actually tour the haunted hot spots. The popular "Ghosts and Legends of the *Queen Mary*" experience takes you deep below deck for a haunting, interactive encounter with the supernatural; call 562-435-3511 or visit ghostsandlegends. com.

If you can't make it to the hotel but want to experience the ghosts, just log on to the ghostsandlegends.com website. Ghost hunters can enter the "Ghostcam Room" and observe the activities in some of the *Queen Mary*'s most haunted areas in real time. Live webcams are posted above the first-class pool, in the boiler room, at Door 13, above the Grey Ghost passageway, and in the engine room.

If you have had an experience at the *Queen Mary*, or if you are curious about the ghostly encounters of others, ghostsandlegends.com has an on-line "Ghost Log," a database of personal paranormal experiences.

The *Queen Mary*
1126 Queens Highway
Long Beach, CA 90802
562-435-3511
e-mail: reservations@queenmary.com
www.queenmary.com

Red Brook Inn

Old Mystic, Connecticut

When the owner of the Crary House was caught with his wife's best friend, he pleaded with his wife to take him back. She agreed, under one condition: never again would her ex-friend enter her house. After her death, her husband broke that promise. Maybe he thought she wouldn't find out. But she did, and she got even. The names in this story have been changed to protect the families involved.

John and Mary Jones had lived in the Crary House for thirty-five years. Jane was Mary's very best friend. The two would huddle around the huge stone fireplace in the keeping room, sipping coffee and sharing the most intimate details of their lives. When Mary contracted cancer, Jane was right there every day, offering support and caring—or so Mary believed. When she learned of the affair between her dearest, closest friend and her husband, she was devastated. Hysterical, she made John promise that he would never again see Jane in the Crary home, HER home.

John did keep that promise, at least for the twelve more

years that Mary was alive. But he didn't waste any time marrying Jane after Mary's death. He moved out of the Crary House to the other side of town, but when Jane booked a party at the old homestead, now the Red Brook Inn, the promise was broken, and Mary got even.

Jane wanted to surprise John on his eightieth birthday, so she decided to book a party at the old Crary House. Big mistake. She defied the fact that she was forbidden by Mary to ever again enter that house.

Jane made an appointment to meet with Ruth Orr, the owner of the inn. As soon as Jane walked through the back door, "strange things began to happen," says Ruth. "First, there was a horrendous odor. It smelled like something died and was rotting in the walls. I was terribly embarrassed," Ruth admits. Ruth assured Jane that the smell had not been there an hour earlier when her overnight guests had breakfast.

After Jane left, Ruth asked her manager to try to find out what was causing such a disgusting odor. He didn't smell anything. After Jane left, the smell was gone.

A week later, Jane returned to make final arrangements. Again, as soon as they walked into the old house, the room reeked with the same foul smell. "It was overpowering," Ruth exclaimed, puckering her face. "Then it hit me that it might be Mary. After all, she hated Jane. My manager thought so, too. Then I started to panic—what if this is really true? What if it is the ghost? What if it happens at the party? Although I really didn't believe it could be John's dead wife, I was really worried."

The night of the party, Ruth meticulously checked and rechecked the house, sniffing everywhere, and it smelled fine. Most of the guests had arrived by the time Jane got there. The presents and the cake were in the back room. However, the second the hostess waltzed into the room, her guests started gagging.

"The odor was horrible," admits Stu, one of the guests that evening. "But Jane seemed oblivious."

Sure enough, wherever the second wife went that evening, the odor accompanied her. She must have wondered why the rooms emptied as she entered. But in spite of the foulness of the odor, she didn't seem to notice.

The worst part of the evening, or maybe the best part, depending on your perspective, came when it was time to cut the cake. The guests all gathered around the table and sang "Happy Birthday" to John as he blew out the candles. Then came time to cut the first piece. Ruth handed him a knife. As the knife cut into the cake, it disintegrated into a million crumbs. There was nothing left to serve.

"It's impossible for a carrot cake to fall apart like that," Ruth remarked. "It had to have been Mary, ruining the party. If you think about it, it's kind of funny."

"Ever since then, I've been reading a lot about ghosts, trying to figure out how it could have happened. Then I read somewhere that spirits can make their presence known through odors," she added.

Was it merely a coincidence, or had a betrayed wife been able to reach out from the other side and get revenge? Both Jane and the foul odor have never returned.

Ruth Orr, a vivacious blond with a twinkle in her eyes, found the Crary House, which she later named the Red Brook Inn, after a year-long search. She knew exactly what she wanted but could not seem to find it. Her real estate agent, Roz, was running out of places to show her. On the verge of giving up, Roz awoke in the middle of the night, thinking of the Crary place. She called Ruth at the break of dawn, convinced she had finally come upon Ruth's house. The pair pulled into the long, maple-lined drive leading up to the house several hours later. Ruth knew before they even entered that this was her home.

Roz says she has seen this phenomenon many times. "After being a real estate agent for so long, you see some things," she admits. "It's that instant recognition, like you found a long-lost friend." Roz also says she immediately knows if a house is haunted. "I can always tell, sometimes just driving up, if a house is haunted. You can just feel it. Sometimes I think people make a connection with the spirit, and that's why they buy the house."

Ruth made an offer that same day. As soon as she moved in, she heard and felt the spirits. Ruth's daughter heard them too. She was helping Ruth unpack, just after she moved in, when they both heard someone coming up the stairs. Knowing they were alone, and not wanting her daughter to be scared, Ruth tried to distract her. But whatever it was just got louder and louder, until her daughter asked, "Is there somebody in the house?"

Ruth now feels totally at peace with her ghosts. "At first, I felt like someone else was here with me all the time. Finally, I just said out loud, 'You can stay, but please don't bother me.' They haven't bothered me since. But they have bothered my guests."

Two years after opening the Red Brook, Ruth purchased the Haley Tavern, another historic home in Old Mystic, scheduled for demolition. She moved it piece by piece to the property adjoining the Crary House. Then she learned that Nancy Crary, born in the Crary home in 1820, married Henry Haley and moved into the Haley home. Together they ran the Haley Tavern. Both of these places now sit together as the Red Brook Inn. Coincidence?

Sightings

After she opened the inn, Ruth said people would come down in the morning and ask if Red Brook had a ghost. "After a while, I noticed that it was always people who stayed on the north side of the house that asked the questions," Ruth says.

One of the ghosts has been credited with saving lives. On two separate occasions, an elderly white-haired woman has startled the occupants of Room 2. Christopher Campbell, a twenty-seven-year-old engineer from New York, claims that a little old lady shook his shoulder until he bolted upright, wide awake.

"Less than six inches from my face was another face that shocked the hell out of me," Chris reports. "By the time I realized what I was looking at, she was gone. Then I noticed that the room was filled with smoke. We forgot to open the flue in the fireplace before starting a fire. We could have died. She saved our lives."

John Clodig, a well-known organist, and his brother Albert, of Crown Point, Indiana, stayed two nights during a cold snap in March 1986. Again, the flue was closed, and the room filled up with smoke. Luckily, something awakened Albert, and through the smoke he saw a figure standing in the corner. He described her as an elderly lady with white hair and a dark shawl.

"I didn't think of her as a ghost, I just felt like she belonged. She was just standing in the corner, watching us. If she hadn't woken us up, we could have suffocated."

Both men felt she was friendly and caring, and both believe she saved their lives.

Even the inn's resident pet, a big lap cat that Ruth brought with her from California, has a definite reaction to the Crary House. "Before coming in, she would poke her head through the door and sniff around," says Ruth. "Once she entered, she would never walk directly through a room. Instead, she crept along the wall's perimeters, walking much farther around than had she just walked across." After Ruth moved the Haley Tavern onto the property, the cat stayed over there and never returned to the Crary House, even to visit Ruth.

Best Rooms/Times

All of the activity takes place at the Crary House rather than the Haley Tavern. The two men who encountered the old woman visited during the cold season, but I would not recommend putting your life in danger just to see if a ghost will save you.

The Inn

The Red Brook Inn is actually comprised of two buildings: the Haley Tavern, circa 1740, with seven guest rooms, and the Crary House, circa 1770, with three guest rooms.

"It was my idea when I started the inn that I wanted to give people the feel of colonial New England history," Ruth explained. "Everything, from the furnishings to the knickknacks, belongs to that period." One of her prized possessions is the Haleys' original waffle iron from the 1700's. Descendants of the family gave it to Ruth as a housewarming gift. It has been sitting on the Haley hearth for over 200 years.

Ruth used period furnishing, stenciling, antique quilts, and decorator sheets in the ten guest rooms to create a feeling of historic luxury. In every room is a fireplace primed, and the innkeeper will light it for you when you are ready to retire.

Dining

A full breakfast is served in the keeping room in front of "the Great Hearth," its crackling fire burning merrily. Breakfasts are served "grandma style," a term Ruth coined, meaning guests are doted upon. They always begin with juice, fresh fruit, and sausage or bacon. Next comes a hearty main course of pumpkin or apple pancakes, fresh garden vegetable quiche, or Red Brook's world-famous walnut waffles. Food is presented on exquisite Victorian china and silver.

A favorite of both inn guests and locals are the authentic colonial dinners, prepared entirely on the authentic brick hearth. Once a month guests step back in time to indulge in a meal prepared as it was two hundred years ago. Even the primitive cooking utensils are authentic to the period. The distinct, fragrant aroma of a leg of lamb or a wild turkey permeates the house as it roasts on the old spit, meticulously spun by a hanging jack from 1850 that still works. Slow-roasted root vegetables, homemade hearth-baked bread, and hearty mincemeat or berry pies complete the experience. "You just can't reproduce the taste of game slow-roasted for hours on an open hearth," one guest claims. Other colonial specialties include beef Wellington or country ham.

Don't Miss

The historic downtown area of Mystic is a charming seaport village. The streets are lined with a collection of carefully restored Victorian homes. The famous Bascule Drawbridge still is raised each hour to accommodate the never-ending parade of boats along the Mystic River.

Red Brook Inn
P.O. Box 237
Mystic, CT 06372
203-572-0349
e-mail: redbrookin@aol.com
www.redbrookinn.com

St. James Hotel

Cimarron, New Mexico

It's no wonder that this boisterous Old West saloon and hotel is haunted. Between 1872 and 1884, no fewer than twenty-six men met violent deaths within its dark adobe walls. Gunfights, brawls, and knifings took their toll on the living, giving a clue as to why so many restless spirits are still checked in as residents of the hotel. The walls were riddled with gunshots, many of which passed through or bounced off their intended target. In the saloon's ceiling, over 400 bullet holes were counted when it was replaced in 1902. A list of people who were killed in the hotel is even posted in the lobby.

The hotel's original guest registers, found during the restoration, contain a who's who of the Wild West. Notable guests include Bat Masterson (1887), Wyatt Earp, who spent three days at the hotel with his family, Doc Holliday (1879), train robber "Black Jack" Ketchum, and Billy the Kid. It was here that Buffalo Bill Cody met up with Annie Oakley and planned their Wild West show. Jessie James would always register under the name "R. H. Howard."

Probably the most notorious criminal to stay at the hotel was Robert Clay Allison, who was said to have danced naked on the bar, taking pot shots at the ceiling. He alone is responsible for eleven of the shootings at the old hotel, and for a large number of the bullet holes.

Frenchman Henri Lambert, former personal chef to President Abraham Lincoln, built the Cimarron saloon along the Sante Fe Trail in 1872. The town already had a long-standing reputation for trouble. Even its name, Cimarron, means "wild and untamed" in Spanish. The adobe structure started out as a gambling hall and saloon that boasted the best whiskey west of the Mississippi. The hotel was added later in 1888, as many of the customers were too drunk (or too injured) to travel elsewhere.

Though Cimarron has tamed down, the spirits at St. James have not. One angry spirit had to be locked away by the owner, who was afraid that he might still hurt the living. The room was shut up and never rented because, as the owner put it, "Bad things happened at the hotel when people ventured into that room, and people had been pushed, and even chased out."

This vengeful spirit is believed to be T. James Wright, a big-time gambler. It's said that he actually won the deed to the hotel on a card bet, but was gunned down before he could collect. He hangs around "his" hotel to collect on the bet, staying in Room 19. "He has been known to chase people out of the room. One employee was even knocked to the floor by a shiny ball of energy," says owner Perry Champion. "We have seen the chandelier spin around and around.

The lights go on and off like a strobe light. He obviously doesn't want anyone in his room."

The Champions, having a healthy respect for the powers of this spirit, have locked up the room and refuse to rent it. It hasn't been renovated or fixed up. Inside, there is a table, playing cards, a shot glass, and a bottle of Jack Daniel's.

"We put some tobacco, rolling papers, and a picture of girls in bikinis in there," admits Champion. "We are hoping that will keep T. J. happy for a little while."

Sightings

The spirits of many other restless souls visit or haunt this hotel. The most famous is Mary Lambert, wife of Frenchman Henri Lambert, who built the saloon and inn. Her presence is marked by her strong perfume, which wafts through the hallway past the upstairs guest rooms. If you sleep in her old room (17), the window must be kept shut completely, as Mary wants it to be safe for everyone. She will tap and beat on the window if it's left open, waking up the hotel patrons sleeping in that room, and won't stop until the window is shut. Perhaps she is still looking after her hotel and her guests.

A mischievous "gnomelike" old man, named Little Imp by the Champions, plays tricks on the living, annoying many, especially new employees. Described as a small man with a pockmarked face, the Little Imp has been sighted in the kitchen and restaurant. He has been known to burst glasses, relight candles, and move objects across the room. His favorite targets are nervous new hires, whom he loves to torture. He once appeared on a bar stool and laughed at the young man hired to clean up the dining room. He is also the one who took a steak knife from the holder in the kitchen and stuck it in the floor between the two owners of the hotel. Evidence points to him as well when lampshades and glasses crack all by themselves, and objects disappear and reappear in other places.

A handsome cowboy also haunts the place. Early one morning, Mrs. Champion walked into the dining room, looked up in the mirror, and saw a pleasant-looking cowboy in a big hat, standing behind her. When she turned around, he vanished.

Cold spots can be felt in various locations throughout the hotel. Phones ring off the hook, even though no one operates the phone lines after 9:00 P.M.

Best Rooms/Times

Rooms 17 and 19 are the most haunted, though Room 19 has been closed off after the spirit became violent. The original saloon and gambling hall, now the restaurant, is also very active.

The Inn/Hotel

Built in 1880, the St. James was considered a luxury hotel in its day, offering the first running water west of the Mississippi. The lobby of this historic adobe structure is adorned with crystal chandeliers, velvet curtains, brocade wallpaper, and sturdy furniture, built to withstand a lot of abuse from rowdy clientele. A steep staircase leads up to the second-floor guest rooms.

During the restoration, the original guest registers were discovered, so it's known who stayed in which rooms. Today the rooms, some with original furniture, are named after the famous or notorious people who once stayed in them.

The thirteen historic rooms in the original hotel are decorated in period furnishings, with antique brass or wooden beds. Twelve new rooms adjoining the hotel offer modern accommodations.

Below these guest rooms, one can find the old 1873 saloon, which is now used as the hotel's dining room and where the original antique bar still exists. Look closely, and you will see the original bullet holes.

Dining

Unfortunately, this hotel does not serve single diners. If you want to eat at this hotel, bring a friend. I went down the road to Lucien Maxwell's Grist Mill, a charming authentic mill restored into a fabulous restaurant—also, by the way, rumored to be haunted.

Don't Miss

To really experience the bawdiness of the Old West, immerse yourself in one of the hotel's murder mystery weekends. Guests come in costume and relive

the lives of some of the hotel's most notorious customers.

St. James Hotel
Route 1, Box 2
17th and Collinson Streets
Cimarron, NM 87714
505-376-2664

Sea Crest by the Sea

❧❧❧

Spring Lake, New Jersey

Since I've experienced so many ghosts at the Myrtles Plantation, it takes a lot to scare me. I was scared out of my wits at the Sea Crest Inn. I was very grateful that my friend Aldine was with me that night, or I probably would have left. This frightening memory still haunts me.

When we checked in, the owner, Tom, joked about the frisky ghost. "I put you in the Yankee Clipper Room. That's where the Captain stays. He has an obvious preference for the ladies." Tom laughed. "If there is another man in the room, the Captain stays away."

The Sea Crest Inn was a favorite haunt for the dashing sea captain, even when he was alive. He stayed at the inn whenever he was in town, until, on one fateful trip, his ship was smashed to bits just off the Jersey coast, not far from Spring Lake. Today the Captain still visits at the Sea Crest Inn, and tries to make contact with nearly every unaccompanied female guest.

When Tom and Marilyn bought the impressive Victorian

inn, the previous owner of twenty-five years warned the couple that the inn had a ghost. He told them that there was a sea captain who was a permanent guest, rattling around on the third floor.

"We thought that was silly," says Tom. "We pooh-poohed the idea, for about two weeks. Then we realized it wasn't nonsense."

The first tip-off that something was not quite right was when their dog wouldn't go up to the top floor. "She always follows us wherever we go, but she would stand at the bottom of the stairs and just growl. Finally we had to take the dog up, but she ran back down. The dog really likes people a lot, so it was very strange," says Tom. "I think animals have a sixth sense. They can see things we can't.

"Then other screwy things happened, like in the Yankee Clipper Room, when the girls clean the room they put everything away, and then when we go back, the binoculars are lying on the bed," the former innkeeper continues. "We put them back on the shelf, and before long, they are back on the bed. In the Victorian Rose Room, the room just below the Captain's room, he goes down and lies on the bed. We can see the imprint."

The family cat, Princess, also sensed the ghost. She sat for hours on the second floor, facing directly into the mirror, looking upward to the third-floor landing. "If we can't find the cat, we go up, and there she is, just staring into the mirror. She seems to know a lot about these things."

Tom reports that the Captain's activities picked up after a captain's log from a ship that sank off the coast was placed in the room. "The log sort of found us," he reports. "We were in an antique shop in Pennsylvania with a large book section. I went to the shelf, picked out this book, and there it was. Then, when we brought it home, I think this guy began to feel more comfortable, and he began to come more often. One guest looked up in the mirror, and saw his face. Another heard him talking in the middle of the night."

Terri Thomson, innkeeper at the Sea Crest for many years, frequently saw the Captain.

When I'm on the second floor, when I pass the staircase going to the third floor, I always see a shadow of a man at the top of the stairs, looking down at me. I don't think he's a bad ghost, but even in the middle of the day, I just walk by really fast, and I don't look up.

It sounds like people are up there walking around. You think maybe it's the heater, but I don't think so. It always feels very cold when I go up. But when I'm here alone, I never go up by myself.

He also comes down to the Victorian Rose Room. I was in there making the bed, and I had to go out for just a minute. When I came back, the bed had a print on it, like someone had sat down. I looked around, but I was the only one here.

I think there may be a ghost in the cellar, because when the owners go away, I always make sure the door is locked, and the knob starts jiggling like someone is trying to get out. Then the dog starts barking. I feel very uneasy when I have to go down.

Sightings

I was fortunate that my friend Aldine went with me to the Sea Crest. It was in the dead of winter. We were the only guests at the inn, so we were all alone up on the third floor. I was upstairs in the Yankee Clipper Room, working on my laptop. Aldine, as usual, was downstairs at the cookie jar. For some reason, I felt uncomfortable, and I kept wishing Aldine would hurry on up. I didn't tell her I was scared, because I didn't want to upset her. Aldine turned on the television, which was odd, because we never watched television when we traveled together. Maybe she felt it too, and wanted the distraction. Eventually we drifted off to sleep.

I woke up to a horrible sound. It was the voice of a man sobbing. I thought, What a horrible movie—I can't take this. I rolled over to turn off the television, which was on my side of the bed. The TV was off.

Oh, my God, I thought, that must be Aldine. How could she make a sound like that? Something must be really wrong. I turned over to face Aldine. She was lying there still, her eyes closed. It wasn't her. I pulled the covers over my head and started silently singing silly songs.

"Do you hear it too?" It was Aldine, nudging me and whispering frantically.

"Yeah. I thought you were asleep," I choked, grateful that she was awake.

"No way."

We both bolted up, braver with the safety of another conscious human.

"Let's get out of here," I whispered.

"No, we can't. 'They' are outside. Didn't you hear the doorknob rattling?"

I hadn't. We talked about the possibility of running downstairs together and sleeping in the car. We were about to make a run for it when we heard footsteps coming up the stairs. Not knowing if it was the innkeeper or the ghost, we waited, panicking. The footsteps stopped outside our door. I looked at Aldine, and she flipped on the lights and got up and turned on the TV. We spent the rest of that night with all the lights blazing, pretending to watch television while we were really trying to block out all the other noises.

I must digress right now. I put off writing the chapter about the Sea Crest because it was so upsetting, and I needed to get some perspective on it. Even though I am safely residing on the opposite coast, sometimes spirits have a way of reaching out and touching you. As I was recounting my experiences at the Sea Crest, my computer froze, and the cursor disappeared. Then even the frozen document closed and disappeared. When I tried to reopen the document, it told me that it didn't exist. I was sick at losing this chapter, because it was so hard for me to write.

My computer has gone crazy several other times while trying to research and write this book (see the Eliza Thompson House, page 140), but with my deadline approaching, I just couldn't afford to waste hours of work. Finally I negotiated out loud, though I don't know to whom: "Please, I know you are there. Please give me back my chapter. I am trying to tell your story." With that said, I tried to open the document again, and I caught a flash of my text display for an instant before the blank page replaced it. "Okay, I saw it, I know it is there," I pleaded. "Please, let me have it back." (I had heard enough stories from inn owners who pleaded with their ghosts to know that talking to them usually works.)

I closed the blank document again. The screen went blank, then out of nowhere my typed chapter came up. The document was restored, up to the point when I had heard the Captain sobbing, and I turned to Aldine. For some unexplainable reason, my description of the rest of that night was not there. However, grateful to be able to recover any of my document, I whispered a quick "Thank You," and saved several copies of the chapter.

Best Rooms/Times

Reports increase dramatically in the winter months. "That's because the Captain is at sea in the summer," Tom explained. "He wanders all around the third floor, but his favorite room is the Yankee Clipper Room, with the ocean views. But he comes down to the Victorian Rose on occasion."

Marilyn confirms this. "The Victorian Rose is the only room I cannot sleep in, even with Tom there. It makes me very uncomfortable."

The Hotel

The Sea Crest Inn by the Sea is a beautiful, gothic Victorian mansion, with the typical Victorian turrets and crannies. There are twelve guest rooms, including two suites. All of the rooms have a queen-size bed, a private bath, and a TV/VCR. Many of the rooms have a fireplace and a Jacuzzi tub. The inn is located just a few hundred feet from the beach.

The following description is from the Sea Crest website:

On arrival you hear soft classical music. Fresh flowers await you in your room. The merriment begins with a few tunes on the player piano at afternoon tea. Your bountiful gourmet breakfast begins at the civilized hour of nine A.M. Candlelit in winter, the antique French sideboard is laden with a sumptuous offering that is both healthy and delicious, including a selection of fresh-from-the-oven buttermilk scones and muffins, fresh fruit, Sea Crest granola, our own special blend of full-bodied, caffeine-reduced coffee, and a wide array of teas. A variety of settings from the family collection of china, crystal and silver complement the table and provide a delightful backdrop for a convivial start to the day.

The Sea Crest is a half-block from a quiet beach and the inviting boardwalk. As you start the day's adventures, a stable of bicycles is provided for your pleasure. Back at the inn, play croquet on the lawn or enjoy soft ocean breezes while relaxing on the veranda.

During a full moon, guests can request the "Full Moon Picnic," which includes champagne, cheese, crackers, fruit, and Godiva chocolates. This can be served on the front veranda or packed, along with a blanket, to take to the beach. Other specials include the Sea Crest Romance Package and the Sea Crest Massage Package.

Dining

Breakfasts at the Sea Crest are fabulous. You may be tempted by the Sea Crest Buttermilk Scones, a seafood casserole, omelets, or another specialty, piña colada French toast. The wonderful scones and the biscotti are available for sale to take home.

Don't Miss

Current owner Art Thomson is a poet laureate and storyteller. His latest project includes a collection of short stories entitled *Bedtime Stories*, which he tells right before bedtime. Many of these tales are reminiscent of Hitchcock or *The Twilight Zone*. Sweet dreams!

Sea Crest by the Sea
19 Tuttle Avenue
Spring Lake, NJ 07762
732-449-9031 or 800-803-9031
e-mail: capt@seacrestbythesea.com
www.seacrestbythesea.com

Simmons Homestead Inn

❦

Hyannis Port, Massachusetts

The ghost of a little girl who drowned in the old Simmons pond in 1833 haunts this stately country inn on Cape Cod.

"When I first moved here, I had never seen, nor did I believe in, ghosts," says owner Bill Putnam. "But one day as I was working upstairs, I felt a strange presence behind me. As I turned, I caught a vision of something white and swirling, and I distinctly heard some giggling. When I turned back, the dresser drawer was opened, and clothes were strewn around the room.

"It seemed as though she wanted to see who was moving into her house and if everything was okay," added Bill. "I've never experienced anything like that," he admits. "When I first moved here and heard her giggles, I got nervous, and started checking to be sure I wasn't screwing up her daddy's house. I was constantly finding things that a seven-year-old would do. She pulls out children's books or toys. Sometimes I can see a tiny imprint on the bed, the size of a child."

Captain Lemuel Simmons, a somewhat famous sea captain, built the stunning Greek Revival mansion in 1820. He had three sons, who all became sea captains, and one daughter. A child named Susan, believed to be Simmons's niece, drowned at the home in 1833.

"Everyone describes her as about three feet tall, with middle-of-the-back-length light brown hair. We all see her in the same white dress, which I assume she was buried in. She giggles, so I assume she is having fun, which is important. It's her house. She was here first. Her name is on the front door. We take care of her."

Bill does watch out for her. House rules, posted at the inn, include the following: "Please do not let Abigail, the cat, inside, and please, don't let Susan, our seven-year-old ghost, outside."

"I'm glad she's here," admits Bill. "I know ultimately you're supposed to send them off, but she seems content here, and I'm happy she's here. I want to try to find out more about her, about why she is here."

Sightings

"A lot of people walk down the hall past her room and feel a blast of cold air hit them in the face, or their hair stands up," says Bill.

My stepson Craig saw her in the upstairs hallway when he was only thirteen. I think it might be easier for children to see ghosts than adults.

One guest was in Room 5 reading a book when she heard a child ask her what she was doing. She jumped up to see where the voice had come from, but no one was there. She had left her book on the bed, but it had flown across the room by itself. Another, braver guest actually carried on a full conversation with the child for about ten minutes.

Often, in the middle of the day, we see a tiny imprint on the bed that looks like a child's outline. Maybe that's because she is taking an afternoon nap.

Samantha, my dog, is testimony to the ghost. She would wake up and appear to be looking for something. Then she would stop and get a contented look, as though someone was petting her.

Best Rooms/Times

"My only experiences with her were when I was working upstairs, or in the attic," says Bill, "so to my knowledge she has never been downstairs. In those days kids loved to go up to the attic. Obviously, it's an area she loved. When children go up there today, they all say she is around. The south wing wasn't built until 1841. Susan died in 1833, so she only roams above the old part."

There are also many sightings in her bedroom, Room 5. You probably will feel like someone is watching you in Susan's room—it's dubbed "Owls, Lots of Hoots," and is filled with dozens of toy owls.

The Inn/Hotel

The inn was built in 1820 by Lemuel Simmons, who, at the age of nineteen, was one of the youngest sea captains on record. He lived at the home until his death in 1890. His estate, which included an impressive amount of acreage and the Simmons pond, was sold to another sea captain, Henry C. Hunt. In 1897 Hunt purchased a windmill in Orleans. To move the giant gristmill, it had to be dismantled piece by piece and moved by barge to Hyannis Port. It was reconstructed where the back of the present parking lot is located, and operated as a gristmill well into the 1900s. This mill remained as a landmark on the property until 1983, when it was donated to the Orleans Historical Society.

In 1919 the property was purchased by Manuel Lombard and renamed the Old Windmill Farm. Three generations of aristocratic Lombards summered in the house until 1983, when Bill Simmons, an ex–race car driver, drove up in the driveway and exclaimed, "This is me."

Bill has turned the old Simmons estate into a whimsical guest inn. Eclectic and fun in decor, all the rooms have animal themes, including the Jungle Room, Geese with a Few Cows, the Fish Aquarium, Cape Cod Critters, and Horse and Hound. Over the years, dozens of critters have been added to the rooms by guests. "By now, it is totally out of control," laughs Bill.

Some of the rooms have fireplaces, and there is a hot tub out back for the cooler months. The second-floor landing is home to the hoods from his old race car and that of Paul Newman. Bill's eyes light up as he tells harrowing stories from his racing days.

"We take kids of all ages and shapes. Same with dogs and small farm animals," says Bill.

Bill's favorite time of day is sunset. Classic white Adirondack chairs and hammocks beckon guests at the back of the house to witness "the best sunset panorama on the Cape." "We stop everything to go watch as the fiery sky turns from gold to crimson and finally to black."

Dining

Breakfast is included with the room. Bill notes that if you don't like the food, "beer is always available."

Bill maintains a notebook with critiques of all the places to eat in town. "If it's not on my restaurant list, don't go there," he claims. "I love the Cape. I send them out to all my hidden treasures."

There is a large bar and billiard room for guests. Bill hosts a single-malt scotch "Tasting Hour" or a "Wine Tasting Party" on weeknights during the cooler months. He says he looks at it as a research project, and he also hates to drink alone. "I'll check you in, get you drunk, and send you to dinner."

Don't Miss

Don't leave home without a Cape Cod ghost map. It marks out over a hundred alleged ghosts on Cape Cod and the islands, including haunted houses and taverns and UFO sightings. The map also points out ancient forests, sea monsters, mermaids, burn circles, ghost ships, and witches. The same company also sells a treasure map, which locates both the shipwrecks and the ship routes around Cape Cod from Plymouth to Provincetown and designates hidden treasure, old forts, taverns, and lighthouses.

If anyone is interested in taking their own self-guided tour in search of treasure or ghosts, the maps are available at Nautical Book Store off Main Street in Hyannis, or by calling 508-362-4908 or 1-800-959-0410.

Simmons Homestead Inn
288 Scudder Avenue
Hyannis Port, MA 02647
508-778-4999 or 800-657-1649
e-mail: SimmonsHomestead@aol.com
Simmonshomesteadinn.com

Thayer's Historic Bed n' Breakfast

❧❀❧

Annandale, Minnesota

The psychic's voice dropped. "Someone close to you is going to die," she flatly pronounced.

Her words hit me like a ton of bricks. The dear faces of my family and friends flashed before me. "Who?" I demanded to know, quickly followed by "When?"

Up until that moment, I had been looking forward to my biannual reading with Sharon Gammel, a noted psychic and tarot reader, and owner of Thayer's Historic Bed n' Breakfast. It's a luxury I've indulged in every January and July, since my friend Aldine introduced me to Sharon and Thayer's.

"Sharon is an incredible psychic. And . . . she owns a haunted hotel," Aldine would say.

Yeah, right. I had met my fill of "psychics" at the Myrtles. We used to call them "seriously psycho." They would show up uninvited, with full entourage, usually wearing gypsy attire or large gold earrings, and proclaim, "Hi, my name is Star, and I'm a psychic. I came to investigate your house." Then they would walk through the house, hands outstretched, picking up "vibes." If they had read the brochure, they might know enough to impress their friends, but I had done enough research on the history of the plantation to know when they were just plain wrong. One Halloween, I watched in amusement as a noted psychic from California channeled Daisy Davis, one of my fictitious murder mystery characters. I could barely keep from laughing out loud as the psychic went deep into a trance, her eyes rolled back into her head, and Daisy "spoke to us." All I wanted was to meet yet another phony psychic.

Still, Aldine was a blast to travel with, so I knew I would have a good time with her at Thayer's, psychic or not. Aldine and I met, as fate determined, when our paths crossed at the Mason House Inn in Bentonsport, Iowa, another haunted inn. It was late in the evening, and I was in the keeping room talking to the owners, when Aldine "arrived." There was a huge commotion in the hallway, followed by loud banging and chattering passing through the inn.

"Oh, Aldine is here," the owner proclaimed. In the midst of this whirlwind was a stunning redheaded beauty, very stately, and quite clumsy. Aldine and I had one of those instant connections, like we had known each other for a long time. We stayed up, like schoolgirls, giggling and whispering until dawn.

"You have to promise to come visit me in Virginia," Aldine pleaded as we clung to each other on the sidewalk before taking off in different directions the next day. And I did. I would visit her in Powhattan, at her plantation, Edgemont (also haunted), and she would visit me in Louisiana. When we weren't in the same state, we burned up the phone lines, talking for hours. Occasionally she joined me as I researched haunted hotels, and several times, when things got really scary, I was very relieved not to be alone. So when she mentioned Thayer's, and the psychic, I knew if nothing else it would be a good time.

Thayer's is darling—very plain on the outside, but the interior of this three-story Victorian hotel is decorated like a movie set, with bold colors and vintage Victorian antiques. Sharon greeted us. She didn't "look" like the psychics I had met at the Myrtles. She was dressed quite normally, and with her carrot-red hair and childlike face, she looked more like a grown-up Annie than a gypsy fortune-teller.

Our readings weren't scheduled until morning, so Aldine showed me around. Maybe it was all the portraits hanging on the walls, or maybe it was just the kitties, I don't know, but everywhere I went inside the hotel, I felt like I was being watched. I caught myself turning around several times to see if someone was behind us. No one was there.

After the champagne breakfast, it was time for our readings. I went first. Sharon led me into the huge, empty formal dining room. More than ever, I had that same feeling of being watched. I brought a piece of paper with the three questions she had asked me to write down prior to the reading, though she never asked to see them. With no fanfare, no eyes rolled back into her head, Sharon simply chatted away while she shuffled and dealt the cards. She told me the usual fortune-teller rhetoric about my love life and my career, but she also gave me some surprisingly specific details. Sure enough, my three questions had been answered without my having to ask. I was a little impressed, but still very skeptical. It wasn't until later that year when I listened to the tape of my session again that I realized that many of her predictions had indeed come to pass.

Since then, partly for amusement, but partly out of curiosity about my future, I booked a reading with Sharon twice a year. Over time, I saw that the most important events in my life were addressed early on in the reading. So when she told me first thing that someone close to me was going to die, I panicked. I needed to know everything.

"Who!"

"Is your mother's health okay?" she timidly asked.

"I think so."

"It is an older female family member," Sharon calmly stated, her coolness in stark contrast to my fear. My mind raced. As the oldest daughter, it couldn't be one of my sisters. That left my mother and my aunts. My heart pounded as I pictured each of them, treasuring them.

I guess Sharon sensed my distress. "Nothing is written in stone," she assured. "The reading shows things as they stand today. This could change. Just know that if this person decides to leave the planet, it is their choice. And passing over is not a bad thing. It's only bad for those left behind."

Sharon's prediction weighed heavy on my mind. I was consumed by it. The very next day I flew to California to visit my parents. I had been planning a fiftieth wedding anniversary party for them. I kept praying my mother would make it to the party. At least all the plans for the event kept my mind somewhat occupied, so I couldn't dwell on Sharon's words.

Aldine called me in California to tell me that she was in the hospital. She had planned to visit me in Louisiana for Christmas, but came down with the flu, and it had not gone away. Doctors came up with a variety of diagnoses, from the flu, or pneumonia, to lung cancer. We never really considered the lung cancer verdict, preferring to believe it was the flu. Two days later, when Aldine took a turn for the worse, I called her daughter Florence, a college student in Minnesota, and made arrangements for Flo to fly out to be with Aldine. I wanted to be there too, but with my parents' gala just three days away, Aldine insisted that I stay for the party. Always the social butterfly, she ordered me to stay put. "I WANT you to be at that party. You know how much I love parties."

I was still fearful about my mother's health, and I had a large number of guests flying in from all over the country for the event, so I finally conceded and agreed to stay. Then I remembered that Sharon had prepared me for this dilemma nearly two years before. I played the tapes from my previous readings until I found it: "Someone very close to you will be ill. You will want to go see them, but you will be far away. It is okay if you don't go." Wow.

The next day, Thursday, Aldine slipped into a coma. I was so glad her daughter had arrived Wednesday night, and got to visit with her mom. The lab results came back that afternoon. Aldine had lung cancer—the fast-acting kind. There was nothing the doctors could do. Friday, February 6, at noon, they planned to turn off her life support. I deeply regretted not being there with my friend. I considered all the places I could go to be with her at noon. I thought about going to a church, or the ocean, but then I knew the perfect place to be. Knowing Aldine, it was the ONLY place to be. At exactly noon on February 6, I was at the mall, in Macy's, way in the back at the sales rack, saying good-bye.

Finally a sales clerk asked me if I was all right. I was standing there, tears streaming down my face, holding up the marked-down outfits and asking aloud Aldine's opinion of this one or that. Anyone observing me probably thought I was nuts. I stumbled out of the store and just drove for hours along the coast. I pulled over once, at a record store, to buy James Taylor's song "Fire and Rain." Why wasn't it raining outside?

Three weeks after Sharon's prediction, I lost one of my very best friends. Aldine was like a big sister to me.

Sightings

Sharon has always been psychic, though as a child she assumed it was a natural phenomenon that everyone possessed. Sharon knew things about people without being told, and knew what was going to happen before it did. Not only did she see dead people, she delighted in playing with her kitties that had long passed.

Sometimes being sensitive was depressing. When Sharon first set foot in Thayer's, she felt an overwhelming sorrow. "A lot of bad things had happened there, not only to the people who owned the hotel, but to the guests as well. It was nasty," claims Sharon. "You could feel all the unpleasantness. The higher I got in the house, the more I realized that it was haunted, but not by happy spirits. I was really on edge.

"The hotel had made it impossible for any owner to be happy there. Everyone had it bad. One guy had a heart attack. Another had trouble with the law. A lot of bad things went on in the hotel: beds would be wet inside the covers; employees were trapped in the freezer. It was nasty. They didn't tell me the stories until after I bought the place, but I knew."

Sharon had been looking for seven years to find a place to open a restaurant. The moment she walked into the hotel, she said, "It was like, okay, now I know why I've been waiting. In spite of the dreadful gloom hanging in the air, I knew in that moment that I would own the hotel.

"Out of desperation I struck a deal with its other occupants. I said, 'Here's how it's going to be. We've got to work things out. You don't like it the way it is. I don't like it either. We will work things out.' And it changed. I know that's why it happened. I didn't do it on my own. They did it."

The day she purchased the hotel, Sharon saw an old lady on the third-floor landing, rocking, and said, "'I know you don't like the changes, that it's difficult for you, but just work with me. This place can be pretty, let's work together.' The lady smiled and vanished." She continued,

> When I first started seeing them, I didn't know who they were. It's like when you meet someone; you really don't get to know them until later. But when you live with them, you learn they are profound. Having a ghost is like having the bully as your friend. Everyone else is scared but you're not.

Thayer's was built in 1895 by Gus and Caroline Thayer. Both Gus and Caroline visit us often. There is a portrait of Caroline in the lobby. She watches us. When she is happy, her portrait is smiling, but when she's not, she frowns. Gus leaves pennies for us to find; I think it's his way of letting us know that he's been here.

There is a little girl who sits on the stairs, about halfway down, with her arms tucked under her knees. She is dressed in a plaid dress. She just sits there and watches us. I spoke to her, to find out what she was doing there, but she speaks in a different language, and I can't understand her.

We have a number of guests from the other side who visit on a regular basis. One is a young lady who spent her wedding night on the third floor. She comes back often. She has blond hair, and wears a stunning white lace duster from around 1910. She usually wears her hair up, but in her room she lets it down. She's cool, just happy to be here.

We have two ghost kitties, also.

Sharon's husband Warren, who passed away, also stays nearby. Before Warren's death, Sharon used to joke to him that she wished Gus would leave quarters, not pennies. Shortly after his death, quarters started dropping out of thin air.

When Sharon learned that two women had visited the hotel and told the ghosts to leave, she was furious. "They did what!" she screeched.

"The ladies came in and told the ghosts they couldn't

stay and they had to go on," reported the bartender, who overheard the ladies speaking to the spirits. "The ghosts are not very happy right now," he added.

"How dare they," Sharon fumed. She stormed into the dining room and passionately addressed the spirits: "You know this is your home, and you can visit any time you want to. I apologize for the rudeness of those people."

"People sometimes ask, 'Why do ghosts haunt?'" says Sharon. "They don't haunt. They visit. Why do they come back? Why do you go visit friends? They know where they are. They come visit, they check in. No big deal.

"It's ridiculous to think that someone has to have died a horrible death to haunt a place. You go see someplace because you want to, not because you are stuck there for eternity. It's odd that someone would think that in order to have guests in your home, they all have to be malevolent. Some are. You talk to them and find out why, just like when friends come over and are nasty. You talk to them and find out why."

One guest, Millie, the mother of one of Sharon's friends, froze as she approached the hotel and could not force herself to enter. She described her experience as "a flashback, like instant recall." She "remembered" being with an older woman with a lot of baggage, wearing a blue dress. She clearly saw herself as an African-American girl of about ten or eleven. Millie shuddered as the flashback continued. A group of men approached and yanked her away, screaming. Millie was terrified.

"What she was witnessing," explained Sharon, "was a memory from a past life, brought on when she returned to the scene of the crime many years before. The Underground Railroad passed by the hotel. Millie had been trying to escape. She was caught, and punishment too horrible to remember awaited her. Even in this life, she was filled with terror as she stood on that sidewalk outside the hotel."

The two kitty-cat ghosts, Sadie and Coco Bear, are also regularly sighted. They are ghost cats that once lived with Sharon but have long since passed over. "Often one will brush up against you, or lie on your feet at night. You can actually see the indentation on the bed. The cats also get the blame when doors open and close on their own."

The Hotel

In the late 1890s Annandale was a bustling frontier town filled with gambling halls, saloons, notorious gunmen, and shady ladies of the night. Gus and Caroline Thayer ran the hotel, a resting point for weary passengers on the Soo Line Railroad. It offered the gentleman traveler a "full range of services."

Completely renovated by Sharon and Warren in 1985, Thayer's Historic Bed n' Breakfast is listed on the National Register of Historic Places and offers guests a taste of its colorful past. Each of the eleven rooms is furnished with period antiques and handmade quilts. Every room has a private bath with an old-fashioned claw-foot tub or a modern whirlpool. At night you can join other guests in the ten-person hot tub outside in the garden.

Best Rooms/Times

The staircase at the hotel is the hub of the spirit activity, as the spirits move up and down the hotel. The higher up in the hotel, the more active the ghosts. As for guest rooms, the third floor is a ghost haven, centering around Room 305.

Dining

A decadent champagne breakfast may include fresh fruits, muffins, breads, waffles, eggs, chocolate-covered strawberries, and of course, champagne. Sharon, who is also an acclaimed gourmet chef, prepares the dinners. The tavern is dark and quaint, the perfect spot to relate the Thayer's ghost stories.

Murder mystery dinners provide guests an opportunity to experience the hotel in another era. Each guest is assigned a character and puts together a period costume. You may be the killer, or you might just be killed! On occasion, period ghosts have been spotted mingling with the guests.

Once a month, you can "Dine with the Psychic." Sharon prepares a delicious gourmet meal, then sits down to dine with the guests. During the course of the meal, each guest may ask the psychic a question, and receives a mini-reading.

Don't Miss

How many inns offer bed, breakfast, and a psychic reading? Thayer's does. Owner Sharon Gammel is chef, bartender, and psychic. Her career as a psychic medium spans thirty years, and she has clients from New York to Los Angeles. Sharon also teaches classes in psychic development. Prior to your reading, Gammel requests that you write down three questions. The written questions are not looked at until the reading is finished. It is unusual for her not to address all of your questions.

When I finally got a book deal with Warner after six years and several agents, I wanted to see if Sharon would pick it up. "This is too big. If she doesn't," I admonished, "I will NEVER believe in a psychic again. I will know it is all a scam." As usual, I did not tell Sharon in advance where I was or what I was doing. I felt a little guilty about setting her up, but I really wanted to know for sure if this was real.

I will never forget what Sharon said. The very first words out of her mouth were, "All your dreams have come true. All your efforts are finally coming to fruition." Without ever knowing there was one, Sharon had passed my test. This WAS real!

Since then, I have come to have the utmost respect for those true, gifted psychics who use their "powers" to help others; people like Larry Montz, who founded the International Society for Paranormal Research, and John Edwards.

You don't have to stay at the hotel to get a reading from Sharon. You can schedule a phone reading by calling the hotel. But be absolutely sure you really want to know your future.

Thayer's Historic Bed n' Breakfast
60 West Elm Street
Highway 55
P.O. Box 246
Annandale, MN 55302
320-274-8222 or 800-944-6595
e-mail: sharongammell@thayers.net
www.thayers.net

The Tides Inn-by-the-Sea

Kennebunkport, Maine

Emma doesn't make any bones about the fact that she doesn't like men very much, especially egotistical or arrogant men. If she doesn't like you, you will know it. Emma went through a really nasty divorce and was forced to give up her beloved hotel, which left her with a tremendous distaste of the opposite sex. Her mission in life—er, death—as described by the owner of the Tides Inn, is to "kick mean men off the planet."

"If you want to know if you've got a good man or not, bring him to the inn. Emma will let you know if she doesn't like him," claims Kristin, part of the mother–daughter team who have owned the Tides since 1972. "She gets them good every time. She always finds a way to make a fool out of them."

Time after time, she has scared the unsuspecting bullies silly, leaving them to whimper like schoolgirls. Several have left in a huff.

Emma was first seen by a painter hired by Marie to paint

murals in the lobby. He was painting a dresser in Room 29 when he looked up and saw her watching him. Unsettled, he ran downstairs to tell Marie. She brought out a bunch of old photos of the hotel and asked him to look through them.

"That's her, that's the woman who was watching me," he pointed.

Marie got the chills. Emma had built the hotel. Marie had felt Emma's presence since she bought the historic inn, watching her every move.

At Marie's request, Emma's portrait was painted into the mural above the staircase. In the attic, Marie found a dress that belonged to Emma. She made a doll in Emma's likeness, and when it was finished, the dress fit perfectly. At first, Marie kept Emma in her bedroom, but Emma was not happy there. She moved Emma downstairs to the lobby and placed her at the piano stool in the bar. From there, she presides over the Tides, carefully watching everyone who enters. Her flimsy head twists and turns, her eyes dart from side to side, if a man passes through its doors. Grandmothers march their grandchildren in just to visit Emma.

"Room 25 is her official room. She is definitely the woman of the house." admits Marie.

When Emma built her seashore resort in 1899, she called it the New Belvidere. For her own amusement, as well as the guests', Emma loved to bring in magicians to put on a show. People would come from far and near to the unique seashore resort. Emma entertained both Theodore Roosevelt and Sir Arthur Conan Doyle.

After Emma's reign, some pretty colorful characters owned the hotel. "Whenever we have guests who have stayed before, we learn so much about the place," says Marie. "This summer we had a fellow stay with us. He was very elderly. He used to come to the hotel years ago. He said the owners of the hotel were real characters. Sometimes, they would be sitting on the floor of the lobby, playing poker. If they were winning, they wouldn't check people in until they were finished. The brother of those innkeepers and the head housekeeper used to work for the famous Guggenheims of New York City. They were living together. It was scandalous in that day. People like that, I can just imagine as ghosts!"

"The hotel should have burned to the ground one year," claims Kristin.

When the Great Fire of 1947 raged across Maine, destroying everything in its path, it looked like the New Belvidere would be ravaged. Miraculously, the fire stopped just two doors from the hotel. The notorious fire burned on for two weeks, and destroyed hundreds of homes and mansions. As it raged toward Goose Neck Beach and the New Belvidere, town residents fled in terror, taking the time to gather up only their most prized possessions.

Everyone except for Mrs. Pate, who lived next door. Instead of fleeing, she sat calmly on her porch, fists clenched, rocking in her rocker on her porch, unwavering in her determination.

"This fire will NOT destroy my home," she proclaimed, over and over. Horrified, friends and neighbors urged her to leave while she still had a chance to save herself. She refused to budge. The fire leveled everything in its three-mile-wide path, closer and closer, until it was just two doors away. It looked as if

Mrs. Pate not only would lose her beloved home, she would lose her life in the unbridled blaze.

Still, she sat steadfast, eyes glazed, repeating her solemn resolution over and over. Suddenly, the ravenous fire stopped. Just two doors away, the remains of once-beautiful estates sat smoldering, the sky dark with ashes and smoke. Mrs. Pate's beloved home, and the New Belvidere, were spared. It was a miracle. Thanks to Mrs. Pate (and possibly Emma), the New Belvidere was still standing amid the ruins!

Today's owners seem more like Thelma and Louise than mother and daughter. They have owned the hotel since 1972. "Things started happening right off the bat," Marie admits.

Right after we bought the hotel, I had an experience on the third floor. I was remodeling, and I felt something push me into the wall. I fell into the corner. I was upset. I felt the presence of a ghost. Something made me stand up and speak; "I am going to be here now. We have to coexist. Please leave me alone."

I don't know what made me do that or say that. I read later that that's the way to control spirits. After that, I had no problem. I talk to her throughout the day. I always tell her when we are going to make changes. When we moved the dining room back to its original location, I took Emma around and showed her all the changes.

The chambermaids always had problems too, in that one area upstairs. Things would disappear, then reappear. A lot of people's hair would stand on end, or they get cold sweats, mostly men.

We've had other people feel as though they were being tucked into bed. She hangs around on the third floor. Men have the most problems. One time, a man staying in Room 29 left before dawn. He didn't know we had a ghost. That evening he called to let me know that he woke up in the middle of the night, looked up, and saw a stern-looking woman glaring at him. Scared out of his wits, he swatted at her. His wife woke up, saw him swatting at the air, and asked him what he was doing. He wasn't trying to get his money back or anything, he mainly just wanted someone to talk to about what happened.

Kristin describes what it was like to grow up in a haunted hotel:

It's like the movie *The Shining*. I was only three years old when my mother bought the hotel. As a child growing up in a house that is haunted, I've just kind of had to adapt to my surroundings. I have been exposed to a lot of different things, and my life experiences have been extraordinary because I have grown up in a house with a ghost.

You hear different things. I was an only child, so many times I would just make my own fun and play in different rooms and talk to my ghost friends. When I had to make up rooms, I would talk to them. When I heard noises or voices, I always hoped it was a ghost, and not a burglar. Once I had an experience in Room 29. The vacuum cleaner would just stop running. I would check it out, and it would start again. I was a little scared at that point, and I just said, "Emma,

stop!" I finished what I was doing, and I was out of
there. Another time, there were glass coffeepots in a
circle on the floor next to Emma. I asked my mother
if she had done it, and she said no. No one else was in
the hotel.

I've definitely experienced Emma, but I also feel
there are other spirits here.

In the winter, when the hotel was closed up, I used
to have to walk through it alone to catch the school
bus. I always ran through the hallways. All the room
doors were open, and it was cold and scary. Sometimes I would hear things, and I would fly down the
stairs to the first floor. I always felt I was being
watched.

I've always had an eerie fascination with the old
hotels. I transform myself back through time. I'm not
afraid to be here anymore. This is my place, and it's
our destiny to stay here. Someday, my mother and I
will haunt this hotel along with Emma.

The Tides Inn-by-the-Sea is one of my favorite spots. I
called Kristin to check some facts and hear the latest ghost
tales. As we were saying good-bye, the computer froze, and
our conversation was lost.

"Emma has spoken!" Kristin declared.

Sightings

No need to hire a private detective to check out your
boyfriend. Emma has little tolerance for uptight men.
"She just has a sense about it," Kristin reports. "If she

doesn't trust a man, she will do something to let you know. It might be nightmares, or she might move something, but she will make a fool out of him. If women report that they've encountered the ghost, usually it's because they are there with a husband or a boyfriend who is nasty. Emma can just sense that mean man thing. When she had to sell the inn to Mr. Allen, that's when the revenge thing came into play. If their soul isn't good, she will let you know."

"Sometimes it's hysterical," giggles Kristin. "We had a guy named Bill Rosenburger staying on the second floor. He was pretty uptight, so I figured Emma would get him good. He came down early the next morning claiming that we had had an earthquake. He told me he was on the toilet, and the toilet started shaking. I could just see this guy on the toilet, so I was trying hard to keep a straight face and not to crack up. He insisted that we turn on the television, to prove there had been an earthquake. Finally I suggested that maybe it was the ghost. 'I don't believe in ghosts,' he bellowed. He was determined to find out what shook the toilet. He came into town this year, but he didn't stay here."

Best Rooms/Times

"We have to be very careful about who we check in to Room 25," admits Marie. "If the man is sweet, we never have any trouble. But if he has a bad attitude, he will have problems. Actually, the entire third floor is haunted. In Rooms 26 and 27, the beds shake. If we aren't sure about a man's personality, we don't put him on that floor."

The Inn

The Tides Inn-by-the-Sea is the last remaining grand hotel overlooking the beach, with magnificent ocean views. It offers the simple mystique of a turn-of-the-century Victorian inn on the beautiful white sands of Goose Rocks Beach.

The twenty-two unique bedrooms on three floors are all decorated with antique furnishings of the period. Here you can wake to the plaintive cries of seagulls; stroll miles of sandy beach and search for shells or sand dollars; settle back in a rocking chair on the veranda and watch lobster men haul traps of fresh lobster in the cove; and sip cocktails at sunset. And depending upon whether Emma approves, your male companion may or may not enjoy these things as well.

Dining

Dubbed the Belvidere Club after Emma's reign, the 1899 dining room serves exceptional regional fare. Specialties include wild rocket, baby spinach, and caramelized pear salad with roasted pecans, pansautéed Timber Island crab cakes, seafood chowder, steamed clams, and of course, Maine lobster.

Or you can join Emma in the vintage Victorian bar for your favorite cocktail or lemonade.

Don't Miss

> After dark, if you dare, take a ghost tour along Maine's mysterious rockbound coast. You will hear chilling tales of intrigue and horror, presented by a costumed guide. Hear ghostly tales of haunted lighthouses, cannibalism, ghost ships, and more. Call Maritime Productions at 207-967-4938 to make your reservations.

Tides Inn-by-the-Sea
Open mid-May to mid-October
252 Kings Highway
Goose Rocks Beach
Kennebunkport, ME 04046
207-967-3757
www.tidesinnbythesea.com

Old Van Buren Inn

❦

Van Buren, Arkansas

After encountering the ghost at the Old Van Buren Inn, one thirteen-year-old girl developed strange psychic powers. Although she had never had any kind of psychic experiences before, as soon as she saw the ghost, her short, sheltered world shattered. She started hearing voices, seeing visions, and having prophetic dreams. She told her mother that she could even see through the walls.

The inn, once the upstanding Crawford Bank, then an illicit speakeasy before changing hands through a number of failed businesses, has long been known for its ghostly activity. It is now owned by Californian Jackie Henningsen; townsfolk tried to keep the secret of its ghosts from her after Jackie bought the ailing building with its marble floors, tin roof, and landmark turret and restored it to its original splendor.

They couldn't keep the secret for long. Jackie had a visit from the ghosts on her very first day.

Wherever I went in the building, I had the creepy feeling that someone was watching me. That night, when I was upstairs, I heard something coming up the staircase. The dogs jumped up and started barking. I opened the door to the hall, but no one was there. The dogs ran down to look, but nothing was there.

No one told me when I was looking at the place that it was haunted. Before I bought it, I went up and down the street, introducing myself to all the shop owners. It wasn't until after I bought it that they all came to visit, one by one, and started telling me the stories.

The most famous story is about a man who murdered his wife on the front steps. Another long-told tale, though not verified, surrounds a crazy lady who was locked in the attic by her husband, rumored to have been the bank president. But I learned that there are lots of other ghosts, too. A lot of different people used to rent the building, and all of them had a hard time with the ghosts. One lady had a dance studio here for six years. I went to see her, and I asked if she had noticed anything. She told me that every night, after the students went home, there would be a woman standing on the landing upstairs. The first night she thought it was one of the mothers, but when she went up, the lady vanished. She always stood on that one landing in the hallway. It's the same place where the workmen wouldn't go. When I asked them why, they said they saw a woman there too, but every time they turned around, no one was there.

For several years it was very very active. I would hear all kinds of noises—footsteps, voices coming from upstairs, even when I knew I was the only person there. My own dog, who used to follow me everywhere, wouldn't go upstairs with me. Neither would my granddaughter. It was scary.

As if things weren't frightening enough, the ghostly activity escalated when Jackie brought in some antique bedroom furniture she had purchased at a yard sale. "It was a local gentleman, whose daughter had murdered someone. He sold his household effects and left town. After I put the furniture up in the bedrooms, I started hearing all kinds of strange noises that I hadn't heard before.

"Things just got crazy. When I would go to bed, the bedcovers were all rumpled, like someone had sat down on the bed. The hot water heater would get turned on and off, the lights would go on, all the fans would start going. Every night, the tape on the telephone recorder would go on. I finally had to unplug the phone at night."

Jackie was finally driven to call the law. One night, when she was all alone in the building, she found muddy boot prints on the upstairs landing. The large prints went from the hall into the Green Room and then just stopped. "I was afraid someone was in that room. But how did he get upstairs without leaving mud on the steps? And there were no footsteps coming back down. I was more afraid a man had broken in." Panicked, Jackie called the police. Even they were baffled by the dark crusts of mud upstairs.

Maybe things have calmed down a bit, or maybe Jackie has just gotten used to her roommates from beyond, but she is finally comfortable with them in her home. "Maybe they aren't as agitated anymore, or maybe they are happy with what I have done to the place."

Sightings

"The story of the little girl is the strangest thing," says Jackie.

A lady came in for lunch one day, and kept saying how much she loved the town. She came back with her daughter two weeks later. It was on a Sunday, and I had already closed. She said she just wanted her daughter to see the extraordinary building. The little girl looked up and saw the ghost lady in the window of the Cranberry Room. Ever since then, the girl has been having visions. She started experiencing psychic stuff. She told her mother there were things in the wall. She started hearing voices and having vivid dreams. The lady called me, and she was very upset. She said the child was only thirteen.

Other people have seen the lady in the window, but they didn't get the powers. One woman was across the street when she looked up and saw the ghost. She came in all shaky. Another lady saw the ghost when she was in her car at the stop sign. She said the apparition stood in the window and stared at her, then faded away. The ghost is always described as a young lady with curly hair and a high lace collar.

One lady saw a man in a mirror, standing behind her. She screamed, but no one else was there. She made herself look back in the mirror. The man was gone.

Another time, a lady was going through a box of pictures I bought at an estate sale. When she got to one old photo, she screamed. She told her husband the eyes in the photo were alive. The photos came from a family where the daughter had killed someone.

One couple with a small baby asked me if I had gotten up and taken a bath at three A.M. The lady claims she got up with the baby and heard someone walking around, and then the bath-water running.

Best Rooms/Times

Although the Green Room and the adjoining bath-room receive most of the ghostly reports, the Cran-berry Room is where the woman is sighted. Ghostly activity seems to pick up after dark.

The Inn/Hotel

The magnificent Old Crawford Bank Building, built in 1889, sits proudly on the corner of Seventh and Main Streets, as did three other banks. There was a bank on each corner, and a total of seven banks in old Van Buren. The Crawford Building, however, was by far the finest. It took seven years to complete, and was the only one of its kind. The wood used in the bank was entirely hand-hewn, and the building had luxurious marble floors, wainscoting, glazed brick, ornate tur-rets, and a variety of other special features. With so much glitter, it's no wonder that it attracted the attention of Jessie James, who kept local accounts in the Crawford Bank.

With the depression in the 1930s, the bank took on a new face. The business was bought out by another bank, but the third floor became a notorious speakeasy, where dancing and carousing went on at all hours. It was during this era that a famous murder took place on the steps of the old bank.

The grisly crime of passion became the talk of this small town in the illicit days when the Crawford Bank served as a speakeasy and dance hall. When an outraged husband learned that his wife was having an affair with his best friend, he followed the unsuspecting couple. He hid in the shadows while the couple dined in a cozy restaurant down the street, then made their way to the speakeasy, laughing and openly affectionate. As the couple went up to join the merriment at the bar, the stewing husband sat on the front steps downstairs, watching and waiting.

He must have waited a long time, because authorities found eleven of his cigarette butts on the sidewalk next to the steps. When the couple finally came down, he shot her as she walked through the door. Her horrified lover looked on in fear.

An ironic twist to this true tale is that the gun used in this murder belonged to Van Buren's presiding mayor, Alan Ray Toothacker. He had loaned out his squirrel gun years before, and had never got it back.

Another owner of the gothic building is rumored to have kept his wife locked upstairs in the attic, claiming she was crazy.

A female apparition haunts the upstairs of the old bank, as do several other entities. Although their identity is not known for sure, it's suspected that the female ghost is one of these two pathetic characters, though why they would want to stay on is unclear.

Though its wild days are long gone, the original door, complete with peephole, still hangs. As recently as 1984, the old dance hall upstairs was rented out to local clubs for parties; the Masons used it for square dancing.

The old bank has been host to a menagerie of floundering businesses, including a flower shop, antique shop, coin shop, T-shirt shop, and dance studio. It then stood vacant for over a year until it was claimed in 1988 by a vivacious Californian, Jackie Henningsen. She was visiting in town, saw the ailing building, and bought it the very next day. She made the room-size vault into her office and opened a restaurant downstairs, then opened two guest rooms on the second floor and made the speakeasy into a large suite for herself.

There are two bedrooms upstairs in the old Crawford County Bank building, the Green Room and the Cranberry Room. Guests share a full bath with two claw-foot tubs. Another half-bath is in the hall. A full home-cooked breakfast is included.

Dining

The downstairs is now a charming café, with oak and ice-cream-parlor chairs and tables, and an assortment of antiques and collectables on the walls. The stained-glass windows reflect a dancing rainbow over the room. Jackie serves lunch and dinner Wednesday through Saturday, and a scrumptious Sunday brunch.

Don't Miss

Catch the Ozark Scenic Railway for a one-day round-trip ride from Van Buren to Winslow, which offers you spectacular views of the Ozark Mountains from the plush velvet bench of a restored 1920s mahogany-paneled passenger car. Embarking from the meticulously restored historic Old Frisco Depot, the train travels over towering trestles and through a remarkable man-made tunnel.

Old Van Buren Inn
633 Main Street
Van Buren, AR 72956
501-474-4202

Epilogue

Wherever You Go, There They Are

"It's TRYING TO KILL ME!" I shrieked, as I frantically pounded on the door of Mike Scheck, the assistant manager, salty smoke, sweat, and tears stinging my face. "Hurry!" I screamed. "My apartment is on fire!"

It was my first night in the summer beachfront apartment. A foul, acidic odor woke me from a deeply groggy state, slowly arousing me to semiconsciousness. I thought the owners must have used some strong oven cleaners or other toxic chemicals when they were cleaning the apartment. When I finally opened my eyes, the room was hazy, and I realized it was filled with waves of smoke. I jumped up to run outside and lost my breath, as if someone had struck me in the stomach. I staggered to the door, gasping for air. I wanted to lie on the ground outside, but I knew I had to get help. When I was able, I ran downstairs for help.

Mike looked groggy as he peered out his door, slinging it wide open when he finally comprehended what I was screaming. He darted out and up the stairs ahead of me to

Apartment 9. Billows of gray smoke were pouring out from the front door, which I had left open. Mike grabbed the bottom of his T-shirt, covered his mouth, and raced in. I took a deep breath, held it, and followed him into the kitchen area. Two of the stove burners were glowing deep red. A charred box of kitchen items next to the burners was still blazing. Remnants of a tape measure I had used earlier that day were slowly smoldering, melting away fiber by fiber. Mike and I glanced at the controls, then back at each other in horror. ALL OF THE BURNERS WERE OFF!

I ran out of the apartment, screaming. Mike bravely grabbed the box and the tiny bits of remaining tape measure and tossed them into the sink, dousing them with water. Tragedy had been averted, but I was hysterical. There was no way the burners could have turned on by themselves. I had almost died from smoke inhalation. Whoever was here was trying to kill me. Then Mike told me that the owners of the apartment had lost their son in a horrible fire. He died from smoke inhalation—in that very apartment!

"It might be better if you don't tell the owners about the ghost," Mike said. "We will just tell them that the burners go on by themselves." That morning, the owner brought in an electrician to check the burners. One was a little hard to turn, so it was replaced. The others, he claimed, worked fine.

I thought about moving out, but I doubted I would be able to get my deposit back. I had waited several months to get this incredible, though somewhat old and tattered, studio at Santa Cruz Beach. It has the most fantastic panoramic 280-degree view of the ocean, the pier, the Santa Cruz Boardwalk, the mission, and the mountains. The building sits high on a cliff above the San Lorenzo River, where the river meets the ocean. Harbor seals with their cubs bask on the rocks right under my balcony. My biggest fear, until then, had been of earthquakes.

I called my friend Paul Manouvrier in New Orleans. "They are trying to kill me," I cried. "It's happening again. What can I do?" I told Paul about the strange blazing burners, and how I had barely escaped suffocation from smoke inhalation, gasping and choking for air. I also told him about the owner's son, who had died in that apartment.

"Did you stop to think that maybe he is not trying to kill you, but he is just trying to get your attention?" Paul asked. "Maybe he has something he wants to say."

"I don't care if he's trying to get my attention or trying to kill me—if I'm dead, I'm dead," I snapped back.

"Don't you think if he wanted to kill you, he could have?" Paul questioned. I don't know the answer to that. All I knew was that I was sharing my apartment with an uninvited roommate.

"Maybe you should talk to him, find out what he wants you to know." I was much too upset at the time to do anything at all.

That evening, a guy named Jason was visiting a couple in an apartment downstairs. He had lived in Apartment 9 for two years. He asked me how I liked the apartment. I told him I didn't like it at all, and I told him about the fire.

"Oh, you met the ghost," Jason smiled. Of course, I couldn't let him stop there. I questioned him incessantly until he told me every last thing that had happened to him. He said many nights he would catch a glimpse of a guy standing in shadow. He would look again, and it would be gone.

"Yeah, it was pretty creepy. Things would just float

across the room. Other things would disappear. I think he liked beer, 'cause I would buy a six-pack, and one or two would be missing. Lots of my friends were scared to come over."

It was of little comfort to me to hear the stories. It took a few nights before I could sleep soundly. I kept my cell phone on my pillow. Maybe I would try talking to him one day and find out what he wanted, but it wouldn't be soon.

The scenario by now was a familiar one to me. When I bought the Myrtles Plantation, things started happening right away too. You try to explain them away, make a practical explanation out of an unexplainable event, but there really is no logical explanation.

You might have heard the adage, "Wherever you go, there you are." It seemed for me it was, "Wherever I go, there THEY are." Looking back, I have been encountering spirits all my life, without realizing it. Even when I was a little girl of three or four, I had an imaginary friend named Mr. Sitarumia. I had always believed that my childhood imagination created him, that as a child, I made him up, but I was shocked to learn recently that he was a real-life holy man from India who had visited my parents years before my birth. Most of my life, I scoffed at such things. As an engineering student and technical nerd, I was able to compartmentalize these events and forget they happened. If you had asked me if I believed in ghosts, I might have said no. Until I bought the Myrtles. Or should I say, until the Myrtles bought me.

I lived at the Myrtles for nine years. Ghosts and sightings were an almost daily occurrence. It changed me in a profound way. I experienced things I did not believe in, things

I did not WANT to believe in. At times, years passed before I could even speak about the events I encountered.

But there is an up side to all this. Anyone who has experienced a ghost will tell you that the experience has instilled a firm belief that life goes on, that the soul exists separate from our bodies. Even those who might explain these spirits as demons are unequivocally convinced of a life after death. The spirit world is real; life does not end. It is a very comforting thought. Maybe not when you are alone in the house and heavy footsteps are coming up the stairs, or someone is pounding on your doors, but at least in retrospect.

My experiences at the Myrtles have created a deep interrogation into the meaning and existence of spirits. In the process of this search, I met Dr. Edith Fiore, author of *The Unquiet Dead*, *You Have Been Here Before*, and *Spirit Releasement Therapy: A Technique Manual*, and guest speaker on the popular made-for-public-broadcasting *Thinking Allowed*. She was the first to point out that my work was very much like hers.

"We do the same thing. Only our method is different," says Dr. Fiore. "I use hypnosis and other means to reach the spirits and allow them to speak. You have visited them in places they haunt. By listening, and telling their story, you accomplish the same thing."

I hadn't even realized that this had become my work, that I was committed to the spirits, that I have an obligation. Every day brings new knowledge. As frightening as the process sometimes seems, I have learned how to communicate with the spirits.

Even as I sit at my computer writing this book, or review printed chapters in my bed at night, pages of manuscript will lift up and float across the room. Lights in my room blink on and off, and I hear strange knockings in my walls. I laugh now at how easily I accept these phenomena as part of my life. I know my pages will be out of order, or that the lights won't go back on until I stop what I'm doing and stand up, but I smile and say aloud, "Yes, I know you're here. Thank you. If you give me some space, I will give you some time later."

Because—wherever you go, there they are.

Postscript

Thanks for reading *Ghostly Encounters*. I hope you enjoyed it. If you have had an experience at a haunted hotel or inn, I would love to hear about it. Please visit the Ghostly Encounters website at www.ghostly_encounters.com to send me an email.

Born in Los Angeles, Frances Kermeen moved with her family to San Jose, California, where she studied computer science and theater. She developed a passion for Victorian architecture, and restored several grand homes. At the age of 22 she received the first award for historic preservation in Los Gatos, California.

It was during a family cruise down the Mississippi River to discover her Louisiana roots (her father grew up in Hammond), that Frances first toured the Myrtles Plantation. When she learned it was for sale, she gave up her high-tech job in Silicon Valley and fulfilled a lifelong dream of living in the south.

After carefully restoring the upstairs and the carriage house, she converted the old cotton plantation into a 10-room guest inn, where she lived for nearly a decade. Fascinated by the rich history and culture of the area, she wrote and produced period murder mystery weekends based on several of the unsolved murders at the Myrtles, which received national acclaim.

Today Frances resides in Natchez, Mississippi and Santa Cruz, California with her puppy dog, Ms. B'havin.